Best of British

A celebration of great British cuisine

AA

The contents of this book are believed correct at the time of printing. Nevertheless, the Publisher cannot be held responsible for any errors or omissions, or for changes in the details given in this Guide, or for the consequences of any reliance on the information provided by the same. This does not affect your statutory rights.

Assessments of AA inspected establishments are based on the experience of the Hotel and Restaurant Inspectors on the occasion(s) of their visit(s) and therefore descriptions given in this Guide necessarily dictate an element of subjective opinion which may not reflect or dictate a reader's own opinion on another occasion. See page 11 for a clear explanation of how, based on our Inspectors' inspection experiences, establishments are graded. If the meal or meals experienced by an Inspector or Inspectors during an inspection fall between award levels the restaurant concerned may be awarded the lower of any award levels considered applicable. The AA strives to ensure accuracy of the information in this Guide at the time of printing. Due to the constantly evolving nature of the subject matter the information is subject to change. The AA will gratefully receive any advice from our readers of any necessary updated information.

Please contact
Editorial Department: lifestyleguides@theaa.com

Front cover photograph courtesy of The Orchid Restaurant at Corbyn Head Hotel

Printed by Canale, Italy

Restaurant descriptions have been contributed by the following team of writers: Cathy Fitzgerald, Sarah Gilbert, David Hancock, Julia Hynard, Denise Laing, Melissa Riley-Jones, Allen Stidwill, Derryck Strachan, Mark Taylor and Kate Trew.

Published by AA Publishing, a trading name of Automobile Association Developments Limited, whose registered office is Fanum House,
Basing View, Basingstoke, Hampshire RG21 4EA.
Registered number 1878835.

A CIP catalogue for this book is available from the British Library.

ISBN-10: 0-7495-5480-0
ISBN-13: 978-0-7495-5480-4
A03592

Best of British

Graffiti at Hotel Felix

Contents

The Best of British

Graffitti at Hotel Felix

There was a time, not that long ago, when British food was regarded as not at its best, especially by foreign visitors looking for an authentic taste of Britain. But then something revolutionary happened. Chefs suddenly woke up to the fact that some of the finest ingredients in the world were being grown or reared on their own doorstep. Even more significantly, these chefs started to use them in place of ingredients imported from the other side of the world and re-learnt a repertoire of British dishes, properly cooked. To demonstrate just how cooking has evolved in this country during the past few years we have produced this guide to restaurants serving the Best of British cuisine.

For the consumer, the return to proper British cooking was a revelation and the gastronomic equivalent of the scene in *The Wizard of Oz* when it changes from black and white into glorious Technicolor. The result was a new generation of chefs who acknowledged Britain's culinary heritage by revisiting classic dishes, adding their own twist and using seasonal, local produce whenever possible.

The Culinary Revolution

It could be argued that the culinary revolution in Britain actually started around 20 years ago. In the mid-80s, the first signs of change happened when a small group of London chefs rebelled against the pretentiousness of nouvelle cuisine and became the architects of what we now call Modern British cooking. Suddenly, a new generation of chefs were ripping up the rulebook by serving their increasingly discerning clientele hearty portions of

Gravetye Manor

Sienna

simple, seasonal dishes with bold flavours. Chefs such as Rowley Leigh, Stephen Bull, Simon Hopkinson and Alastair Little may have had their culinary roots in Mediterranean cooking and the writings of Elizabeth David and Jane Grigson, but they were using seasonal British produce to conjure up simple, honest dishes where flavour was more important than fancy presentation and elaborate, superfluous garnishes.

The Birth of Modern British Cuisine

This change kick-started what was to become known as a Modern British style of cuisine, and it is a cooking style that continues to this day in hundreds of restaurants up and down the country, many of them featured in this book.

The influence of chefs like Stephen Bull and Rowley Leigh is still prevalent in kitchens all over Britain. Both chefs were schooled in classic French cooking techniques but they combined them with their own interpretations of British dishes. Many of their dishes have become permanent fixtures on menus up and down Britain. For example, there can be few restaurants around that haven't served their own versions of Leigh's famous griddled scallops with pea purée and mint or Bull's classic twice-cooked goats' cheese soufflé.

The rise and rise of great British cuisine has continued with a number of other chefs flying the flag for the farmers and artisans who provide them with seasonal home-grown produce. These are chefs working within British culinary traditions and providing customers with what they expect to find in such establishments – straightforward classic dishes.

In London, a number of restaurants are leading this British renaissance, each with its own take on what Modern British cuisine means three decades after the term was created.

It could be a contemporary, buzzy place like the Rivington Bar & Grill where a typical menu could include roast Lancashire suckling pig with greens and quince sauce followed by Bakewell tart or a world-renowned hotel restaurant such as The Grill at the Dorchester, where innovative head chef Aiden Byrne serves pan-fried John Dory served with celeriac, apple and horseradish.

Established British chefs such as Gary Rhodes, Richard Corrigan and Mark Hix are now being joined by a new generation of young chefs who want to cook seasonal British food, whether it's in a AA five-Rosette restaurant in the West End of London or a local gastro-pub in Cumbria, making the most of produce being grown by farmers and suppliers in the surrounding fields.

Perhaps one of the strongest proponents of British cooking is Fergus Henderson of the fashionable St John restaurant near London's Smithfield Market. Henderson's 'nose to tail' cooking philosophy majors on simple, robust dishes that utilise the whole animal. He has also championed the resurrection of long-lost traditional British dishes to the extent that his menu might include tripe served with chips or boiled ox tongue. Henderson has inspired a number of chefs to revisit old British dishes from the Mrs Beeton era and give them pride of place on their menus. After years of chefs trying to reinvent the culinary wheel when it comes to flavours and fancy presentation, suddenly it's cool to put jugged hare, mince and tatties or rice pudding on your menu.

Pushing the Culinary Boundaries

Modern British cooking isn't simply about recreating long-lost dishes from a bygone era. For every chef dusting off a Mrs Beeton book for inspiration, there will be another who wants to push the culinary envelope by experimenting with new flavour combinations and techniques.

Modern British cuisine doesn't get more innovative or cutting-edge than Heston Blumenthal's scientific approach to cooking at Britain's top restaurant, The Fat Duck in Bray, where dishes can raise eyebrows for their inventiveness. In the same way that Fergus Henderson's St John restaurant has made many chefs want to turn back the clock to wartime dishes, Blumenthal has inspired another band of chefs to experiment with food.

The Fat Duck

Such innovation and experimentation is not just the preserve of a few select restaurants in central London. There are a number of dazzling chefs dotted all over Britain, from Adam Simmonds' stunning cuisine at the Oak Room at Danesfield House, Buckinghamshire, to the imaginative cooking of Hywel Jones at Lucknam Park in Wiltshire.

Britain hasn't always been renowned for its cuisine but it currently offers some of the best cooking in the world. There has never been a better time to enjoy the Best of British

Heston Blumenthal,
The Fat Duck

Using the Guide

In celebration of the rise of great British cooking, this comprehensive guide includes restaurants serving the best of modern and traditional British cuisine. British food has been revisited by today's chefs offering old English dishes alongside modern interpretations and presentation of classic fare. Experimenting with new flavour combinations and techniques and the sourcing of seasonal home-grown produce has created innovative Modern British dishes, often with influences from around the world. This collection of restaurants, reviewed and rated by professional AA inspectors, offers inspirational British cuisine at its very best.

The following features will help you to use this guide.

The AA Rosette Award: This guide includes restaurants serving Best of British cuisine with 1, 2, 3, 4 and 5 AA Rosettes (see also page 11).

Notable Wine List symbol: Denotes a wine list that has been judged to be a high quality, well presented listing, with diversity/coverage across grapes and /or countries and style, and the best individual growers and vintages.

V   **Vegetarian symbol:** Denotes the restaurant has a separate vegetarian menu.

Chef and Owner: The names of the chef (s) and owner(s) are as up to date as possible at the time of going to press, but changes in personnel often occur, and may affect the style and quality of the restaurant.

Times: Daily opening and closing times, plus seasonal information, are included. However these times are liable to change without notice. It is wise to telephone in advance to avoid disappointment.

Prices: These are given for fixed dinner and à la carte main course. Prices quoted are a guide only, and are subject to change with out notice.

Book Order: The restaurants are listed in region, county, town and then alphabetically within each town.

Rosette Awards

The AA's Rosette award scheme was the first nationwide scheme for assessing the quality of food served by restaurants and hotels. The Rosette scheme is an award, not a classification, and although there is necessarily an element of subjectivity when it comes to assessing taste, we aim for a consistent approach throughout the UK. Our awards are made solely on the basis of a meal visit or visits by one or more of our hotel and restaurant Inspectors, who have an unrivalled breadth and depth of experience in assessing quality. They award Rosettes annually on a rising scale of one to five.

So what makes a restaurant worthy of a Rosette Award?

For our Inspectors, the top and bottom line is the food. The taste of a dish is what counts, and whether it successfully delivers to the diner the promise of the menu. A restaurant is only as good as its worst meal. Although presentation and competent service should be appropriate to the style of the restaurant and the quality of the food, they cannot affect the Rosette assessment as such, either up or down. The summaries below indicate what our Inspectors look for, but are intended only as guidelines. The AA is constantly reviewing its award criteria, and competition usually results in an all-round improvement in standards, so it becomes increasingly difficult for restaurants to reach award level. For more detailed Rosette criteria, please visit www.theAA.com.

◉ One Rosette
- Excellent restaurants that stand out in their local area
- Food prepared with care, understanding and skill
- Good quality ingredients

◉◉ Two Rosettes
- The best local restaurants
- Higher standards
- Better consistency
- Greater precision apparent in the cooking
- Obvious attention to the quality and selection of ingredients

◉◉◉ Three Rosettes
- Outstanding restaurants demanding recognition well beyond local area
- Selection and sympathetic treatment of highest quality ingredients
- Timing, seasoning and judgement of flavour combinations consistent
- Excellent intelligent service and a well-chosen wine list

◉◉◉◉ Four Rosettes
Dishes demonstrate:
- intense ambition
- a passion for excellence
- superb technical skills
- remarkable consistency
- appreciation of culinary traditions combined with desire for exploration and improvement
- Cooking demands national recognition

◉◉◉◉◉ Five Rosettes
- Cooking stands comparison with the best in the world
- Highly individual
- Breathtaking culinary skills
- Setting the standards to which others aspire
- Knowledgeable and distinctive wine list

Any restaurant without Rosettes has had a recent change of chef and/or owner and is awaiting an inspection.

South West England

Mousehole, Cornwall

The Wellington Hotel

Modern British

Imaginative cooking in quaint Cornish village

The Harbour, BOSCASTLE,
Cornwall PL35 0AQ
Tel: 01840 250202
Email:
info@boscastle-wellington.com
Website:
www.boscastle-wellington.com
Chef: Scott Roberts
Owners: Paul Roberts

Following the devastation of the Boscastle floods in 2004, the Roberts family has brought this old lady of a hotel back from ruin. The stylish, modern Waterloo Restaurant, with a little help from the BBC's 'Changing Rooms' team, provides the perfect setting for son Scottie's imaginative cooking driven by quality produce from the abundant local larder. Take herb-baked cod served with roast fennel, crispy potato cake and dill butter, or perhaps roast pork loin with carrot purée, rösti potato and a cider jus. Service is friendly and relaxed without losing any efficiency. Booking is essential as the restaurant has a fairly limited number of tables, though bar meals are also available.

Times: 6.30–9.30, Closed Thu
Prices: Main £10–£20
Directions: M5, A30, A39 to Camelford, then B3266 to Boscastle. Hotel is situated at the base of village by the harbour
Parking: 15

Harbourside Restaurant

Modern British

Contemporary-style restaurant with harbour views

The Greenbank, Harbourside,
FALMOUTH, Cornwall TR11 2SR
Tel: 01326 312440
Email:
sales@greenbank-hotel.co.uk
Website:
www.greenbank-hotel.co.uk
Chef: Keith Brooksbank
Owners: Greenbank Hotel
(Falmouth) Ltd

Once a base for packet ship captains, this lovely old hotel still has its own private pier for guests arriving by boat. Its airy restaurant makes the most of the spectacular waterside views with its huge picture windows, and sustains the maritime theme. Accomplished cooking is the order of the day here: sea salt-roasted chump of lamb with a kidney skewer perhaps, served with hotpot potatoes, seasonal vegetables and red wine sauce, or spiced pollack fillet with Puy lentil and smoked bacon salsa, roast red pepper sauce, and an oyster and nettle emulsion. Desserts are creative and might include rhubarb and vanilla bavarois with deep-fried custard and roasted rhubarb, or apple jelly with parsnip ice cream and mint syrup.

Times: 12–2/7–9.30, Closed L Sat
Prices: 3 Course Fixed D £24.50–£27
Directions: Approaching Falmouth from Penryn, take left along North Parade. Follow sign to Falmouth Marina and Greenbank Hotel
Parking: 60

New Yard Restaurant

Modern British

Fresh local food in an 18th-century stable yard

Trelowarren, Mawgan, HELSTON,
Cornwall TR12 6AF
Tel: 01326 221595
Email: newyardrestaurant@
trelowarren.com
Website: www.trelowarren.com
Chef: Greg Laskey
Owners: Sir Ferrers Vyvyan

The stunning medieval manor house on the Trelowarren estate near the Lizard peninsula provides the backdrop for this restaurant, which occupies a delightful carriage house in the stable yard next to a gallery, pottery and weaving studio. Most of the ingredients are sourced within a 10-mile radius, with an emphasis on local fish and shellfish, plus game, herbs and fruit supplied by the estate. Typical dishes include fresh fish of the day, a salad of local meat, smoked fish and cheeses, or New Yard burger with fries. Afternoon tea is also served.

Times: 12–2.15/7–9.30,
Closed Mon, D Sun
Prices: 3 Course Fixed D £20
Main £11.50–£15
Directions: 5m from Helston
Parking: 20

Meudon Hotel

Traditional British

Accomplished cooking at a friendly Cornish hotel

MAWNAN SMITH, Cornwall
TR11 5HT
Tel: 01326 250541
Email: wecare@meudon.co.uk
Website: www.meudon.co.uk
Chef: Alan Webb
Owners: Mr Pilgrim

A family of hoteliers now in their fifth generation have run the Meudon for 41 years – their fourth hotel in the village. Dine beneath a fruiting vine in a conservatory restaurant with views of sub-tropical gardens that run down to a private beach. Fresh seafood comes daily from Newlyn, oysters from Helford and cheese from a farm 2 miles away. A classic fixed-price menu of English fare might include grilled fillet of bass with crabmeat and rosemary crust, or pan-sautéed suprême of wild Duchy pheasant over mushroom duxelle with cranberry, in a Merlot and game sauce. Finish with frangipane tart served with a pearl of vanilla ice cream, or choose from the range of Cornish cheeses.

Times: 12.30–2/7.30–9,
Closed Jan
Prices: 3 Course Fixed D £29.50–£33 Main £15–£18
Directions: From Truro take A39 towards Falmouth. At Hill Head rdbt turn left. Hotel is 4m on left
Parking: 30

The Cornish Range

Modern British

Atmospheric restaurant with great seafood

6 Chapel Street, MOUSEHOLE,
Cornwall TR19 6SB
Tel: 01736 731488
Email: info@cornishrange.co.uk
Website: www.cornishrange.co.uk
Chef: Keith Terry
Owners: Richard O'Shea,
Chad James & Keith Terry

A vibrant restaurant with rooms, this former pilchard processing factory has a long-standing association with the sea and, as you would expect, fish and seafood play a prominent part on the menu, with the freshest produce landed locally at Newlyn and delivered daily. Interiors are decorated with earthy tones, with sturdy chairs and tables, soft lighting, flowers and local contemporary artwork giving a rustic, almost Mediterranean feel to the dining room. The accomplished kitchen's modern approach delivers consistency, interest and diner appeal; take roast turbot fillet teamed with a smoked bacon and mussel stew and buttered new potatoes, or perhaps whole grilled Dover sole served with crab and dill butter. Sub-tropical garden for alfresco dining available.

Times: 10.45–2.15/6–9.30
Prices: 2 Course Fixed D £17.50
Main £12–£22.50
Directions: Mousehole is 3m S
from Penzance, via Newlyn. Follow
road to far side of harbour

The Old Coastguard Hotel

Modern British

Popular summer alfresco destination with sea views

The Parade, MOUSEHOLE,
Penzance, Cornwall TR19 6PR
Tel: 01736 731222
Email: bookings@
oldcoastguardhotel.co.uk
Website:
www.oldcoastguardhotel.co.uk
Chef: Barnaby Mason,
Jonathan Blair
Owner: Simon Harris

As the name might suggest, this commanding hotel and restaurant overlooks the sea – but what the name doesn't reveal is how splendid those sea views are and just how quaint and absorbingly lovely the location is, situated in what Dylan Thomas described as 'the most beautiful village in England'. The simple, clean-lined, contemporarily styled décor inside provides a suitably unobtrusive backdrop to enjoy those views over Mount's Bay and the accomplished cuisine. Fish – most from nearby Newlyn – features heavily on a modern menu that might include dishes such as lobster ravioli with a spiced guacamole and tomato and tarragon consommé, or perhaps wild sea bass fillet with a brandade of cod, roasted salsify and broccoli purée.

Times: 12–2.30/6–9.30, Closed
25 Dec (reservations only)
Prices: Main £9.50–£19.50
Directions: A30 to Penzance then
take coast road through Newlyn.
On entering Mousehole hotel is
1st large building on left, after car
park Parking: 15

Margot's

Modern British

Friendly family-run bistro serving good fresh food

11 Duke Street, PADSTOW,
Cornwall PL28 8AB
Tel: 01841 533441
Email: enquiries@margots.co.uk
Website: www.margots.co.uk
Chef: Adrian Oliver
Owners: Adrian & Julie Oliver

There are just nine tables in this cheerful little shop-fronted bistro, with the genial chef-proprietor combining serving and cooking, a formula that's proven both efficient and popular. The restaurant walls are hung with paintings by local artists, most of them for sale. The menu changes constantly according to the local produce available, and includes fish fresh from the harbour. Cooking is accurate and straightforward, with dishes such as Devon smoked duck breast with truffle oil and cucumber, or guinea fowl with spring onion mash and mustard cream sauce. Save room for dessert – sticky toffee pudding with butterscotch sauce perhaps, or saffron-poached pear with jelly and clotted cream.

Times: 12–2/7–9, Closed Nov,
Jan, Sun–Mon
Prices: 3 Course Fixed D £26.95
Main £14–£20
Directions: Telephone for
directions

No. 6

Modern British v

Contemporary surroundings meet modern cuisine

Middle Street, PADSTOW,
Cornwall PL28 8AP
Tel: 01841 532093
Email: enquiries@
number6inpadstow.co.uk
Website: number6inpadstow.co.uk
Chef: Paul Ainsworth,
David Boulton
Owners: Paul Ainsworth,
David Boulton, Chris Mapp,
Molly Christensen

Smack bang next to Rick Stein's Café, No. 6 is certainly a worthy addition to Padstow's culinary heritage. This Georgian townhouse, once known as a smugglers' den, has been stylishly refurbished in contemporary style, with polished-wood tables, smart cutlery and glassware and white linen napkins. Service is friendly and unstuffy, the atmosphere relaxed and informal. Paul Ainsworth (who previously worked at London high-flyer Pétrus) shows his kitchen pedigree in accomplished, attractively presented modern dishes that use top-notch ingredients. Expect a starter like Looe Bay scallops served with Stornoway black pudding, carrots, star anise, vanilla and foraged herbs, perhaps followed up by glazed 'Jimmy Butler' belly pork and cheek, with king prawns, rosemary, butternut squash and shallots.

Times: 6.30–10, Closed Jan,
23-27 Dec, L Easter, Mother's and
Father's Day
Prices: 3 Course Fixed D £25–£30
Main £16.50–£25
Directions: A30 follow signs for
Wadebridge then sign to Padstow

Whitsand Bay Hotel & Golf Club

Modern British

Luxurious setting to dine in style

PORTWRINKLE, Cornwall
PL11 3BU
Tel: 01503 230276
Email:
whitsandbayhotel@btconnect.com
Website:
www.whitsandbayhotel.co.uk
Chef: Tony Farmer
Owners: Chris, Jennifer, John,
Tracey & Paul Phillips

Times: 12–3/7–9
Prices: 3 Course Fixed D £26.95
Directions: A38 towards Plymouth,
continue over Tamar Bridge into
Cornwall. At Trerulefoot rdbt
turn left to Polbathic. After 2m
turn right towards Crafthole,
Portwrinkle Hotel on right

This imposing Victorian stone hotel, resplendent with oak panelling, stained-glass windows and a sweeping staircase, was moved brick by brick from Torpoint and retains many original features. The elegant dining room doesn't disappoint as comfortable high-backed leather chairs and subtle cream and brown décor give a restrained air of luxury. The modern British menu focuses on Cornish local produce including excellent fish from Looe. Starters might include pan-fried Cornish scallops, black pudding, cauliflower fritters and oxtail sauce. Main courses feature the likes of roast saddle of Cornish lamb, leek and pistachio farle, colcannon and glazed carrots and turnips.

St Martin's on the Isle

Modern British v

Highly accomplished cooking in idyllic island paradise

Lower Town, ST MARTIN'S,
Cornwall TR25 0QW
Tel: 01720 422092
Email: stay@stmartinshotel.co.uk
Website:
www.stmartinshotel.co.uk
Chef: Kenny Atkinson
Owners: Peter Sykes

Times: 12.30–2/7–10, Closed
Nov-Feb, L all week
Prices: 3 Course Fixed D £39.50
Directions: By helicopter or boat
from Penzance to St Mary's
- flights from Bristol, Exeter,
Southampton, Newquay or Land's
End. Then 20 min launch transfer
to St Martin's

This waterfront hotel, complete with its own sandy beach, enjoys an idyllic position overlooking the islands of Teän and Tresco. The elegant, first-floor Teän restaurant – decked out in natural tones to reflect the surroundings – has a split-level lounge where guests and diners can also enjoy those stunning views. A highly accomplished kitchen team provides cuisine to match the location, with daily-changing menus driven by the abundance of the local larder, particularly fish and seafood, where freshness, quality and seasonality are showcased. Expect a light modern touch that allows intense, clean flavours to shine in dishes like line-caught sea bass with butter-roasted local lobster and a pea velouté, or perhaps best end and braised shoulder of Bodmin lamb with pea and mint purée, baby leeks and a rosemary sauce, and to finish, maybe an iced apricot parfait with toasted almond ice cream.

Probus Lamplighter Restaurant

Modern British **v**

Local favourite with a sound reputation

Fore Street, Probus, TRURO,
Cornwall TR2 4JL
Tel: 01726 882453
Email: maireadvogel@aol.com
Website:
www.lamplighter-probus.co.uk
Chef: Robert Vogel
Owners: Robert & Mairead Vogel

This veteran establishment has fed locals and tourists alike since the 1950s, and has a reputation for top-notch cooking. It's a warm and cosy venue with log fires, beams, comfy sofas, and two candlelit dining areas – a harmonious mix of old and new. Modern British dishes predominate; expect good-quality local ingredients brought together in combinations designed to tempt and intrigue, while offering clean, balanced flavours. Think line-caught turbot teamed with champ potato and a spinach and wild mushroom broth, or perhaps Gressingham duck breast with crisp confit leg served with a soy, honey, whisky and ginger glaze and Sarladaise potatoes on a fixed-price repertoire.

Times: 7–10, Closed Sun-Mon, L all week
Prices: 3 Course Fixed D £28.90
Directions: 5m from Truro on A390 towards St Austell

St Martin's on the Isle

Tabb's Restaurant

Modern British

Contemporary dining championing local produce

85 Kenwyn Street, TRURO,
Cornwall TR1 3BZ
Tel: 01872 262110
Website: www.tabbs.co.uk
Chef: Nigel Tabb
Owners: Nigel & Melanie Tabb

Husband-and-wife team Nigel and Melanie Tabb have moved their eponymous restaurant to this city-centre location from its previous incarnation (in an old blacksmith's shop on the coast at Portreath) with great effect. The one-time pub has been completely refurbished and now offers a very contemporary vibe; think black slate floors, lilac walls, high-backed leather chairs in cream and lilac, and white linen-clothed tables. The cooking is cranked up a gear too in line with the surroundings, and takes an exciting modern approach with emphasis on using quality local produce (suppliers come credited on the appealing menu). Expect pan-fried loin of wild Cornish venison with creamed leeks, fricassée of wild mushrooms and rosemary jus, or perhaps grilled fillet of brill with home-made black pasta.

Times: 12–2.30/6.30–9.30,
Closed 25 Dec, 1 Jan, 1 wk Jan,
Sun, Mon, L Sat
Prices: Main £12.50–£20.50
Directions: Down hill past train station, right at mini rdbt, 200yds on left

---

Hell Bay

Modern British v

Stunning location, stunning seafood

BRYHER, Isles of Scilly, Cornwall
TR23 0PR
Tel: 01720 422947
Email: contactus@hellbay.co.uk
Website: www.hellbay.co.uk
Chef: Glenn Gatland
Owners: Tresco Estate

Located on the smallest of the Scilly Isles, and perfect for a relaxing break, this hotel overlooks the constantly changing Atlantic seascape. Subtle lighting creates a warm atmosphere in the evenings, and the cream walls are a perfect foil for the original oil paintings. The freshest of island and Cornish produce appears on the menu, from top-quality seafood (perhaps pan-fried sea bream accompanied by a bubble-and-squeak potato cake, creamed Savoy, shallots and a vermouth fondue) to the likes of a rump of lamb served with Parmentier potatoes, baby beetroot and a port and apricot jus. The daily-changing fixed-price menu might also feature a fig and frangipane tartlet with Chantilly cream and red wine reduction to close.

Times: 12–3/6.30–9.30,
Closed Jan-Feb
Directions: Helicopter from Penzance to Tresco, St Mary's. Plane from Southampton, Bristol, Exeter, Newquay or Land's End

The Island Hotel

British
Island living, seafood a speciality

This delightful colonial-style hotel is uniquely situated on its own private island, offering a truly memorable seaside location. Furnished in contemporary style, the restaurant is light and airy, enjoying stunning sea views and forming an elegant backdrop for displays of original art. Carefully-prepared, imaginative modern British cuisine is the order of the day, drawing inspiration from international sources and local ingredients, particularly seafood. Think grilled marinated Scottish salmon with olive oil, basil and caramelised vinegar as a starter, while for mains why not make the most of the superb locally-caught fish and go for poached fillet of brill in red wine with pomme purée and wild mushrooms. For dessert, succumb to warm chocolate tart with orange and mascarpone ice cream, or if you have room, a selection of West Country cheeses with tomato and sultana chutney.

TRESCO, Isles of Scilly,
Cornwall TR24 0PU
Tel: 01720 422883
Email: islandhotel@tresco.co.uk
Website: www.islandhotel.co.uk
Chef: Peter Marshall
Owners: Mr R Dorrien-Smith

Times: 12–2.30/7–9, Closed
5 Nov-1 Mar, L all week
Prices: 3 Course Fixed D £38
Directions: 20 minutes from
Penzance by helicopter

Hell Bay

St Mary's, The Scilly Isles

Holne Chase Hotel

Traditional British NOTABLE WINE LIST

Peaceful country retreat offering fine dining

An original Domesday manor, Holne Chase was used as a hunting lodge for Buckfast Abbey for many years until it became a hotel in 1934. The traditionally styled restaurant offers fantastic views over the lawn and terrace, while in winter log fires burn and candlelight casts a warm glow over the soft décor. Seasonally influenced menus make full use of local ingredients, including fish from Brixham and Looe, local game, home-grown vegetables from the Victorian walled kitchen garden and produce from the owners' farm. Expect clean flavours in appealing dishes, like braised and glazed blade of Widecombe beef with mash potato and honey-glazed vegetables, or perhaps a pan-fried fillet of red mullet layered with ratatouille and served with baby leaf spinach and a balsamic reduction.

Two Bridges Road, ASHBURTON, Newton Abbot, Devon TQ13 7NS
Tel: 01364 631471
Email: info@holne-chase.co.uk
Website: www.holne-chase.co.uk
Chef: Joe Bartlett
Owners: Sebastian & P Hughes
West Country Hotels Ltd

Times: 12–2/7–8.45, Closed L Mon
Prices: 3 Course Fixed D £35
Directions: Travelling N & E, take 2nd Ashburton turn off A38. 2m to Holne Bridge, hotel is 0.205m on right. From Plymouth take 1st Ashburton turn
Parking: 40

Blagdon Manor Hotel & Restaurant

Traditional British v

Confident cooking in delightful Devon retreat

Dating back to the 16th century, this Grade II listed traditional Devon longhouse on the Devon/Cornwall border has been added to over the years and is now a relaxed country-house hotel. Set within 20 acres, the hotel retains many original features, including heavy oak beams, slate flagstones and a freshwater well. Service is formal but friendly and the atmosphere is relaxed. Popular with locals, the main restaurant is candlelit and cosy, and leads through to the light and airy conservatory extension. The traditional British cuisine makes the most of high-quality local produce, as in a tian of Dorset coast crab with smoked salmon roulade and avocado, followed by a tasting of West Country lamb. Tempting desserts include hot chestnut soufflé with cranberry sorbet.

ASHWATER, Beaworthy, Devon EX21 5DF
Tel: 01409 211224
Email: stay@blagdon.com
Website: www.blagdon.com
Chef: Stephen Morey
Owners: Stephen & Liz Morey

Times: 12–2/7–9, Closed 2 wks Oct, 2 wks Jan, Mon (ex residents), L Tue, D Sun
Prices: 3 Course Fixed D £35
Directions: From A388 towards Holsworthy, 2m N of Chapman's Well take 2nd right towards Ashwater. Next right by Blagdon Lodge. Hotel 2nd on right
Parking: 12

Combe House Hotel

Modern British V ▮NOTABLE WINE LIST

Fine-dining experience in Elizabethan mansion

An Elizabethan mansion at the end of a winding mile-long drive provides a grand setting for this country-house hotel. The interior is hugely atmospheric, with ornate ceilings, ancestral portraits, fine antiques, fresh flowers and blazing log fires throughout the panelled public rooms. Dining is equally impressive, with a skilled kitchen using the best of local, seasonal and home-grown produce to underpin contemporary British dishes with French influences. There's a good choice for vegetarians (open cep raviollo with braised baby vegetables and Madeira cream), and vegans are willingly catered for. Brixham fish, bought daily at auction, might include roast monkfish medallions and fresh lobster tail with a foaming bisque sauce, followed by dark Valhrona chocolate tart with lime ice cream.

Gittisham, HONITON, Nr Exeter, Devon EX14 3AD
Tel: 01404 540400
Email: stay@thishotel.com
Website: www.thishotel.com
Chef: Hadleigh Barrett, Stuart Brown
Owners: Ken & Ruth Hunt

Times: 12–2/7–9.30, Closed 2 wks end Jan
Prices: 3 Course Fixed D £39.50
Directions: M5 junct 28/29, A373 to Honiton. Right in High St and follow signs for Sidmouth A375, then brown tourist signs for Combe
Parking: 35

The Quay

Modern British

Exciting food in an 'upturned boat'

Owned by artist Damien Hirst and adorned with his work, you wouldn't expect a traditional restaurant and you won't be disappointed – it's a first-floor dining room in the shape of a fish, but with the appearance of an upturned boat! The white-painted boards, clothed tables, banquette seating and chairs are all pretty straightforward however, as is the traditional British cooking, with a modern emphasis. The Taste Menu also comes with the option of selected wines. If you prefer to get a bit more involved, choose the likes of crab and tarragon risotto to start, followed by Gressingham duck breast with red cabbage, vanilla mash and five-spice jus from the Dining Menu, or maybe salmon Wellington with red onion confit and cauliflower purée.

11 The Quay, ILFRACOMBE, Devon EX34 9EQ
Tel: 01271 868090
Email: info@11thequay.com
Website: www.11thequay.com
Chef: Lawrence Hill-Wickham
Owners: Simon Browne & Damien Hirst

Times: 10–3/6–9.30, Closed 25-26 Dec, 2-25 Jan
Prices: Main £15.95–£22.95
Directions: Follow signs for harbour and pier car park. Restaurant on left before car park

Lewtrenchard Manor

Modern British v

Fine food in Jacobean splendour in a secret valley

LEWDOWN, Okehampton,
Devon EX20 4PN
Tel: 01566 783222
Email: info@lewtrenchard.co.uk
Website: www.lewtrenchard.co.uk
Chef: Jason Hornbuckle
Owners: von Essen Hotels

Once the home of the celebrated hymn writer and novelist Reverend Sabine Baring-Gould of 'Onward Christian Soldiers' fame, this magnificent Jacobean manor house is secreted away in a quiet valley on the fringe of Dartmoor, surrounded by idyllic gardens and peaceful parkland. Seemingly untouched by time, the interior oozes understated charm and wonderful period detail, complete with oak panelling, beautifully ornate ceilings, stained-glass windows, large fireplaces, period furnishings and family portraits. The candlelit, panelled dining room continues the theme – it's a relatively intimate affair overlooking the pretty colonnaded courtyard, bedecked with flowers in summer and providing the perfect setting for alfresco dining. The kitchen takes a modern approach with the focus on top-quality fresh local produce and seasonality, including Devonshire game (you can pre-book a specially prepared Gastro Game Menu), fish from the quayside at Looe, and herbs and vegetables from the hotel's own walled garden. Deceptively and intelligently simple-themed dishes conceal a flair and confidence to allow clear, clean flavours to shine, as in seared scallops with sweet pickled vegetables and mackerel jelly, or perhaps pan-fried pollack with split green pea purée, sautéed scallops, roast salsify and beurre noisette jus with rosemary, while a delightful crème brûlée served with passionfruit and banana sorbet and coconut and butterscotch sauce might prove a fitting dessert. Service is expectedly formal, but with a friendly yet professional approach, while a good-value wine list bolsters the package.

Times: 12–1.30/7–9, Closed L Mon
Prices: 4 Course Fixed D £40
Directions: Take A30 signed Okehampton from M5 junct 31. Continue for 25m and exit at Sourton Cross. Follow signs to Lewdown, then Lewtrenchard
Parking: 40

Dartmoor Inn

Modern British v

Stylish, rural gastro-pub

LYDFORD, Devon EX20 4AY
Tel: 01822 820221
Email: info@dartmoorinn.co.uk
Website: www.dartmoorinn.com
Chef: Philip Burgess &
Andrew Honey
Owners: Karen & Phillip Burgess

Old-fashioned charm at this smart country inn is successfully balanced by modern interior décor, with influences from Sweden and New England. There's a tiny bar, with a log fire and real ales, while the restaurant comprises a series of small dining rooms with well-spaced tables and upholstered chairs. Cooking is consistent and menus are tightly aligned to seasonal produce. A set menu is offered alongside a simpler carte of perennial favourites (fish and chips, or oxtail and Madeira). Impressive dishes include potted pork rillettes, or fillet of organically farmed salmon with crayfish and saffron butter, the organic credentials evident in both the superb colour and flavour of the fish.

Times: 12–2.15/6.30–9.30,
Closed Mon, D Sun
Prices: Main £12.75–£22.50
Directions: On A386, Tavistock
to Okehampton road
Parking: 35

Lynton Cottage Hotel

Modern British v

Stunning views and carefully cooked food

North Walk, LYNTON, Devon
EX35 6ED
Tel: 01598 752342
Email:
enquiries@lynton-cottage.co.uk
Website: www.lynton-cottage.co.uk
Chef: Allan Earl
Owners: Allan Earl,
Heather Biancardi

With the sea pounding 500 feet below, this country house hotel, perched on the hillside, offers understandably marvellous views. The restaurant has a fresh and vibrant feel with colourful artworks and makes the best of the magnificent outlook, while friendly, caring staff encourage relaxation. The short carte is well balanced, with local, organic and seasonal produce making their own positive statement. Expect modern presentations and careful cooking that shows maturity and a deft touch. Start with timbale of crab, crayfish and chorizo with avocado purée, follow with roast rump of lamb with confit of winter greens and a red wine sauce, and round off with hot chocolate fondant with vanilla ice cream and date purée.

Times: 12–2.30/7–9.30, Closed
Dec & Jan
Prices: 4 Course Fixed D
£24.95–£29.95
Directions: M5 junct 27, follow
A361 towards Barnstaple. Follow
signs to Lynton A39. In Lynton turn
right at church. Hotel on right
Parking: 18

Artillery Tower Restaurant

British

Accomplished cooking in a unique waterside setting

Firestone Bay, PLYMOUTH, Devon
PL1 3QR
Tel: 01752 257610
Website: www.artillerytower.co.uk
Chef: Peter Constable
Owners: Peter Constable

This circular 16th-century stone-built tower looks out across Plymouth Sound towards Drakes Island and was once part of the strategic sea defences in Plymouth. The restaurant is simply furnished with wooden tables set against stone walls in a round room. As a champion of local produce, the kitchen offers unfussy dishes prepared with respect for the excellent quality of the ingredients. An impressive starter of roast monkfish with provençale tomatoes and salsa verde might be followed by a tender, accurately cooked loin of venison with celeriac mash and pepper sauce, and crème brûlée with mulled pears for dessert.

Times: 12–2.15/7–9.30, Closed
Xmas & New Year, Sun-Mon, L Sat
Prices: 3 Course Fixed D
£25.50–£35
Directions: 1m from city centre
and train station
Parking: 20

Barbican Kitchen

Modern British

A stylish brasserie serving contemporary food

Plymouth Gin Distillery,
60 Southside Street, PLYMOUTH,
Devon PL1 2LQ
Tel: 01752 604448
Email: info@barbicankitchen.com
Website:
www.barbicankitchen.com
Chef: Lee Holland
Owners: Christopher &
James Tanner

Housed in the Plymouth Gin distillery, the oldest surviving industrial building in Plymouth, the Barbican Kitchen might be a new restaurant but it was in this building that the Pilgrim Fathers ate their last meal before setting sail on the Mayflower. The open-plan kitchen and vibrant brasserie fuse old and new with grey and pink colour schemes and clever use of light and space. Come for lunch, a pre-theatre meal, dinner or a Sunday roast. Dishes are simple and well-executed and the menu offers a flexible feast with main courses like seared calves' liver with confit garlic mash and crispy pancetta or try 'create your own steak' – the cut, sauce and starch.

Times: 12–3/5–10, Closed 25-26
& 31 Dec, D Sun
Prices: Main £6.95–£14.95
Directions: On Barbican, 5 mins
walk from Bretonside bus station

Tanners Restaurant

Modern British v

Exciting, modern cuisine in a medieval setting

Housed in Plymouth's oldest surviving building, this restaurant offers modern style in an impressive and ancient setting that blends flagstones, beams, vaults and an old stone well with contemporary art. Built in 1498, there has been over five hundred years of food history in this building but it's a forgone conclusion that past occupants have never seen such imaginative dishes cooked with so much flair. Think roast partridge served with bubble-and-squeak and a thyme sauce, or perhaps seared fillet of brill teamed with smoked salmon croquettes and a horseradish velouté. This continues to be a popular venue thanks to consistent standards and the owners' TV appearances: the Tanner brothers have also now opened a sibling contemporary brasserie – the Barbican Kitchen (see entry) – on the city's Southside Street.

Prysten House, Finewell Street, PLYMOUTH, Devon PL1 2AE
Tel: 01752 252001
Email: tannerbros@aol.com
Website: www.tannersrestaurant.co.uk
Chef: Christopher & James Tanner
Owners: Christopher & James Tanner

Times: 12–2.30/7–9.30, Closed 25, 31 Dec, 1st wk Jan, Sun & Mon
Prices: 3 Course Fixed D £30
Directions: Town centre. Behind St Andrews Church on Royal Parade

---

The Jack In The Green Inn

Modern British

An informal setting for some serious cooking

A popular dining pub with a great atmosphere, the restaurant at The Jack In The Green Inn is contemporary and relaxed, happily accommodating all comers, whether in jeans or suits. There is great emphasis on using fresh local produce wherever possible and menus change every six weeks to make best use of seasonal fare. Dishes are traditional using French principles of cooking, as in a starter of crispy Crottin Chavignol with beetroot fondant and saffron shallots, a main course of pan-fried fillet of brill with provençale vegetables and pistou and a dessert of apple and Calvados brûlée. There is also a tasting menu, impressive choice of bar meals, and private rooms are available for celebrating special occasions.

ROCKBEARE, Exeter, Devon EX5 2EE
Tel: 01404 822240
Email: info@jackinthegreen.uk.com
Website: www.jackinthegreen.uk.com
Chef: Matthew Mason, Craig Sampson
Owners: Paul Parnell

Times: 12–2/6–9.30, Closed 25 Dec–5 Jan
Prices: 3 Course Fixed D £25
Main £10.50–£19.50
Directions: 3m E of M5 junct 29 on old A30
Parking: 120

Soar Mill Cove Hotel

Soar Mill Cove Hotel

Modern British **v**

Stunning coastal views and superb local ingredients

Set amid spectacular Devon countryside with dramatic sea views, this family-owned hotel's elegant restaurant and lounge make the most of their location in an enviable position above the lovely tranquil cove. Glorious sunsets are just one of the benefits, and the comfortable restaurant has a relaxing neutral-themed décor with polished wood tables, and local artists' paintings on display. The outside terrace is also perfect for alfresco dining. The cooking is ingredient-led, with an emphasis on quality produce from the abundant West Country larder. The accomplished kitchen's approach is via a fixed-price menu and tasting option, and not surprisingly fresh fish and seafood is a speciality on the seasonal menus. Watch the lobster pots being emptied in the bay, and then enjoy the catch served with queen scallops and a saffron reduction, or simply grilled with garlic butter.

Soar Mill Cove, Marlborough,
SALCOMBE, Devon TQ7 3DS
Tel: 01548 561566
Email: info@soarmillcove.co.uk
Website: www.soarmillcove.co.uk
Chef: I Macdonald
Owners: Mr & Mrs K Makepeace
& family

Times: 7.15–9, Closed Jan,
L all week
Prices: 3 Course Fixed D £38
Main £10–£20
Directions: A381 to Salcombe,
through village follow signs to sea
Parking: 25

The Salty Monk

Modern British

Talented cooking in 16th-century ecclesiastical building

Originally a salt house used by Benedictine monks, this roadside building dates from the 16th century and is kept in immaculate condition. The lounge and bar are full of original character, while the L-shaped restaurant at the rear has a more contemporary feel with rich opulent colours; light and airy with views over the award-winning gardens. Tables are well spaced and West Country artists' work adorns the walls. Good use is made of local produce, especially fresh fish with dishes changing regularly to make the best of market availability. Take pan-fried fillets of line-caught sea bass on leek rösti with a casserole of mussels, while alternatives might include a filo parcel of braised ruby red brisket with honeyed root vegetables garnished with sirloin on a red wine and beef jus. Alfresco summer dining proves an added bonus.

Church Street, Sidford,
SIDMOUTH, Devon EX10 9QP
Tel: 01395 513174
Email: saltymonk@btconnect.com
Website: www.saltymonk.co.uk
Chef: Annette & Andy Witheridge
Owners: Annette &
Andy Witheridge

Times: 12–1.30/7–9, Closed 3 wks
Jan, 2 wks Nov, L Sun–Wed
Prices: 3 Course Fixed D £32.50
Directions: From M5 junct 30
take A3052 to Sidmouth, or from
Honiton take A375 to Sidmouth,
left at lights in Sidford, 200yds
on right
Parking: 18

Sidmouth

The Elephant Bar & Restaurant

Modern British

Contemporary harbourside restaurant

Housed in two stylishly converted Georgian houses overlooking the bustling harbour, the Elephant is a smart, contemporary restaurant that continues to impress. There are plans to open a first-floor fine-dining restaurant - The Room - which will showcase the cuisine of Simon Hulstone and his accomplished team, set against the backdrop of spectacular bay views. Downstairs, the more informal Elephant Brasserie, offering simple brasserie dishes, is also to be refurbished. At the stove is a chef with a strong pedigree, whose growing reputation for precise and confident cooking sees the popularity here continue to blossom. Quality West Country ingredients and vibrant flavours shine through well-constructed dishes. Pan-roasted John Dory on parsnip purée with a verjus and spring onion butter sauce, or loin of Haldon Estate venison with vanilla-roasted butternut and baby beetroot jus might jostle for your attention.

3/4 Beacon Terrace, TORQUAY, Devon TQ1 2BH
Tel: 01803 200044
Email: info@elephantrestaurant.co.uk
Website: www.elephantrestaurant.co.uk
Chef: Simon Hulstone
Owners: Peter Morgan

Times: 11.30–2.30/6.30–9.30, Closed 1st 2 wks Jan, Sun (Wed in Feb-Mar)
Prices: 3 Course Fixed D £22.50 Main £13–£22
Directions: Follow signs for Living Coast, restaurant opposite

Orchid Restaurant

Modern British

Superb views combine with superlative cooking

Renowned fine-dining restaurant in a luxurious resort hotel overlooking Torbay. Smartly refurbished in simple style, the Orchid has an upmarket ambience with well-spaced, elegantly clothed tables and stunning views. Service is similarly formal and mainly French, while the food is refreshingly simple and modern. There's a confidence to the cooking that impresses, with dishes notable for both imagination and local produce: you might start with marinated salmon, oyster beignet, pickled cucumber and horseradish cream, and then tuck into a pavé of halibut with vanilla, peas à la française, pomme dauphinoise and a red wine reduction, or South Devon beef fillet with fried organic egg, pomme Pont-Neuf and Dijon foam. Desserts are similarly divine and ancillaries like canapés, bread and petits fours maintain the form through to the end.

Corbyn Head Hotel, Sea Front, TORQUAY, Devon TQ2 6RH
Tel: 01803 296366
Email: dine@orchidrestaurant.net
Website:
www.orchidrestaurant.net
Chef: Daniel Kay & Marc Evans
Owners: Rew Hotels Ltd

Times: 12.30–2.30/7–9.30,
Closed 2 wks Jan, 2 wks Nov,
1wk Apr, Sun-Mon, Tue
Prices: 3 Course Fixed D £35.95
Directions: Follow signs to Torquay seafront, turn right, hotel on right on the edge of Cockington Valley, on seafront
Parking: 50

Mortons House Hotel

Traditional British

Notable dining in Elizabethan surroundings

With the ruins of Corfe Castle as a backdrop and set in delightful gardens and grounds, this impressive Tudor house was built in an 'E' shape to honour Queen Elizabeth I. Beautifully updated and stylishly furnished, it retains a timeless feel. The serene oak-panelled dining room may have formal table settings, but service is friendly and knowledgeable. Classical in style, the British and international cooking is skilful and accomplished, with well-executed dishes utilising produce of high quality, sourced locally whenever possible. Seared scallops with Jerusalem artichoke risotto and hazelnut sauce, or braised shin of beef with parsnip purée, cep boudin and baby beetroot are fine examples of the fare. For dessert, why not try Grand Marnier soufflé, served with a mandarin granité.

East Street, CORFE CASTLE, Wareham, Dorset BH20 5EE
Tel: 01929 480988
Email: stay@mortonshouse.co.uk
Website: www.mortonshouse.co.uk
Chef: Ed Firth
Owners: Mr & Mrs Hageman, Mr & Mrs Clayton

Times: 12–1.45/7–9
Prices: Main £15–£25
Directions: In centre of village on A351
Parking: 40

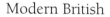

The Coventry Arms

Modern British

Local delicacies in popular country pub

Mill Street, CORFE MULLEN, Dorset BH21 3RH
Tel: 01258 857284
Chef: Ian Gibbs
Owners: John Hugo & David Armstrong Reed

Ideally situated by the river, this converted 15th-century watermill oozes rustic, old world charm with its original flagstone floors, large open fireplace, low ceilings and exposed beams. The fishing paraphernalia reflects the interests of the proprietor, who supplies the menu with local rod-caught trout. Local produce also includes a variety of game when in season and venison, pigeon and pheasant are sourced from local estates. The modern British menu includes the likes of terrine of crab and lobster with langoustines, followed by fillet of John Dory with mussels, clams and saffron chowder.

Times: 12–2.30/6–9.30
Prices: Main £10–£19
Directions: A31 2m from Wimborne
Parking: 50

Sienna Restaurant

Sienna Restaurant

Modern British

Small but beautifully formed restaurant of real class

This unassuming, shop-fronted restaurant at the top of the high street is run by delightful husband-and-wife team, Russell and Elena Brown. With just 15 covers, there's an obvious intimacy; the décor is suitably understated, with a restful 'sienna' colour scheme. Unclothed wooden-topped tables and modern artwork all add to the contemporary feel. Elena delivers a charming front-of-house presence, while Russell's elegant and well-conceived cooking offers beautifully balanced combinations and clear flavours. Underpinned by high-quality produce, the cooking intelligently flourishes without over embellishment. Take a truffle-crusted medallion of Limousin veal served with potato purée, sautéed girolle mushrooms and a summer truffle sauce perhaps followed by a glazed coffee tart with espresso ice cream, maple syrup and walnut sauce. Sit back and enjoy a highly personal and memorable experience.

36 High West Street,
DORCHESTER, Dorset DT1 1UP
Tel: 01305 250022
Email:
browns@siennarestaurant.co.uk
Website:
www.siennarestaurant.co.uk
Chef: Russell Brown
Owners: Russell & Elena Brown

Times: 12–2/7–9.30, Closed 2 wks Feb/Mar, 2 wks Sep/Oct, Sun-Mon
Prices: 3 Course Fixed D £33.50
Directions: Near top of town rdbt in Dorchester

Summer Lodge Country House

Summer Lodge Country House ❀❀❀

Modern British 🍷NOTABLE WINE LIST

Idyllic, intimate retreat meets refined cooking

This former dower house turned country-house hotel can be found nestling in a pretty fold of the Dorset Downs, and there's an air of luxury and quality about the interior, decked out in classic, chintz country-house style. Service is on the formal side (with cheese trolley, dessert wine trolley and roast trolleys for Sunday lunch), but friendly too, while the sommelier brings serious expertise to the classy wine list. The spacious, split-level dining room is elegant with fine table appointments and views over the gardens, while the rose- and honeysuckle-covered gazebo offers an enchanting alfresco summer option. The accomplished kitchen's modern focus, underpinned by a classical theme, uses prime local goods to produce refined dishes with clean, clear flavours. Think Cornish turbot served with confit pork belly, herb-crushed potatoes and creamed leeks. There's a tasting menu option available too.

EVERSHOT, Dorchester, Dorset DT2 0JR
Tel: 01935 482000
Email:
summer@relaischateaux.com
Website:
www.summerlodgehotel.com
Chef: Steven Titman
Owners: Red Carnation Hotels

Times: 12–2.30/7–9.30
Prices: Main £19.95–£26.95
Directions: 1.50m off A37
between Yeovil and Dorchester
Parking: 60

The Museum Inn

Modern British

Great gastro-pub with accomplished cooking

This red-brick and thatched inn stands in an idyllic village setting and makes a charming statement. Sympathetic refurbishment has retained original flagstones and fireplaces, but pastel tones, a light-and-airy feel and stylish country furnishings add a modern, upmarket vibe, albeit with a relaxed, friendly atmosphere. Eat from the same menu in a variety of comfortable bar rooms or in the more formal Shed restaurant at weekends. Driven by judiciously sourced quality produce (meats are fully traceable and traditionally reared, many other ingredients are organic or free range, while fish is delivered daily from the south coast), the accomplished kitchen takes a modern British line; think slow-roast belly pork with cider apple sauce, spinach and colcannon potatoes. There's also a sunny terrace.

FARNHAM, Dorset DT11 8DE
Tel: 01725 516261
Email:
enquiries@museuminn.co.uk
Website: www.museuminn.co.uk
Chef: Daniel Turner
Owners: Mark Stephenson,
Vicky Elliot

Times: 12–2/7–9.30, Closed
25 & 31 Dec
Prices: Main £14–£17
Directions: 12m S of Salisbury, 7m
N of Blandford Forum on A354
Parking: 20

Hotel Alexandra & Restaurant

Modern British v

Attractively presented food in an elegant setting

The plethora of model sailing ships, and marine and local pictures around this Grade II listed hotel leave you in no doubt that this elegant restaurant is by the sea, even if you miss the amazing view over Lyme Bay. The good-value menu also leans towards the sea, though you'll find meaty choices too among the accomplished repertoire. Take grilled whole lemon sole served with a fennel risotto and courgette ribbons, while meat-lovers might opt for roasted rack of lamb with dauphinoise potatoes and a panaché of green vegetables. If you have room, finish with a selection of West Country cheeses served with home-made walnut bread.

Pound Street, LYME REGIS,
Dorset DT7 3HZ
Tel. 01297 442010
Email:
enquiries@hotelalexandra.co.uk
Website:
www.hotelalexandra.co.uk
Chef: Ian Grant
Owners: Kathryn Richards

Times: 12–2/7–8.30, Closed last
Sun before Xmas-end Jan
Prices: 4 Course Fixed D £29.95
Directions: From Bridport take A35
to Lyme Regis, through Chideock,
Marcombe Lake, past Charmouth,
turn left at Charmouth rdbt, follow
for 2m
Parking: 26

Le Petit Canard

Modern British

Pretty village restaurant, delicious dining

Dorchester Road, MAIDEN NEWTON, Dorchester, Dorset DT2 0BE
Tel: 01300 320536
Email: craigs@le-petit-canard.co.uk
Website: www.le-petit-canard.co.uk
Chef: Gerry Craig
Owners: Mr & Mrs G Craig

Set in a conservation area, this pretty, 350-year-old building contains a small but charming dining room with exposed brickwork and old beams highlighted by sensitive décor and lighting and crisp white linen. Service is professional and attentive with a good knowledge of ingredients and the wine list. Fixed-priced menus are modern focused, the repertoire bolstered by daily specials. Expect a loin of local lamb served with pea purée and a lemon garlic reduction, or perhaps pan-fried sea bass with fennel mash and a red wine dressing, while a blueberry crème brûlée might head-up desserts.

Times: 12–2/7–9, Closed Mon, L all week (ex 1st and 3rd Sun in month, D Sun
Prices: 3 Course Fixed D £29–£33
Directions: In centre of Maiden Newton, 8m W of Dorchester

The Green

Modern British

Modern cooking in a popular West Country location

3 The Green, SHERBORNE, Dorset DT9 3HY
Tel: 01935 813821
Website: www.thegreensherborne.co.uk
Chef: Michael Rust
Owners: Michael & Judith Rust

The smart green-painted woodwork makes this attractive old stone Grade II listed property easy to spot. Inside, the character of the old building is retained in the exposed beams, wooden floor and antique wooden tables and chairs. Relaxed, friendly service and atmosphere – there's a real buzz – establishes this as a popular venue. Cooking is modern in style with simple but stylish presentation from a talented team. You might try monkfish tails with salsify, buttered leeks, asparagus, fir apple potatoes, shrimps and basil, and perhaps an iced mascarpone parfait finish, served with honey, toasted almonds and apricots. (The period ground-floor room is complemented by private dining on the first floor.)

Times: 12–2/7–9, Closed 2 wks Jan, 1 wk Jun, 1 wk Sep, BHs, Xmas, Sun-Mon
Prices: 3 Course Fixed D £28.95
Directions: Town centre, just off the A30 at the top of Cheap St.

Perry's Restaurant

Modern British

NOTABLE WINE LIST

Satisfying food in a pleasant harbourside location

4 Trinity Road, The Old Harbour, WEYMOUTH, Dorset DT4 8TJ
Tel: 01305 785799
Email: enquiries@perrysrestaurant.co.uk
Website: www.perrysrestaurant.co.uk
Chef: Andy Pike
Owners: Matt & Liz Whishaw

Set on the charming quayside and occupying a former merchant's house, this long-established and unpretentious eatery specialises in local fish and seafood. Book a window table to watch the maritime manoeuvres in the harbour and tuck into pan-fried scallops with Jerusalem artichoke purée, or Portland crab ravioli with saffron mussel sauce, spring onion and chilli to start. Follow with baked brill, served with warm smoked haddock and potato mousse and dill cream, or perhaps grilled fillet of wild sea bass with crab and potato cake, stir-fried greens with ginger, and lime butter sauce. If you still have room, round off with passionfruit brûlée.

Times: 12–2/7–9.30, Closed 25-27 Dec, 1 Jan, Mon (winter)
Prices: Main £11.50–£18.95
Directions: On western side of old harbour - follow signs for Brewers Quay

---

Cavendish Restaurant

Modern British

Georgian splendour meets highly creative cooking

Dukes Hotel, Great Pulteney Street, BATH, Somerset BA2 4DN
Tel: 01225 787960
Email: info@dukesbath.co.uk
Website: www.dukesbath.co.uk
Chef: Richard Allen
Owners: Alan Brookes, Michael Bokenham

An elegant, charming Grade I listed Georgian building, just a few minutes walk from the city's Pulteney Bridge, Dukes Hotel cuts a stylish stance. The elegant Cavendish Restaurant is at its heart – a garden room, light and airy and understated, with white table linen, botanical prints and attentive and friendly staff. The kitchen delivers a highly creative and appealing menu that reflects the seasons, the modern approach underpinned by a classical theme and driven by high-quality West Country produce, with an emphasis on organic and free-range ingredients. Dishes showcase skill, a clean style and light touch, with excellent presentation and flavour combinations. Take confit belly and roast loin of Chew Valley pork served with black-pudding croquette, or perhaps line-caught sea bass with fennel and crab tortellini, and to finish, a coconut pannacotta with lychee sorbet and roasted banana tart.

Times: 12–2.30/6.30–10, Closed Mon, D Sun
Prices: Main £14.95–£21.95
Directions: M4 junct18 take A46 to Bath. At lights turn left towards A36, at next lights turn right and right again into Gt Pulteney St

The Olive Tree

Modern British 🍷 NOTABLE WINE LIST

Fresh, vibrant cooking in stylish hotel restaurant

The Queensberry is a stylish, 18th-century townhouse hotel hidden in the centre of Georgian Bath. Less formal than the hotel, The Olive Tree restaurant combines Georgian opulence with contemporary simplicity, with wooden floors and soft grey walls hung with modern artworks. Brown leather banquettes and unclothed tables add to the relaxed feel. Attentive service from polo-shirted staff is a real strength. Innovative modern British menus are based on quality ingredients and competent cooking with creative flair. Particular attention is paid to seasonality. Expect a starter of pork belly with plum fritters and pickled vegetables, with mains such as partridge casserole with parsnip purée and chorizo dumplings, or Cornish sea bass on crab, leek and basil risotto. Flavours are well managed and clear throughout.

Queensberry Hotel, Russel Street, BATH, Somerset BA1 2QF
Tel: 01225 447928
Email: reservations@thequeensberry.co.uk
Website: www.thequeensberry.co.uk
Chef: Marc Salmon
Owners: Mr & Mrs Beere

Times: 12–2/7–10, Closed L Mon
Prices: Main £16–£27
Directions: City centre. 100yds N of Assembly Rooms in Lower Lansdown

---

Bruton House Restaurant

Modern British v

Fine dining and contemporary style in historic village

The spacious bar and drawing room area are comfortably furnished with sofas and armchairs so you can relax before or after dining. The elegant restaurant retains character features including a large stone fireplace and oak beams, along with more contemporary touches such as bright artwork, wood flooring, and leather chairs. Service is formal and discreet but also friendly. The accomplished and passionate chef-proprietors are making a strong reputation for themselves here, and there is a clear focus on simple, seasonal cuisine with commitment to local produce. Expect a loin of Clarendon Estate venison served with a thyme and juniper sauce, or line-caught sea bass with fennel and orange sauce, and perhaps poached pear with caramelised brioche and fig sorbet to finish.

High Street, BRUTON, Somerset BA10 0AA
Tel: 01749 813395
Email: info@brutonhouse.co.uk
Website: www.brutonhouse.co.uk
Chef: Scott Eggleton & James Andrews
Owners: Christie-Miller Andrews Ltd

Times: 12–2/7–9, Closed 1-16 Jan, 16 Aug-1 Sep, Sun-Mon
Prices: 3 Course Fixed D £36–£39.50 Main £23.50–£25
Directions: A303, exit signed Bruton, follow signs to Bruton, restaurant at end of High St, opposite pharmacy

Truffles Restaurant

British

Creeper-clad, intimate restaurant

95 High Street, BRUTON,
Somerset BA10 0AR
Tel: 01749 812255
Email: mark@trufflesbruton.co.uk
Website: www.trufflesbruton.co.uk
Chef: Mark Chambers
Owners: Mr & Mrs Chambers

It may have two floors but this pleasant rural restaurant is economical with its tables, no doubt to ensure that guests have a comfortable dining experience and the proprietors have more time to spend giving an extremely friendly service. There's a personal touch to the accomplished cooking too, being intelligently straightforward, and modern British in style that showcases quality local ingredients, seasonality and clear flavours. There could be slow-roasted belly of Bronham pork served with dauphinoise potato and Somerset Pomona sauce, and perhaps a white peach tart Tatin finish, delivered with Somerset dairy cream. Look out for special events.

Times: 12–2/7–9.30, Closed Mon,
L Tue–Wed, D Sun
Prices: 3 Course Fixed D £29.95
Directions: From A303, follow signs to Bruton, in town centre at start of one-way system, on left

---

Woods Bar & Dining Room

British 🍷 NOTABLE WINE LIST

Unpretentious setting for accomplished cooking

4 Banks Square, DULVERTON,
Somerset TA22 9BU
Tel: 01398 324007
Chef: Olivier Certain
Owners: Paddy Groves,
Sally Harvey

Food-lovers are beating a path to this charming pub/restaurant (once an old bakery), where the passion for good food and wine is obvious. Inside, a lovely log fire warms the cosy interior, which is split-level with a popular bar at the top of the restaurant and a refined barn-style feel, with beams, exposed timbers and hand-made wood furniture. Clean, accurate, straightforward modern British cooking with French influences – using quality West Country produce – is the draw here with a great choice of eating options from simple light lunches to the full carte, which might include roast tenderloin of Somerset pork and slow-cooked belly stuffed with boudin noir. Ask for help in choosing a wine and you won't be disappointed either.

Times: 11–3/6–11.30,
Closed 25 Dec
Prices: Main £10–£18.50
Directions: Telephone for directions

The Moody Goose

Modern British v

Historic setting for innovative modern cooking

The Old Priory, Church Square,
MIDSOMER NORTON, Somerset
BA3 2HX
Tel: 01761 416784
Email: info@theoldpriory.co.uk
Website: www.theoldpriory.co.uk
Chef: Stephen Shore
Owners: Stephen Shore

Dating from 1152, The Old Priory is one of the oldest houses in Somerset, complete with inglenook fireplaces, flagstone floors and oak beams. The Moody Goose restaurant is decorated to complement the building's character, period features and contemporary cuisine, with beautiful modern watercolours displayed alongside a 100-year-old cooking range. Menus are designed around fresh seasonal produce, locally sourced where possible, and herbs, fruit and vegetables come from the Priory's own kitchen garden. Dishes are cooked to order with the emphasis on simplicity – maybe pressed terrine of red mullet, aubergine and baby leek with basil vinaigrette, followed by poached rabbit saddle with confit leg, tarragon sauce and herb gnocchi.

Times: 12–1.30/7–9.30, Closed 1 Jan, BHs except Good Friday, Sun
Prices: 3 Course Fixed D £25 Main £18.50–£22
Directions: Down Midsomer Norton High Street, right at lights, right at rdbt in front of church
Parking: 14

Charlton House

Modern British 🍷 NOTABLE WINE LIST

Innovative cuisine in wonderfully elegant surroundings

Charlton Road, SHEPTON MALLET, Somerset BA4 4PR
Tel: 01749 342008
Email: enquiries@charltonhouse.com
Website: www.charltonhouse.com
Chef: Elisha Carter
Owners: Roger Saul

It's no surprise that this chic country-house hotel set in delightful grounds exudes style and atmosphere, owned as it is by the founders of the internationally acclaimed design label Mulberry. Decorated with imagination and theatrical panache, exquisite Mulberry fabrics and leather furnishings abound. The kitchen pays due respect to high-quality local produce, much from the hotel's own organic and rare breed farm, Sharpham Park. Dishes impress with their artistry, flavour and modern stylish presentation; take slow-cooked loin of Sharpham lamb served with braised artichokes and cassoulet of beans, and a fig tart with roasted fig purée and tobacco ice cream finish. A seven-course tasting menu bolsters carte and lunch offerings, while the wine list is extensive and personally chosen by the proprietor. Service is attentive and professional.

Times: 12.30–2.30/7.30–10.15
Prices: 3 Course Fixed D £52.50
Directions: On A361. Hotel is located 1m before Shepton Mallet
Parking: 70

The Priory House Restaurant

Modern British

Enjoyable dining at a smart high-street restaurant

1 High Street, STOKE SUB
HAMDON, Somerset TA14 6PP
Tel: 01935 822826
Email: reservations@
theprioryhouserestaurant.co.uk
Website: www.
theprioryhouserestaurant.co.uk
Chef: Peter Brooks
Owners: Peter & Sonia Brooks

A high-street restaurant decked out in smart contemporary shades of blue and beige. Take a drink in the bar or on the pretty garden terrace in summer, and then move through to the restaurant for some accomplished modern British cuisine, distinguished by technical mastery, attentive sourcing of ingredients, and plenty of flavour. Dishes are gutsy, yet refined, and deliver on both taste and texture: start with pork and herb terrine perhaps, served with beetroot chutney and pickled gooseberries, followed by pink-roasted breast of Devonshire duckling with braised red cabbage and apricot sauce, or Somerset beef fillet with seared foie gras, wild mushrooms, and béarnaise sauce. Wines are supplemented by an interesting selection of Somerset cider brandies.

Times: 12–2/7–9.30, Closed 25
Dec, BHs, 2 wks May, 2wks Nov,
Sun & Mon, L Tue–Fri
Prices: Main £18–£19.50
Directions: 0.50m from A303 in
the centre of Stoke Sub Hamdon

The Willow Tree Restaurant

Modern British

Imaginative regional cooking in a period restaurant

3 Tower Lane, TAUNTON,
Somerset TA1 4AR
Tel: 01823 352835
Chef: Darren Sherlock
Owners: Darren Sherlock
& Rita Rambellas

Having worked for the Roux brothers for 12 years and run a successful restaurant in London, Darren Sherlock delights in sourcing the finest ingredients from local suppliers. Everything is made in-house — stocks, bread, pasta, pastry and ice cream — and is served in the delightful little restaurant in a Grade II listed building, originally a moat house. Exposed beams and an inglenook fireplace set the scene alongside white-linen dressed tables and bright artwork, while outside there is a charming waterside terrace. The menu makes good reading, the kitchen's modern approach underpinned by a classical French influence; take a navarin of lamb served on Puy lentils with confit shallot and sautéed spinach, or chocolate tart with beetroot ice cream to finish.

Times: 6.30–10, Closed Jan,
Aug, Sun-Mon, L all week
Prices: 3 Course Fixed
D £22.50–£29.50
Directions: 200 yds from Taunton
bus station

43

The Tollgate Inn

Modern British

Traditional character inn offering notable cooking

A roadside inn with two restaurant areas – downstairs, once a weavers' shed, is an intimate dining room with a wood burning stove, furnished with pews and cushions. The first-floor restaurant is larger with an open fire, wooden beams and high-backed leather chairs, and was the adjoining Baptist church for the workers. The fine modern British cuisine with Mediterranean influences specialises in local produce and each item is carefully sourced – beef from Church Farm, Broughton Gifford; game from local shoots; village-grown vegetables. All this makes for some excellent dishes, perhaps crab soufflé with bisque sauce to start, followed by roast venison with juniper and port sauce, and sticky toffee pudding to finish.

Ham Green, BRADFORD-ON-AVON, Wiltshire BA14 6PX
Tel: 01225 782326
Email: alison@tollgateholt.co.uk
Website: www.tollgateholt.co.uk
Chef: Alexander Venables
Owners: Alexander Venables & Alison Ward-Baptiste
Times: 11–2.30/5.30–11, Closed Dec 25-26, Mon, D Sun
Prices: Main £13.50–£19.50
Directions: M4 junct 18, take A46 and follow signs for Bradford-on-Avon, take A363 then turn left onto B3105, in Holt turn left onto B3107 towards Melksham. The Tollgate Inn is 100 yds on right
Parking: 40

Castle Combe, Wiltshire

*The Bybrook at
the Manor*

The Bybrook at the Manor

Modern British

Innovative cooking in imposing surroundings

Dating back to the 14th century, this charming manor house sits in peaceful grounds complete with Italian gardens and lawns sweeping down to the Bybrook river. The restaurant boasts many original features including stained-glass windows and carved stonework, and expect artful modern dishes from a kitchen that consistently impresses with its imaginative approach, quality ingredients, and clever combinations. Local produce is used where possible, with vegetable and herbs often arriving courtesy of the manor's gardens. A salad of hand-dived roast scallops is a typical starter, served with salt cod crème fraîche, cauliflower pannacotta and three preparations of lemon, followed by slow-roast belly of Gloucestershire Old Spot pork with prune purée, confit potatoes, red cabbage jam, liquorice jus and crackling, and desserts such as warm caramelised pear tart with caramel ice cream and pear foam.

Manor House Hotel, CASTLE COMBE, Chippenham, Wiltshire SN14 7HR
Tel: 01249 782206
Email: cdumeige@manorhouse.co.uk
Website: www.exclusivehotels.co.uk
Chef: David Campbell
Owners: Exclusive Hotels

Times: 12–2/7–10, Closed L Sat
Prices: 3 Course Fixed D £49.50
Directions: M4 junct 17, follow signs for Castle Combe via Chippenham
Parking: 175

Lucknam Park

Modern British

Faultless country-house cuisine

Set in 500 acres of beautiful grounds, this magnificent Palladian mansion is now a luxury country-house hotel. The formal dining room is an elegant bow-fronted affair with views across the estate. Well-spaced tables, crisp napery and fine glassware fit the bill, as does the attentive and knowledgeable service, while chef Hywel Jones's highly accomplished, clean-cut cooking more than matches expectations. The approach is modern-focused, underpinned by a classical French theme, with emphasis placed on quality seasonal ingredients. The fixed-price menus come dotted with luxury; think caramelised veal sweetbreads, lasagne of wild mushrooms, langoustines, Sauternes and rosemary foam to start, followed by loin of Brecon venison with creamed cabbage, oxtail and sloe gin sauce, or perhaps roast fillet of Cornish John Dory with braised free-range pork belly, white onion purée and baby leeks.

COLERNE, Chippenham, Wiltshire SN14 8AZ
Tel: 01225 742777
Email: reservations@lucknampark.co.uk
Website: www.lucknampark.co.uk
Chef: Hywel Jones
Owners: Lucknam Park Hotels Ltd

Times: 12.30–2.30/6.45–10, Closed L Mon–Sat
Prices: 3 Course Fixed D £60
Directions: From M4 junct 17/ A350 to Chippenham, then A420 towards Bristol for 3m. At Ford turn towards Colerne. After 4m turn right into Doncombe Ln, then 100yds on right
Parking: 80

The Harrow at Little Bedwyn

Modern British v 🍷NOTABLE WINE LIST

Emphasis on stunning seafood and wine

A classy country restaurant of some note, the Harrow's dining room is bright and contemporary, featuring dark-leather high-backed chairs and neatly dressed tables. Service is led by Sue Jones, while husband Roger mans the stove. There's also a small garden at the rear for summer alfresco dining and aperitifs. Roger's approach in the kitchen is modern, with emphasis placed on the freshness and quality of ingredients. Fish is sourced daily from Brixham, while meat is from specialist farmers and butchers and salads and herbs are specifically grown in North Devon. Roger's cooking style is intelligently straightforward, allowing ingredients to shine with clean-cut flavours. Expect the likes of grilled diver-caught scallops with chorizo, pea purée and pea shoots, a roast faggot and caramelised suckling pig with apple sauce and perhaps a treacle tart to finish. There is also an excellent wine list.

LITTLE BEDWYN, Marlborough, Wiltshire SN8 3JP
Tel: 01672 870871
Email: bookings@harrowinn.co.uk
Website: www.harrowinn.co.uk
Chef: Roger Jones
Owners: Roger & Sue Jones

Times: 12–3/7–11, Closed 3 wks Jan & Aug, Mon-Tue, D Sun
Prices: 4 Course Fixed D £40 Main £22–£25
Directions: Between Marlborough and Hungerford, well signed

Compasses Inn

Traditional British

Carefully prepared, quality produce

This 14th-century thatched inn comes brimful of character and atmosphere. Its original beams derive from decommissioned galleons, while stone walls, uneven flagstones and high settle booths add further charm, and, with only two windows, candle-light adds to the timeless quality, punctuated with helpings of relaxed and friendly service. The cooking's certainly not stuck in a time warp though, the modern approach making intelligent use of carefully sourced produce, including fish from Brixham. Menus come chalked up on blackboards, changing regularly to focus on seasonal and local availability; perhaps sea bass fillet with scallops and a crabmeat sauce, or slow-roast pork belly served with an apricot and apple compôte and cider sauce.

LOWER CHICKSGROVE,
Tisbury, Wiltshire SP3 6NB
Tel: 01722 714318
Email: thecompasses@aol.com
Website:
www.thecompassesinn.com
Chef: Ian Evans, Ian Chalmers
Owners: Alan & Susie Stoneham

Times: 12–3/6–11, Closed 25 & 26 Dec
Prices: Main £9–£18
Directions: On A30 W of Salisbury, take 3rd right after Fovant, after 1/2m turn left into Lagpond Lane, Inn 1m on left
Parking: 35

The Wheatsheaf Inn

Modern British

Friendly gastro-pub in tranquil village setting

Dating back to the 14th century, this Cotswold stone pub in the pretty village of Oaksey has a big inglenook fireplace, a wooden-fronted bar and dark beams. The restaurant has a light, modern feel with sisal carpet, wooden tables and painted walls decorated with wine racks and jars of preserved vegetables. Modern British pub food is the order of the day, from a kitchen team with a strong commitment to local produce. Starters include salmon fishcake with a sweet-and-sour sauce, which may be followed by guinea fowl with fondant potato and bacon, or sea bass with crab and basil terrine, and a mussel and herb sauce.

Wheatsheaf Lane, OAKSEY,
Wiltshire SN16 9TB
Tel: 01666 577348
Chef: Tony Robson-Burrell/
Guy Opie
Owners: Tony & Holly Robson-Burrell

Times: 12–2/6.30–9.30,
Closed Mon
Prices: Main £10.25–£17.95
Directions: Off A429 towards Cirencester, near Kemble
Parking: 15

The Pear Tree at Purton

Modern British

Charming Cotswold-stone hotel with superior food

Church Fnd, PURTON, Swindon,
Wiltshire SN5 4ED
Tel: 01793 772100
Email: stay@peartreepurton.co.uk
Website:
www.peartreepurton.co.uk
Chef: Alan Postill
Owners: Francis and Anne Young

Surrounded by rolling Wiltshire farmland, this 15th-century former vicarage, once belonging to the unique twin towers church of St Mary's in Purton, looks out over 7.5 acres of well-tended gardens. The airy conservatory restaurant perfectly complements the serene setting, with fine linen and elegant tableware adding to the air of genteel refinement. The kitchen takes a suitably modern approach using quality ingredients – many locally sourced – cooked simply, marrying flavours with obvious expertise and flair. Take a starter of crispy sea bass with chilli and peanut salad, followed by steamed halibut with crispy bacon and an olive and caper salsa, or perhaps a rack of lamb partnered with a tomato and basil jus, and to finish, a prune and almond tart served with caramel ice cream.

Times: 12–2/7–9.15, Closed 26-30 Dec, L Sat
Prices: 4 Course Fixed D £34.50
Directions: From M4 junct 16, follow signs to Purton. Turn right at Spa shop, hotel 0.25m on right
Parking: 70

George & Dragon

Modern British

Charming old pub with a relaxed atmosphere

High Street, ROWDE, Wiltshire
SN10 2PN
Tel: 01380 723053
Email: thegandd@tiscali.co.uk
Website: www.
thegeorgeanddragonrowde.co.uk
Chef: Christopher Day
Owners: Mr & Mrs Hale &
Mr C Day

This charming old inn mixes original features with a relaxed gastro-pub atmosphere. With dark wooden beams throughout, a log fire strikes a homely note in the bar, while the restaurant is decked out with wooden furniture and simple table appointments. The carte is supplemented by blackboard specials, plus a separate fish menu featuring the likes of whole grilled lemon sole, or Scottish langoustines with mayonnaise. Expect mains such as rack of lamb with garlic mash, or warm duck breast salad with onion marmalade and sautéed potatoes, then finish with an old fashioned pudding: treacle tart with clotted cream for example, or chocolate bread-and-butter pudding.

Times: 12–3/6–11, Closed 1-8 Jan, Mon, D Sun
Prices: Main £9.50–£18.50
Directions: 1.50m out of Devizes towards Chippenham on A342
Parking: 12

Kent countryside

South East
England

The Fat Duck

Modern British v 🌹 NOTABLE WINE LIST

The epitome of contemporary dining

Who could have predicted that the well-groomed, Thames-side village of Bray would become home to British gastronomy. Heston Blumenthal's Fat Duck is leading the way in innovative gastronomy. Two small cottages on the main village road seem an unassuming and unlikely international destination of culinary discovery and home to one of the world's best chefs, but The Fat Duck oozes understated quality and chic. Oak beams and low ceilings are complemented by modern art and coloured-glass screens, which combine effortlessly with the Tudor building. Comfortable chairs and white napery are backed by impeccable service (a real feature of The Fat Duck experience), which is professional, enthusiastic and friendly – with staff eager to share their knowledge without a hint of condescension. Blumenthal is a chef par excellence as well as a true culinary pioneer, and a leading exponent of the scientific approach to cuisine. Whilst there's nothing bizarre about the ingredients he uses, it's this combination of flavours that sometimes raises eyebrows or catches the headlines; witness a new tasting-menu dish called Sound of the Sea (a seafood offering eaten while listening to an iPod playing just that). But it's not just the exciting combinations that are a hallmark of this stunning experience, it's Heston's absolute precision and clarity of flavour and balance that sets him apart. For the full-on show, look to the tasting menu with its eight or so courses and various head-turning tasters and inter-courses, though there is also a good-value lunch option and carte, which might deliver a best end of lamb with purée of onion and thyme, hot pot of lamb neck, sweetbread and oyster, or perhaps a galette of rhubarb with neroli-scented yogurt mousse, crystallised coconut and rhubarb sorbet. Wow! An extensive wine list rounds off the package in style. So just sit back and enjoy the journey with a culinary alchemist at the helm.

High Street, BRAY,
Berkshire SL6 2AQ
Tel: 01628 580333
Website: www.fatduck.co.uk
Chef: Heston Blumenthal
Owners: Fat Duck Ltd

Times: 12–1.45/7–9.45, Closed 2 wks at Xmas, Mon, D Sun
Prices: Fixed D £80–£84.75
Directions: M4 junct 8/9 (Maidenhead) take A308 towards Windsor, turn left into Bray. Restaurant in centre of village on right

Hinds Head Hotel

British

Fine British pub food, destination dining

The Hinds Head wants to be a local village pub, but as part of Heston Blumenthal's stable it will always invite interest from much further afield as gastronomes beat a path to its 15th-century door. A fascinating place with uncertain origins, perhaps a former hunting lodge or guest house for the local Abbot, the inn was no stranger to celebrity in the past with guests including Prince Philip on his stag night. The main dining area on the ground floor is a light restaurant, and there's plenty of oak panelling, beams, leather chairs and real fires too. The menu is quite different to that at the Fat Duck – make no mistake, this is pub food – with traditional British dishes like pea and ham soup, oxtail and kidney pudding, Lancashire hot pot, and puddings like sherry trifle, treacle tart and banana Eton Mess.

High Street, BRAY, Berkshire SL6 2AB
Tel: 01628 626151
Email: info@hindsheadhotel.co.uk
Website: www.hindsheadhotel.co.uk
Chef: Heston Blumenthal
Owners: Heston Blumenthal & James Lee

Times: 12–2.30/6.30–9.30, Closed 25-26 Dec, D Sun
Prices: Main £10.50–£18.50
Directions: M4 junct 8/9, at rdbt take exit to Maidenhead Central, next rdbt take exit Bray & Windsor, after 0.50m take B3028 to Bray

---

The Crab at Chieveley

Modern British v

Award-winning seafood restaurant

A deceptively simple cooking style belies the abundance of skill to be found in the kitchen at this former downland pub, but don't be fooled – expect top-notch cooking conjured from the freshest fish and seafood available. Tastefully transformed into a well-appointed hotel, there's a cosy bar and two dining areas: a formal room with red and chocolate coloured leather seating, and a more relaxed space with polished wooden tables. This former winner of the AA award for best seafood offers an extensive menu that will delight fish fanciers. Typically dishes include baked monkfish with lentils and pancetta, whole plaice with caper beurre noisette, or roast turbot with red wine jus. Finish with vanilla pannacotta and passionfruit jelly with a refreshing blackcurrant sorbet.

Wantage Road, CHIEVELEY, Berkshire RG20 8UE
Tel: 01635 247550
Email: info@crabatchieveley.com
Website: www.crabatchieveley.com
Chef: David Horridge
Owners: David & Jackie Barnard

Times: 12/11
Prices: 3 Course Fixed D £29.50–£33
Directions: M4 junct 13 to Chieveley, School Rd to B4494, turn right to Wantage
Parking: 80

Sir Christopher Wren's House

Sir Christopher Wren's House

Modern British

Relaxed fine dining with unbeatable views

Wren himself may well have approved of the Thames-side views from Strok's Restaurant overlooking Eton Bridge at his one-time home; watch the sun set behind the riverbank trees from the champagne terrace. Soft downlights, flickering candles, modern and contemporary with a hint of traditional elegance is the style. The European menu with Mediterranean twists takes a modern approach with classical influences. Quality ingredients meet skilful, balanced dishes with understated presentation; think a tian of goat's cheese and roasted pepper with shaved truffle salad to open, perhaps followed by a seared scallop and crayfish risotto with Avruga caviar, or noisettes of lamb served with confit celeriac and carrots and veal sweetbreads.

Thames Street, WINDSOR,
Berkshire SL4 1PX
Tel: 01753 861354
Email:
reservations@wrensgroup.com
Website:
www.sirchristopherwren.co.uk
Chef: Stephen Boucher
Owners: The Wrens Hotel Group

Times: 12.30–2.30/6.30–10
Prices: 3 Course Fixed D £28.80
Main £18.75–£23.25
Directions: Telephone for directions
Parking: 14

Villiers Hotel Restaurant & Bar

Modern British

Stylish brasserie-style restaurant

3 Castle Street, BUCKINGHAM,
Buckinghamshire MK18 1BS
Tel: 01280 822444
Email:
reservations@villiershotels.com
Website: www.oxfordshire-hotels.
co.uk
Chef: Paul Stopps
Owners: Oxfordshire Hotels Ltd

Originally a coaching inn dating back to Cromwellian times, the hotel comes steeped in history and has been tastefully modernised over the years. A completely new look sees the restaurant achieving a modern, brasserie style and vibe. Simple modern cooking to match provides some classics, alongside new and interesting combinations, with pasta and rice options available as starter or main portions. Expect to kick off with the likes of crispy pork belly teamed with seared scallops and apple purée or a classic chicken liver and foie gras parfait with pear chutney and sultana toast, perhaps followed by seared lamb's liver served with celeriac purée, smoked bacon and Savoy cabbage. Dessert might feature an Indian vanilla crème brûlée or prune and Armagnac tart with praline cream.

Times: 12–2.30/6–9.30
Prices: Main £8.95–£21.50
Directions: Town centre - Castle Street is to the right of Town Hall near main square
Parking: 46

Annie Baileys

Modern British

Ever-popular rural restaurant

Chesham Road, Hyde End,
GREAT MISSENDEN,
Buckinghamshire HP16 0QT
Tel: 01494 865625
Email: david@anniebaileys.com
Website: www.anniebaileys.com
Chef: Andrew Fairall
Owners: Open All Hours (UK) Ltd

Named after a local Victorian landlady, this popular rural restaurant is an informal and friendly place to take a relaxing meal or enjoy a drink at the bar or by the fire. The interior has a country-cottage feel, combined with a Mediterranean colour scheme. The Mediterranean theme extends to the food, presented on a brasserie-style menu with something for everyone. Starters double as light bites and might include slow-roasted tomatoes with grilled goat's cheese or honey-roast figs in Parma ham. Follow with sea bass served with a crayfish risotto, and be sure to leave room for desserts such as Annie Baileys 'Baileys' crème brûlée or caramel fudge brownie with honeycomb ice cream.

Times: 12–2.30/7–9.30,
Closed D Sun
Prices: Main £10.50–£18.95
Directions: Off A413 at Great Missenden. On B485 towards Chesham
Parking: 40

Oak Room at Danesfield House

Oak Room at Danesfield House ❀❀❀

Modern British v

Stunning cuisine in fairytale surroundings

Overlooking the Thames in a fantastic location, Danesfield, with its castellated towers, tall chimneys and raised terraces, has all the hallmarks of a fairytale castle – while the Oak Room Restaurant, redesigned by Anouska Hempel, is all luxury and relaxation. Nothing prepares you, however, for the stunning culinary experience, where new chef Adam Simmonds shows off his fine kitchen pedigree with top-quality, innovative cooking using the best seasonal produce and some serious technical skill. Clean flavours and presentation allow each dish a unique taste experience; take pan-fried fillet of cod served with parsnip purée, braised salsify, razor clams, curry jelly and goat's cheese, and to finish, perhaps a wild strawberry mousse with ice cream, nettle pannacotta, meringue and crystallized nettle leaves. Once you've eaten here, you'll certainly want to repeat the experience.

Henley Road, MARLOW,
Buckinghamshire SL7 2EY
Tel: 01628 891010
Email:
adooley@danesfieldhouse.co.uk
Website:
www.danesfieldhouse.co.uk
Chef: Adam Simmonds

Times: 12–2/7–9.30, Closed
Xmas, New Year, BHs, Sun,
L Mon–Wed, D Sun
Prices: 3 Course Fixed D £55
Directions: M4 junct 4/A404
to Marlow. Follow signs to
Medmenham and Henley. Hotel
is 3m outside Marlow
Parking: 100

Starr Restaurant

Starr Restaurant

Modern British **v**

Skilful cooking in a stable conversion

Market Place, GREAT DUNMOW,
Essex CM6 1AX
Tel: 01371 874321
Email:
starrrestaurant@btinternet.com
Website: www.the-starr.co.uk
Chef: Mark Pearson
Owners: Terence & Louise George

The Starr is a timber-framed, 15th-century coaching inn
overlooking the village market place. Billed as a restaurant with
rooms, it has built up a loyal following for its smart décor, good
food and friendly service. The restaurant occupies a converted
stable block to the rear of the main building and, together with the
conservatory, makes an excellent venue for serious dining. A skilful
kitchen team produces modern British dishes with some French
influences. House favourites include pan-seared Lyme Bay scallops
with parsnip purée and parsnip crisps, and Suffolk pork belly 'four
ways' with caramelised endive, fondant potato and apple velouté.
Another multi-faceted dish is a pudding of lemon 'three ways'.

Times: 12–1.30/7–9.30, Closed
27 Dec-6 Jan, D Sun
Prices: 3 Course Fixed D £45
Directions: M11 junct 8, A120
7m E towards Colchester. In town
centre
Parking: 16

The Woolpack

Modern British

Modern dining in traditional inn

There has been a Woolpack Inn since the 1100s, but the current building is 19th century. A contemporary interior features polished oak floors, oak beams, ivory-coloured half panelling and luxurious leather seating. Smoked glass, wooden blinds and 1950s fashion photographs complete the look. The kitchen brigade delivers accomplished modern British cooking offering clean, clear flavours from excellent produce. Hand-dived scallops, nicely caramelised, are served on a full-flavoured pea purée with mixed leaves drizzled with truffle oil, followed by braised shin of beef with stilton dumpling and port jus. Finish with freshly baked rich chocolate fondant and home-made vanilla ice cream.

Mill Green Road, INGATESTONE, Essex CM4 0HS
Tel: 01277 352189
Email:
info@thewoolpack-fryerning.co.uk
Website:
www.thewoolpack-fryerning.co.uk
Chef: Ben Horle
Owners: John & Lisa Hood

Times: 12–4/7–12.30, Closed 2 wks in Aug, 2 wks after Xmas, Mon, L Tue & Sat, D Sun
Prices: 3 Course Fixed D £20.95 –£29.95 Main £12.95–£16.95
Directions: M25 junct A12, between Brentwood & Chelmsford
Parking: 20

Rhinefield House

Modern British **v**

Impressive dining in magnificent surroundings

The Italianate ponds and ornamental gardens are nearly as stunning as the Alhambra and Parliament inspired décor at this impressive baronial-style hotel. The elegant Armada Restaurant is richly furnished and features a huge Elizabethan-style carved fireplace, which took several years to complete. Imaginative modern British and European dishes range from New Forest fur and feather game pie to Poole scallops with warm smoked salmon, artichoke stew and sweet curry emulsion, to start. Main courses include a tasting of free-range local lamb with thyme galette, or pan-fried John Dory with clam bubble-and-squeak. Earl Grey tea ravioli with frozen whisky mousse and almond cake makes an intriguing dessert. There is a delightful terrace for alfresco dining.

Rhinefield Road, BROCKENHURST, Hampshire SO42 7QB
Tel: 01590 622922
Email:
info@rhinefieldhousehotel.co.uk
Website: www.
rhinefieldhousehotel.co.uk
Chef: Kevin Hartley
Owners: Hand Picked Hotels Ltd

Times: 12.30–2/7–9.30
Prices: 3 Course Fixed D £37.45
Directions: From M27 junct 1 take A337 to Lyndhurst, follow A35 W towards Christchurch. 3.50m from Lyndhurst, turn left into the Forest at sign for Rhinefield House. Hotel 1.50m on right
Parking: 150

The Star Inn Tytherley

Modern British

English inn with modern, heart-warming food

This 16th-century coaching inn has a quintessentially English feel with views of the village cricket green, a pretty courtyard garden and a traditional theme to the décor. The atmosphere is cosy, with warm colours, exposed beams and open log fires, while the restaurant occupies a separate wing and is a light and airy space with smartly dressed tables and subdued lighting. Modern and imaginative menus come underpinned by traditional and classic dishes, delivered in refined mode with plenty of care taken over presentation. Fresh local produce with a strong emphasis on fish and game is the style; take poached halibut fillet with red rice, braised fennel and sauce gribiche, or supreme of guinea fowl and confit leg with bubble-and-squeak, while desserts could deliver glazed lemon tart with raspberry coulis.

EAST TYTHERLEY, Nr Romsey, Hampshire SO51 0LW
Tel: 01794 340225
Email: info@starinn-uk.com
Website: www.starinn-uk.com
Owners: Allan & Lesley Newitt

Times: 11–2.30/6–11, Closed Mon winter, D Sun
Prices: Main £13.50–£17.95
Directions: Romsey A3057 N, left to Awbridge, Kents Oak, through Lockerley on right
Parking: 60

Hour Glass

Modern British

Rustic charm blended with modern designs

From the outside it epitomises rural England, with its low walls and thatched roof. Inside, though, it's a surprising mixture of styles: a modern bar area, with smart black leather sofas and informal tables attracting casual diners, leads into a warren of beamed alcoves that show the building's 16th-century origins. A huge inglenook fireplace dominates, and tables set in nooks and crannies ensure privacy. Tantalising dishes from every corner of the globe appear on menus that are full of interest. Despite the wide scope of the dishes, most ingredients are firmly local, with traditional vegetable paella a typical cosmopolitan offering.

Burgate, FORDINGBRIDGE, Hampshire SP6 1LX
Tel: 01425 652348
Email: hglassrestaurant@aol.com
Website: thehourglassrestaurant.co.uk
Chef: Daniel Towell
Owners: Hannah & Charlotte Wiggins

Times: 12–2/7–10, Closed 25 Dec, 1 Jan, Mon (incl BHs), D Sun
Prices: Main £14.95–£20.95
Directions: 1m from Fordingbridge on A338 towards Salisbury
Parking: 30

Chewton Glen Hotel

Chewton Glen Hotel

Modern British **v**

Impeccable, Palladian style country-house dining

Set in landscaped grounds, this outstanding, internationally renowned country-house hotel is a haven of luxury and tranquillity. The renowned and stylish restaurant has a contemporary feel, while the chic conservatory impresses with a tented ceiling. Plenty of luxury also graces the menus, and carefully sourced, top-quality produce is the key to success here; the kitchen's suppliers are chronicled at the back of the menu. Classical dishes form the backbone, with the accomplished, refined cooking delivering clear, clean and well-balanced flavours on a repertoire of fixed-priced options and five-course Menu Gourmand. Start with a terrine of game and follow with turbot fillet served with horseradish mashed potato, baby onions, white wine jus and truffle cream or Quantock duck breast with parsnip purée salsify, butternut squash and blueberry sauce. The dazzling wine list has more than 500 bins.

Christchurch Road, NEW MILTON,
Hampshire BH25 6QS
Tel: 01425 275341
Email:
reservations@chewtonglen.com
Website: www.chewtonglen.com
Chef: Luke Matthews
Owners: Chewton Glen Hotels Ltd

Times: 12.30–1.45/7.30–9.30
Prices: 3 Course Fixed D 62.50
Main £24.50–£32.50
Directions: Off A35 (Lyndhurst)
turn right through Walkford,
4th left into Chewton Farm Rd
Parking: 150

JSW

Modern British **v**

Quality and élan are the bywords of this restaurant

There's a relaxed, contemporary vibe in this former pub, with light-oak beams, cream walls – still featuring those thoughtful line drawings of nudes (by the chef-proprietor's sister) – and well-spaced tables. Service is skilled and attentive with a young, knowledgeable team on hand. Quality ingredients and superb flavours are at work throughout, with Jake's deceptively simple, sophisticated modern approach well thought out. There's bags of self-assured confidence and great balance of flavour, delivered by set menu, carte and eight-course tasting option. Take scallops with pea purée and bacon to start, perhaps followed by turbot with asparagus, wild garlic pesto and tagliatelle, or loin of lamb with root vegetable and Hampshire hot pot, while salted caramel mousse with hazelnut praline might head-up desserts. One to watch, with an inspired kitchen at work in their new surroundings.

20 Dragon Street, PETERSFIELD, Hampshire GU31 4JJ
Tel: 01730 262030
Chef: Jake Watkins
Owners: Jake Watkins

Times: 12–1.30/7–9.30, Closed 2 wks Jan & summer, Sun-Mon
Prices: Fixed D £32.50–£42.50
Directions: A3 to town centre, follow signs to Festival Hall car park. Restaurant 80yds from car park
Parking: 19

Tylney Hall Hotel

Bertie's

Modern British

Lively converted inn with French atmosphere

80 The Hundred, ROMSEY,
Hampshire SO51 8BX
Tel: 01794 830708
Email: sales@berties.co.uk
Website: www.berties.co.uk
Chef: David Heyward
Owners: David Birmingham

This converted, one-time coaching inn continues to offer a relaxed, bistro-style experience, with its friendly and attentive front-of-house team proving a real bonus. There's a warm, cosy character to the original building, while a conservatory extension at the back adds a contemporary edge. Original artworks and mirrors decorate light walls, while polished-wood furniture and blue carpet add to the comforts. The kitchen's modern British cooking ideally suits the surroundings, with clear-flavoured, cleanly presented, straightforward dishes. The choice might include a braised blade of beef with roasted onion mash and braised chicory, and perhaps a fig and almond tart with clotted cream and red wine syrup to finish.

Times: 12–2.30/6.30–10, Closed
26-30 Dec, BHs, Sun
Prices: 3 Course Fixed D £15.95
Main £11.95–£18.95
Directions: 200yds from
Broadlands' gate in town centre
Parking: 10

Tylney Hall Hotel

Modern British

Smart formal dining in opulent surroundings

ROTHERWICK, Hook, Hampshire
RG27 9AZ
Tel: 01256 764881
Email: sales@tylneyhall.com
Website: www.tylneyhall.com
Chef: Stephen Hine
Owners: Elite Hotels

An imposing, 19th-century, red-brick mansion set in 66 acres of grounds, with fine Gertrude Jekyll gardens that include cascading waterfalls, ornamental lakes and woodland walks. Within, expect oak panelling, ornate ceilings, log fires, an old-fashioned style of service and a sense of grandeur, with the glass-domed Oak Room restaurant overlooking the garden. The modern cooking focuses on quality (and often luxurious) British produce, dishes have a refreshing simplicity, based on classical roots with an innovative modern twist. Think porcini ravioli on creamed Savoy cabbage, followed by breast of chicken with truffle mousse. Finish with pomegranate pannacotta. Daily dish from the carving trolley is a must.

Times: 12.30–2/7–10
Prices: 3 Course Fixed D £35
Main £23–£27
Directions: M3 junct 5 take A287
(Newnham). From M4 junct 11
take B3349 (Hook), at sharp bend
left (Rotherwick), left again & left
in village (Newnham) 1m on right
Parking: 150

The Essex

Modern British v

Thatched restaurant with modern seasonal cooking

High Street, GODSHILL,
Isle of Wight PO38 3HH
Tel: 01983 840232
Email:
info@godshillparkfarm.uk.com
Website:
www.godshillparkfarm.uk.com
Chef: Steve Harris
Owners: K A & M J Domaille

Set in the picturesque village, this Grade II listed cottage comes thatched and redecorated. There are leather sofas in the lounge area, while wooden flooring, upholstered chairs and white linen characterise the comfortable, light and airy dining area. Plain walls are hung with local prints and there's a patio area to the rear. Service is suitably relaxed and friendly. The kitchen takes a modern line with its seasonal-changing, fixed-price menus making the best of local organic produce. Lunch is bolstered by a light-bite medley, while dinner cranks things up a gear, with the likes of seared Aberdeen Angus fillet and braised shin served with summer greens, dauphinoise and Madeira jus, or venison Wellington, with perhaps a chocolate fondant tart finish, accompanied by champagne sorbet and iced doughnuts.

Times: 12–4/6–11, Closed L Mon–Tue (winter), D Sun
Prices: 3 Course Fixed D £32
Directions: On A3020 6m S of Newport

The Royal Hotel

Modern British

Sophisticated cuisine in smart surroundings

Belgrave Road, VENTNOR,
Isle of Wight PO38 1JJ
Tel: 01983 852186
Email: enquiries@royalhoteliow.co.uk
Website: www.royalhoteliow.co.uk
Chef: Alan Staley
Owners: William Bailey

High ceilings, crystal chandeliers, heavily draped curtains, large oil paintings and candles add to the stately, old-fashioned ambience of this Victorian seaside hotel. It is quite formal, with a sophisticated atmosphere and smartly attired staff. Modern British and French influenced cuisine makes the best use of fine local produce like asparagus from the Arreton Valley, local Ventnor lobster and Godshill free-range chicken. You could try a starter of chicken liver and foie gras parfait, served with apricot and ginger chutney. Main courses might take in pancetta-wrapped monkfish with wild mushroom, chorizo and pea risotto or chargrilled beef fillet with Madeira sauce, with hot chocolate fondant among the puddings.

Times: 12–1.45/6.45–9, Closed 2 wks Jan, Closed L Mon–Sat in Apr–Oct
Prices: 3 Course Fixed D £35–£50
Directions: On A3055 coastal road, into Ventnor. Follow the one way system, turn left at lights into Church St. At top of hill bear left into Belgrave Rd, hotel on right
Parking: 50

The George Hotel and Brasserie

Modern British

Charming restaurant with great local reputation

This Cranbrook landmark combines period and contemporary style, and has a long tradition of hospitality dating back to the 14th century and lists Queen Elizabeth I among its former guests. The tempting menu can be taken either in a vibrant new brasserie overlooking the local church, or in the more formal restaurant, a striking contemporary room with opulent chandeliers, an imposing inglenook fireplace and comfortable leather chairs. Ingredients come courtesy of the Kent and Sussex coast and countryside wherever possible, and arrive at the table in tasty modern British dishes such as devilled mackerel with crushed new potatoes and a tomato and mint salad, or pot-roasted Park Farm lamb with braised couscous, Mediterranean vegetables and yoghurt.

Stone Street, CRANBROOK, Kent TN17 3HE
Tel: 01580 713348
Email: reservations@thegeorgehotelkent.co.uk
Website: www.thegeorgehotelkent.co.uk
Chef: Paolo Fernandes
Owners: Mark & Sara Colley

Times: 12–3/6–9.30, Closed 25-26 Dec
Prices: Main £9.50–£17
Directions: A229 into Cranbrook and Stone St, on left.
Parking: 12

Oakley & Harvey at Wallet's Court

Modern British

Historic manor not far from the white cliffs

Set in pretty gardens in a peaceful location on the outskirts of town, this country-house hotel is based around a lovely Jacobean manor. The cosy lounge bar has a buzzy atmosphere, while the restaurant – a dinner-only affair – is formally laid with white linen and high-backed chairs, set to a backdrop of oak beams, inglenook fireplaces and evening candlelight. Walls are hung with original art, and there are carved pillars dating back to 1627. But there's nothing remotely historic about the cooking, the accomplished modern British repertoire – driven by a commitment to quality local seasonal produce, including ingredients from the hotel's kitchen garden – comes fashionably dotted with European influences. Take locally-landed cod with aubergine caviar, chorizo and sautéed potatoes, or perhaps a rack of Kentish lamb served with ratatouille, rosemary and fondant potatoes.

Wallet's Court, West Cliffe, St Margarets-at-Cliffe CT15 6EW
Tel: 01304 852424
Email: dine@wallettscourt.com
Website: www.wallettscourt.com
Chef: Stephen Harvey
Owners: Gavin Oakley

Times: 12–2/7–9, Closed 25–26 Dec, L Mon–Sat
Prices: Fixed D £40
Directions: M2/A2 or M20/A20, follow signs for Deal (A258), 1st right for St Margarets–at–Cliffe. Restaurant 1m on right.
Parking: 50

Read's Restaurant

Read's Restaurant

Modern British ▮ NOTABLE WINE LIST

Distinctive cuisine in an elegant Georgian manor house

Read's Restaurant serves distinctive cooking of passion and simplicity using home-grown herbs and vegetables, local game and fresh fish. Modern British cuisine is the order of the day, with dinner a grander affair than lunch. The menu offers a choice of dishes with detailed descriptions and quotations to accompany them, like the words of Miss Piggy – 'Never eat more than you can lift'. With that in mind, you could try the seven-course tasting menu, or order from the carte. Expect the likes of roasted cannon of Kentish lamb served with a hazelnut crust, braised button onions, dauphinoise potatoes and a thyme jus, while a roasted pineapple tart with a peppered coulis, vanilla caramel and pineapple sorbet might catch the eye at dessert. The equally accomplished wine list has an extensive choice (over 250 wines) with many heavyweights and a good selection by the glass, too.

Macknade Manor, Canterbury
Road, FAVERSHAM, Kent
ME13 8XE
Tel: 01795 535344
Email: enquiries@reads.com
Website: www.reads.com
Chef: David Pitchford &
Ricky Martin
Owners: David & Rona Pitchford

Times: 12–2.30/7–10, Closed BHs,
Sun, Mon
Prices: 4 Course Fixed D £48
Directions: From M2 junct 6 follow
A251 towards Faversham. At
T-junct with A2 (Canterbury road)
turn right. Hotel 0.5m on right
Parking: 30

Rankins Restaurant

Modern British

Bistro-style cuisine in rustic surroundings

The Street, SISSINGHURST,
Kent TN17 2JH
Tel: 01580 713964
Email: rankins@btconnect.com
Website:
www.rankinsrestaurant.com
Chef: Hugh Rankin
Owners: Hugh & Leonora Rankin

A one-time saddler's and general store, this timber-framed building dates from 1898 and found a new lease of life as a restaurant in 1971. The beamed interior has the intimate feel of a cottage, with well-spaced tables offering a certain privacy, while the cooking is bistro-style with an emphasis on quality ingredients and simple but attractive presentation. Specialities of the house include seared scallops with buttered leeks and mustard sauce, and roast confit of duck with cassoulet sauce. A masterful dessert is chocolate nemesis, a rich chocolate cake lightened with a compôte of raspberries, blackberries and redcurrants.

Times: 12.30–2/7.30–9, Closed
BHs, Mon, Tue, L Wed–Sat, D Sun
Prices: 3 Course Fixed D £32.50
Directions: Village centre, on A262

The Spa Hotel

Modern British

Serious cuisine in fine-dining environment

Mount Ephraim, ROYAL
TUNBRIDGE WELLS, Kent TN4 8XJ
Tel: 01892 520331
Email: info@spahotel.co.uk
Website: www.spahotel.co.uk
Chef: Steve Cole
Owners: Goring Family

The restaurant at this imposing Georgian country house – set in 14 acres of landscaped grounds – provides a grand, spacious backdrop for elegant dining. Sparkling chandeliers, high ceilings, freshly cut flowers and quality tableware set the scene, complemented by suitably formal table service. The menu offers a range of modern British dishes featuring seasonal local produce and traditional techniques. Think guinea fowl 'en crepinette' with Mediterranean vegetables and rosemary polenta, or perhaps medallion of pancetta monkfish served with braised oxtail, vegetables and crispy brisket, and to finish, a caramelised apple sponge with sauce anglaise and sweet basil syrup.

Times: 12.30–2/7–10, Closed
L Sat
Prices: 3 Course Fixed D £29.50
Directions: On A264 leaving
Tunbridge Wells towards East
Grinstead
Parking: 140

The Swan

British

Brasserie cooking in lively, modern setting

A radical conversion of a 15th-century coaching inn brings a contemporary, brasserie-style vibe to this pretty Kent village. Wood, granite and stainless steel are softened by fashionable neutral tones, banquette seating and modern artwork and mirrors. It's lively and vibrant, with two sleek bars, dining on two levels, a smart lounge and a paved and shaded terrace for alfresco dining. Youthful, black-clad staff provide attentive service, while the accomplished kitchen's simple, modern, clean-cut, brasserie-inspired dishes hit all the right notes, too. Expect a menu offering fish pie with crab mash and greens, or confit belly pork with celeriac mash and apple sauce.

35 Swan Street, WEST MALLING, Kent ME19 6JU
Tel: 01732 521910
Email: info@theswanwestmalling.co.uk
Website: www.theswanwestmalling.co.uk
Chef: A Clarke, S Goss
Owners: Fishbone Ltd

Times: 12–2.45/6–10.45, Closed 26 Dec, 1 Jan, L 27 Dec, 2 Jan
Prices: 3 Course Fixed D £16 Main £10–£20
Directions: M20 junct 4 follow signs for West Malling

The Sportsman

Modern British

Superb fresh fish in unpretentious surroundings

Relaxed and cheery gastro-pub with a modern colonial cum shaker style – stripped wooden floorboards, half wood-clad walls, reclaimed timber tables, local art on the walls and a couple of open fireplaces. The daily-changing modern menu offers a good choice of mainly fish, but also plenty of other local produce, much of it from the surrounding countryside. Presentation is simple – almost rustic – letting the quality and freshness of the ingredients speak for themselves. A good example would be a starter of half a dozen Whitstable native oysters, followed by roast leg and braised shoulder of Monkshill Farm lamb with mint sauce and warm chocolate mousse with salted caramel and milk sorbet.

Faversham Road, Seasalter, WHITSTABLE, Kent CT5 4BP
Tel: 01227 273370
Website: www.thesportsmanseasalter.co.uk
Chef: Stephen Harris
Owners: Stephen & Philip Harris

Times: 12–3/6–11, Closed 25-26 Dec, Mon, D Sun
Prices: Main £13.95–£19.95
Directions: 3.50m W of Whitstable
Parking: 20

Bignell Park Hotel & Restaurant

Modern British v

Creative cooking in country setting

Chesterton, BICESTER,
Oxfordshire OX26 1UE
Tel: 01869 326550
Email: enq@bignellparkhotel.co.uk
Website:
www.bignellparkhotel.co.uk
Chef: Chris Coates
Owners: Caparo Hotels

Sixteenth-century charm and character combine well with modern facilities at this small hotel situated in a peaceful country setting near Bicester Shopping Village. Housed in a converted barn, with a dramatic gallery as a backdrop, the oak-beamed restaurant adorned with paintings is the setting for imaginative fixed-price dinners. Daily menus offer value for money and a varied choice of confidently cooked modern dishes and traditional favourites. Examples include confit belly pork, with prune compôte, lamb rump with roasted root vegetables and lentil and chorizo casserole, and sticky toffee pudding with caramel foam and vanilla bean ice.

Times: 12 2/7–9.30, Closed D Sun
Prices: 3 Course Fixed D
£24.95–£27.95
Directions: M40 junct 9, follow
A41 towards Bicester, turn off at
Chesterton and hotel is signed
at turning
Parking: 50

The Lamb Inn

Traditional British

Traditional coaching inn with imaginative menu

Sheep Street, BURFORD,
Oxfordshire OX18 4LR
Tel: 01993 823155
Email: info@lambinn-burford.co.uk
Website: www.cotswold-inns-
hotels.co.uk/lamb
Chef: Sean Ducie
Owners: Cotswold Inns & Hotels

Dating from 1420, the inn was originally built as weavers' cottages. The spacious restaurant overlooks a lovely courtyard with Cotswold stone walls and a sitting area that positively buzzes in the summer. Inside, cream walls, mullioned windows and frosted skylights make for a bright, cheerful room decorated with food-related pictures, wooden tables and chairs and large floral displays. The food is imaginative and the flavours concise and well balanced using the best of local produce, such as Gloucestershire Old Spot pork, Hereford beef, Bibury trout and Cerney goat's cheese. House specialities include fried lamb's sweetbreads with rosemary biscuit, or perhaps a duo of beef, followed by chocolate torte with rum-and-raisin ice cream.

Times: 12–2.30/7–9.30
Prices: 3 Course Fixed D £32.50
Directions: 1st left as you descend
on the High St

Macdonald Randolph

Traditional British

Classic Oxford dining experience

Situated in the heart of Oxford opposite the Ashmolean Museum, this neo-Gothic hotel was built in 1864 and recently underwent a £6 million refurbishment. The richly furnished, high-ceilinged restaurant combines tradition with elegance, while its large picture windows offer diners wonderful views of the city. British cuisine – underpinned by a classical base – is on offer using quality seasonal ingredients, simply prepared and beautifully presented. Take baked fillet of sea bass served with baby gem lettuce and seared scallops, or seared loin of venison with spinach and chestnuts, and to finish, perhaps a classic crêpe Suzette or apple and redcurrant sponge with vanilla ice cream.

Beaumont Street, OXFORD, Oxfordshire OX1 2LN
Tel: 0870 400 8200
Email: randolph@macdonald-hotels.co.uk
Website: www.macdonaldhotels.co.uk
Chef: Tom Birks
Owners: Macdonald Hotels
Times: 12–2.30/5.30–10

Prices: 3 Course Fixed D £29.50
Main £18–£24.95
Directions: M40 junct 8 onto A40 towards Oxford, follow signs towards city centre, leads to St Giles, hotel is on right
Parking: 50

The Swan at Tetsworth

Modern British

Elizabethan coaching inn with a timeless atmosphere

Tracing its history back to 1482, The Swan retains all its old-world and rustic charm, and today combines its business as both a restaurant and renowned antiques centre. There's nothing at all dated about the menus however. Whether eating in the garden in the summer or enjoying a cosy candlelit dinner, diners can expect an internationally inspired, seasonal menu underpinned by quality ingredients. Think roast crown of poulet noir with roasted foie gras and carrot purée, and to finish, perhaps a sticky toffee pudding – this version delivered with praline ice cream and a miniature apple tart.

High Street, Tetsworth, THAME, Oxfordshire OX9 7AB
Tel: 01844 281182
Chef: Derek Muircroft
Owners: Solution Culinaire

Times: 12–3/7–9.30, Closed D Sun
Prices: Main £15–£22
Directions: 3m from M40 junct 6. 5m from M40 junct 8
Parking: 120

St Mark's, Thame

The Feathers

Modern British v

Accomplished cuisine at a sophisticated hotel

Formed from five townhouses dating from the 17th century, this luxurious hotel set in a busy market town not far from Blenheim Palace offers a choice of two eateries. For grazing or light meals, try the bar or bistro, but for most the restaurant is the main draw – a chic, wood-panelled affair made up of three interconnecting rooms decorated in rich plums and creams, with traditional fittings and elegantly appointed tables. Choose from the three-course Market Menu or à la carte, both offering an interesting take on a modern British theme. Start with velouté of white onion, thyme and cider, for example, then progress with confidence to slow-cooked pig's cheeks, kohlrabi and sauce hollandaise, with vanilla pannacotta and spiced quince to finish.

Market Street, WOODSTOCK, Oxfordshire OX20 1SX
Tel: 01993 812291
Email: enquiries@feathers.co.uk
Website: www.feathers.co.uk
Chef: Simon Garbutt
Owners: Empire Ventures Ltd

Times: 12.30–2.30/7–9.30, Closed D Sun
Prices: 3 Course Fixed D £37.50–£46
Directions: 8m from Oxford on A44, follow signs for Evesham & Blenheim Palace. In Woodstock take 2nd left into the town, hotel 20mtrs on left

---

Drakes on the Pond

Modern British

Skilful cooking in a classy village restaurant

Personally run by the friendly proprietors, this cottage-style building is situated on the edge of the village with views across the Surrey hills. The décor is kept simple, with primrose yellow walls creating a light and airy feel, set off by white-clothed tables, blue glassware and fresh flowers. Good, honest cooking makes the most of quality, fresh ingredients, and service is formal but friendly. The seasonally-changing menu includes the likes of tian of fresh white crab and creamed coconut for starters, followed by a mains of fillet of sea bass with caramelised onion and tomato Tatin. And for dessert, perhaps try almond and treacle tart served with salt caramel ice cream.

Dorking Road, ABINGER HAMMER, Dorking, Surrey RH5 6SA
Tel: 01306 731174
Website: www.drakesonthepond.com
Chef: John Morris
Owners: John Morris & Tracey Honeysett

Times: 12–2/7–10, Closed 2 wks Aug-Sep, Xmas, New Year, BHs, Sun, Mon, L Sat
Prices: Main £21–£24
Directions: On the A25 between Dorking and Guildford
Parking: 20

The Brasserie

Modern British

Skilful modern cooking in five-star hotel setting

The more informal option to the smaller, sister fine-dining Latymer restaurant at this renowned five-star hotel, The Brasserie has a wall of windows overlooking manicured lawns and the grand spa. There's a spacious lounge for pre- or post-meal drinks, while the décor of the restaurant has something of a Mediterranean tone, the large open room decked out with marble floor, big leather arm chairs and well-spaced darkwood tables, all set around a central white statue. The dinner carte offers an eye-catching modern approach driven by tip-top produce; think seared fillet of halibut with fennel and apple salad, basquaise and a mussel curry sauce, and perhaps a prune and Armagnac tart finish, served with crème fraîche.

Pennyhill Park Hotel & Spa, London Road, BAGSHOT, Surrey GU19 5EU
Tel: 01276 471774
Email:
enquiries@pennyhillpark.co.uk
Website:
www.exclusivehotels.co.uk
Chef: Andrew Turner,
Graham Chatham
Owners: Exclusive Hotels

Times: 12–2.30/7–10.30
Prices: Main £15–£32
Directions: M3 junct 3, continue through Bagshot village & turn left onto A30. Hotel is 0.50m past Notcutts on right
Parking: 500

The Oak Room at Great Fosters

Modern British ▲ NOTABLE WINE LIST

Regal Elizabethan setting for accomplished cuisine

Steeped in history, this former royal retreat, and now majestic Elizabethan manor hotel, sits in acres of celebrated landscaped grounds. Dark woods, deep sofas and magnificent tapestries blend with exquisite period features in its stately interior, while the elegant Oak Room restaurant cleverly blends modern design with more traditional features. Think vaulted oak-beamed ceiling, ornate wood-carved fireplace and mullioned windows versus high-backed chairs, large contemporary tapestry and friendly, polished service. The kitchen's modern approach delivers accomplished dishes showcasing quality produce. Expect the likes of confit Cornish mackerel with celeriac remoulade, seed mustard potatoes and a purée of autumn roots, followed by pan-seared brill with razor clams and cockles, herb spätzle and shellfish consommé, with hot cherry soufflé and mulled cherry sauce to finish.

Stroude Road, EGHAM, Surrey TW20 9UR
Tel: 01784 433822
Email:
enquiries@greatfosters.co.uk
Website: www.greatfosters.co.uk
Chef: Christopher Basten
Owners: Great Fosters (1931) Ltd

Times: 12.30–2/7–9.30,
Closed L Sat
Prices: 3 Course Fixed D £33
Main £23–£25
Directions: 1m from town centre
Parking: 200

Kinghams

Modern British

Local produce in attractive cottage surroundings

Built in the 1620s, this pretty red-brick cottage enjoys a picturesque Surrey village setting. The interior has a welcoming, relaxed feel with low ceilings and beams, crisp white linen and well-trained staff attending to customers' needs. There is a heated gazebo in the garden for the summer months. Cooking is imaginative with excellent presentation and uses lots of quality local, seasonal farm produce. Fresh fish is delivered daily, so expect the likes of a fillet of wild sea bass with roasted tomatoes, shallots and creamed artichokes on the fish board, or alternatively, try roasted venison served with fig stuffing and a pear and pickled ginger sauce. To finish, perhaps a white chocolate and Bailey's bread-and-butter pudding with a dark chocolate velouté.

Gomshall Lane, SHERE,
Surrey GU5 9HE
Tel: 01483 202168
Email:
paul@kinghams-restaurant.co.uk
Website: www.kinghams-restaurant.co.uk
Chef: Paul Baker
Owners: Paul Baker

Times: 12.15–2.30/7–9.30,
Closed 25 Dec–4 Jan, Mon, D Sun
Prices: 3 Course Fixed D £22.45
Main £12.95–£21.95
Directions: On A25 between
Guildford and Dorking. 12 mins
from M25 junct 10
Parking: 16

Due South

British

Seaside dining, committed to organic and local produce

139 Kings Road Arches,
BRIGHTON, East Sussex BN1 2FN
Tel: 01273 821218
Email: eat@duesouth.co.uk
Website: www.duesouth.co.uk
Chef: Roz Batty
Owners: Robert Shenton

Once a fishermen's net-mending shed, this modern glass-fronted restaurant is set in an old archway right on the seafront, with an outside terrace for alfresco dining. Inside, the style is modern with banquette seating and polished pine tables. The restaurant's strong commitment to the environment and renewable resources is reflected in local, seasonal produce from organic and free-range sources, 80% of which is sourced within a 20-mile radius. Take for example Ditchling Court Farm Garden lamb or whole baked sea bass stuffed with lemon and herbs. Wines are also English and European to cut down on import distances.

Times: 12–4/6–10, Closed 2 wks
Xmas & New Year
Prices: Main £11.50–£18.95
Directions: On seafront, beneath
cinema

Horsted Place

Modern British

Opulent country house restaurant, formal but friendly

Little Horsted, UCKFIELD, East
Sussex TN22 5TS
Tel: 01825 750581
Email: hotel@horstedplace.co.uk
Website: www.horstedplace.co.uk
Chef: Allan Garth
Owners: Perinon Ltd

Built in 1850, the house has interiors designed by Augustus Pugin, and is set in its own 1,100-acre estate. It celebrated its 20th anniversary as a country-house hotel in 2006, and the elegant, traditional restaurant was tastefully redesigned to mark the occasion. The kitchen's modern approach produces plenty of interest in generously proportioned dishes; take medallions of local organic veal served with spétzle noodles and girolle mushrooms, or perhaps halibut with a herb and brioche crust and vermouth sauce. A Kirsch and vanilla pannacotta might provide the finish, served on a compôte of English strawberries.

Times: 12–2/7–9.30, Closed L Sat
Prices: Main £19.50
Directions: 2m S on A26 towards Lewes
Parking: 50

Millstream Hotel & Restaurant

Modern British

Indulgent dining in a gorgeous village setting

Bosham Lane, BOSHAM,
West Sussex PO18 8HL
Tel: 01243 573234
Email: info@millstream-hotel.co.uk
Website:
www.millstream-hotel.co.uk
Chef: James Fairchild Dickson
Owners: The Wild Family

Lying in the heavenly little village of Bosham, this popular hotel lures a well-heeled sailing crowd from nearby Chichester, thanks to a picture-perfect location and accomplished cooking. At dinner, the ambitious kitchen pulls out all the stops to deliver a luxurious meal. The chef here clearly has high aspirations – the food is both imaginative and technically accomplished with quality ingredients used with care and sensitivity throughout this large menu. Try Shetland scallops with a hazelnut and coriander crust to start followed by a main course of sea trout with almond butter, spinach and shrimp risotto.

Times: 12.30–2/6.45–9.15
Prices: 3 Course Fixed D £30–£36
Main £10.50–£13.95
Directions: Take A259 exit from Chichester rdbt and in village follow signs for quay
Parking: 40

Bailiffscourt Hotel & Spa

Modern British

Fascinating architectural folly offering creative cooking

Set in 30 acres of parkland with moats and small streams, this architectural gem was built in 1927 by Lord Moyne in the style of an authentic medieval manor house, using reclaimed stone and woodwork. Gothic-style mullioned windows overlook the rose-clad courtyard, while narrow passageways lead you through a series of intimate lounges and sitting rooms. The restaurant, with its heavy wooden ceiling, stone window frames with leaded lights, and walls adorned with rich tapestries, continues the medieval illusion. The cooking style, however, is definitely in the present, concentrating on simple flavour. Starters might include crisply-baked Crottin goat's cheese with tomato and pepper coulis, while main courses range from roasted sea bass with fondant potato, black olive tapenade and scallop velouté, to grilled fillet of beef with creamed celeriac, horseradish and red wine and shallot sauce.

CLIMPING, Littlehampton, West Sussex BN17 5RW
Tel: 01903 723511
Email: bailiffscourt@hshotels.co.uk
Website: www.hshotels.co.uk
Chef: Russell Williams
Owners: Pontus & Miranda Carminger

Times: 12–1.30/7–9.30
Prices: 3 Course Fixed D £45.50–£57.50
Directions: From A27 (Arundel), take A284 towards Littlehampton. Continue to the A259, Bailiffscourt is signed towards Climping Beach
Parking: 60

The Old House Restaurant

Modern British

Fine dining in surroundings of great character

A converted 16th-century house is the venue for this homely restaurant, which is bright and sunny with plenty of charm. The décor is Tudor-style, with white walls, black painted beams, diamond-leaded windows and an inglenook fireplace. The dining room is suitably grand, in gold, cream and navy, without being intimidating. There's an emphasis on good quality ingredients, locally sourced wherever possible. The creamy crab and tiger prawn risotto is a good example of the dish, while the main course of poached salmon arrives fresh and tender served with a selection of mini vegetables. An enjoyable dessert is the chef's own version of bread-and-butter pudding, using chocolate and Bailey's but dispensing with the fruit, served with cookie dough ice cream.

Effingham Road, COPTHORNE, West Sussex RH10 3JB
Tel: 01342 712222
Email: info@oldhouserestaurant.co.uk
Website: www.oldhouserestaurant.co.uk
Chef: Alan Pierce
Owners: Mr & Mrs C Dormon

Times: 12.15–2/6.30–9.30, Closed Xmas, New Year, 1 wk spring, BHs, Mon
Prices: 3 Course Fixed D £35–£45 Main £19–£35
Directions: From M23 junct 10 follow A264 to East Grinstead, take 1st left at 2nd rdbt, left at x-rds, restaurant 0.75m on left

Gravetye Manor Hotel

Gravetye Manor Hotel

Modern British

Fabulous country-house hotel with memorable cuisine

No visit to Gravetye Manor would be complete without exploring its gardens, created by Victorian William Robinson as the Natural English Garden. Equally lovely, the traditional oak-panelled restaurant here has a carved white ceiling and winter log fires. Chef Mark Raffan has his culinary roots in classical French cuisine from his time with the Roux brothers, plus a stint as personal chef to the late King Hussein of Jordan. This background and experience ensure an interesting and eclectic menu of broadly modern English cuisine delivered with high skill and top-class local ingredients. Typical dishes include roast fillet of West Coast turbot served with braised oxtail, parsnip purée and cockles marinière, or perhaps braised cheek of veal with roasted sweetbreads, a cassoulet of beans with pancetta, braising juices and sage butter. Top desserts could feature a hot banana soufflé with pistachio ice cream.

EAST GRINSTEAD, West Sussex
RH19 4LJ
Tel: 01342 810567
Email: info@gravetyemanor.co.uk
Website:
www.gravetyemanor.co.uk
Chef: Mark Raffan
Owners: A Russell & M Raffan

Times: 12.30–1.45/7–9.30, Closed D 25 Dec (ex residents)
Prices: 3 Course Fixed D £34 Main £28
Directions: From M23 junct 10 take A264 towards East Grinstead. After 2m take B2028. After Turners Hill, follow signs
Parking: 45

London

Tower Bridge

St John Bread & Wine

British

Unpretentious restaurant, bakery and wine shop

94-96 Commercial Street,
LONDON E1 6LZ
Tel: 020 7251 0848
Email: reservations@
stjohnbreadandwine.com
Website: www.
stjohnbreadandwine.com
Chef: James Lowe
Owners: Trevor Gulliver &
Fergus Henderson

Tucked behind the old Spitalfields Market, this no-frills sibling to big brother St John is a resolutely British affair. Whitewashed walls, parquet flooring and simple wooden tables and chairs set a wholly unpretentious, utilitarian edge. The British food is flavour-driven and unfussy, using quality produce while delivering some earthy dishes using humble ingredients. Ox faggot and mash, brawn and pickled cucumber, Blackface lamb and fennel or sea bass, ruby chard and green sauce set the style. Service is attentive, friendly and informed, while wines, like the wonderful breads, are on sale to take out.

Times: 9/11, Closed 24 Dec
–2 Jan, BHs, D Sun
Prices: Main £11–£15

Canteen

Modern British

All-day eatery in Spitalfields

2 Crispin Place, Spitalfields,
LONDON E1 6DW
Tel: 0845 686 1122
Email: info@canteen.co.uk
Website: www.canteen.co.uk
Chef: Cass Titcombe,
Patrick Clayton-Malone, Dom Lake
Owners: Patrick Clayton-Malone,
Dom Lake

This unpretentious eatery in Spitalfields Market opened in 2006 to rave reviews and has heaved with an eclectic mix of foodies, locals and city types ever since. Glass-walled on three sides, it teams retro booth seating with long shared tables and prides itself on offering high-quality cuisine at reasonable prices. A lengthy all-day menu includes breakfast items and designated 'fast service' dishes, as well as a daily roast, home-made pies and fish options. Expect British classics conjured from the freshest of ingredients – macaroni cheese, for example, or pie, mash, greens and gravy – plus a diet-busting array of homely desserts such as steamed syrup pudding and custard, or orange jelly with ice cream and shortbread.

Times: 8/11, Closed 25-26 Dec
Prices: Main £4.50–£13.50
Directions: Overlooking Spitalfields
Market

The Narrow

British

Gordon Ramsay's inaugural waterside pub

44 Narrow Street, LONDON
E14 8DP
Tel: 020 7592 7950
Email:
thenarrow@gordonramsay.com
Website: www.gordonramsay.
com/thenarrow
Chef: John Collin & Mark Sargeant

Gordon Ramsay's first excursion into the pub market saw him open The Narrow on London's Limehouse back in April 2007. Set on the edge of the Thames, this Grade II listed building – formerly the dockmaster's house – commands wonderful river views. The ground floor is divided into a bar area, a relaxed section for eating, and a dining room. Sympathetic renovation has retained bags of character, with half-wall panelling, fireplaces and black-and-white vintage photography and prints. ('The Captain's Table' private dining room is on the first floor.) The food focuses on classic British dishes based around quality seasonal produce; take cock-a-leekie pie and mash, or perhaps braised Gloucestershire pig cheeks with mashed neeps.

Times: 11.30am–10.30pm
Prices: Main £9–£14.50
Parking: 20

St John

British

The best of British nose-to-tail cooking

26 St John Street,
LONDON EC1M 4AY
Tel: 020 7251 0848
Email:
reservations@stjohnrestaurant.com
Website:
www.stjohnrestaurant.com
Chef: Christopher Gillard
Owners: T Gulliver & F Henderson

Fergus Henderson's stark, utilitarian-styled former smokehouse sits across the road from Smithfield Market and continues to draw the crowds. Upstairs, above the bustling bar and bakery, the high-ceilinged dining room is an equally pared-down affair of coat-hook-lined white walls, white-painted floorboards, white paper-clothed tables and wooden café-style chairs, set in serried ranks that echo the rows of industrial-style lights above. The kitchen's open to view, staff are knowledgeable, friendly and relaxed, in tune with the robust, honest, simplistic, bold-flavoured British food that utilises the whole animal. Menus change twice daily and there's plenty of humble ingredients; think roast bone marrow and parsley salad, perhaps tripe and chips or beef and squash, or bread pudding and butterscotch sauce. (See also Spitalfields spin-off, St John Bread & Wine.)

Times: 12–3/6–11, Closed Xmas, New Year, Easter BH, Sun, L Sat
Prices: Main £12.80–£28
Directions: 100yds from Smithfield Market, northside

81

Rhodes Twenty Four

Modern British

Truly classic Rhodes cuisine overlooking the City

Set on the 24th floor of the tallest building in the Square Mile, this ear-poppingly high restaurant has stunning take-your-breath-away views over London by day or night. There is a separate bar while the sophisticated dining room, dressed in its best white linen armed with stylish appointments, allows all tables to enjoy the spectacular panoramas. Service is slick and friendly, with good attention paid to wine, while the cuisine is Gary's hallmark modern British with a twist. As you'd expect, impeccable ingredients, crystal-clear flavours, perfect balance and sharp presentation parade on exciting dishes. Clearly defined menus might feature roast beef fillet with red wine onions, oxtail hash and poached egg béarnaise, and to finish, it has to be the bread-and-butter pudding. Do leave time for security check-in at this important tower block.

Tower 42, Old Broad Street,
LONDON EC2N 1HQ
Tel: 020 7877 7703
Website: www.rhodes24.co.uk
Chef: Gary Rhodes & Adam Gray
Owners: Restaurant Associates

Times: 12–2.30/6–9, Closed BHs, Xmas, Sat-Sun
Prices: Main £17.50–£24
Directions: Telephone for directions, see website

Rivington Bar & Grill

British **v**

Straightforward, best of British classics in buzzy setting

28-30 Rivington Street,
LONDON EC2A 3DZ
Tel: 020 7729 7053
Email:
shoreditch@rivingtongrill.co.uk
Website: www.rivingtongrill.co.uk
Chef: Damian Clisby
Owners: Caprice-Holdings Ltd

A combined restaurant, bar and deli, this buzzy place is tucked away down a narrow side street in fashionable Hoxton. White walls and wooden floors make for a suitably relaxed backdrop to a parade of simple, confident, seasonal, no-frills modern British cooking using top-notch produce. Think roast Lancashire suckling pig with greens and quince sauce, or fish fingers and chips with mushy peas, while comforting desserts might feature Bakewell tart with vanilla ice cream. Nice touches include chips served in little buckets and your own small loaf of bread.

Times: 12–3/6.30–11, Closed Xmas & New Year, L Sat
Prices: Main £9.25–£25.50
Directions: Telephone for directions

Chamberlains Restaurant

Modern British, Seafood

Market-fresh fish beloved of City slickers

23/25 Leadenhall Market,
LONDON EC3V 1LR
Tel: 020 7648 8690
Email: info@chamberlains.org
Chef: Glen Watson
Owners: Chamberlain & Thelwell

Colourful Leadenhall Market, thronging with City workers at midday and early evening, makes a relaxed setting for this seafood restaurant. It sits beneath the restored Victorian glass roof of the old market, alongside the cobbled walkway, with excellent views of the exquisite architecture from the first floor and mezzanine dining areas. You can also eat more casually in the basement wine bar, or bag a table outside on warmer days. Fish from owners Chamberlain and Thelwell (suppliers to the trade) is delivered right up to opening times, with freshness guaranteed. Try a starter of lobster bisque with collops of lobster and chopped dill, followed by sesame seared tuna with caponata and grilled Mediterranean vegetables. There's plenty of meat too, though the speciality fish and chips remains popular.

Times: 12/9.30, Closed Xmas, New Year & BHs, Sat & Sun
Prices: 3 Course Fixed D £19.95
Main £19–£35
Directions: Telephone for directions

White Swan Pub & Dining Room

Modern, Traditional British

Busy, upmarket gastro-pub with a smart dining room

108 Fetter Lane, LONDON
EC4A 1ES
Tel: 020 7242 9696
Email: info@thewhiteswanlondon.
com
Website: www.
thewhiteswanlondon.com
Owners: Tom & Ed Martin

Beyond the bar of this tastefully restored pub is a mezzanine area, available for drinks parties, and a formal first-floor dining room. Decked out with white-clothed tables, its handsome wooden floors, contemporary chairs, banquettes and mirrored ceiling cut an upmarket edge. Friendly, attentive and relaxed French service adds to the experience. The menu combines classics alongside more esoteric dishes; think braised rabbit tortellini with cep foam and vichy carrots, or red wine braised monkfish cheeks with gremolata mash and deep-fried leeks. Desserts might feature chocolate sponge with hot fudge and white chocolate sorbet, while daily specials provide additional interest.

Times: 12–3/6–10, Closed 25 Dec, 1 Jan and BHs, Sat-Sun (except private parties)
Prices: Main £15–£18.50
Directions: Fetter Lane runs parallel with Chancery Lane joining Fleet St with Holborn

---

The House

Modern British

Enjoyable, simple cooking in a relaxed environment

63-69 Canonbury Road,
LONDON N1 2DG
Tel: 020 7704 7410
Email: info@inthehouse.biz
Website: www.inthehouse.biz
Chef: Jeremy Hollingsworth
Owners: Barnaby &
Grace Meredith/Jeremy

Behind a maroon awninged, redbrick façade lies this cosy neighbourhood restaurant which has quite a local following. Wooden floors, whitewashed walls and simple artwork give the dining room a light and airy feel during the day. In the evening, locals gather around the comfortable bar sofas and well-spaced dining tables. Simple dishes prove very satisfying in this setting, using organic produce wherever possible. Try Loch Fyne smoked salmon with buckwheat blinis to start, then maybe sea bass with a ragout of borlotti beans and baby onions with braised fennel, and finish with warm Valrhona chocolate pudding served with espresso ice cream. Everything from the breads to ice creams is home made.

Hollingsworth
Times: 12–2.30/6–10.30,
Closed L Mon
Prices: Main £12.95–£22.50
Directions: Behind town hall on Upper St Islington. Between Highbury Corner and Essex Rd

The Lock Dining Bar

Modern British

Great value destination

Heron House, Hale Wharf,
Ferry Lane, LONDON N17 9NF
Tel: 020 8885 2829
Email: thelock06@btconnect.com
Website: thelock-diningbar.com
Chef: Adebola Adeshina
Owners: Adebola Adeshina,
Fabrizio Russo

Just a few minutes walk from Tottenham Hale station, this chic eatery has the feel of a New York loft house, its North African furnishings teamed with pine flooring, chocolate leather sofas and works of art by local painters. An open-plan kitchen delivers a menu of modern British dishes with a focus on seasonal produce. Starters might include the likes of baked polenta fritter and Crottin goat's cheese dressed with truffle emulsion, or pan-fried scallops with plantain, and garlic froth, followed by pan-fried fillet of dorade with sautéed potatoes and slow caramelised onions. Finish with deep-fried rice pudding beignets with mixed berry sauce. It's all reasonably priced, particularly at lunchtime, and great value for money.

Times: 12–2.30/6.30–10,
Closed L Sat (except match days),
D Mon, Sun
Prices: 3 Course Fixed D £19.50
–£25 Main £10.50 £22
Directions: Telephone for
directions
Parking: 20

Dorset Square Hotel

Modern British

Relaxed bar-restaurant with cricketing roots

39-40 Dorset Square,
LONDON NW1 6QN
Tel: 020 7723 7874
Email: info@dorsetsquare.co.uk
Website: www.dorsetsquare.co.uk
Chef: Martin Halls
Owners: LHP

Standing on the original site of Lords cricket ground, this smart Regency townhouse hotel is home to the popular lower-ground floor Potting Shed Restaurant and Bar – a split-level affair with skylights and a warm, sunny feel. The gardening theme is developed with an array of terracotta pots and seed boxes across one wall, while a cricketing mural adorns another wall. The cooking is predominantly British with contemporary twists. The seasonal menu is kept simple and wholesome, focusing on accurate flavours. Tuck into a tender rump of lamb with garlic cream potatoes, or a Dorset blue cheese and leek tart with grape chutney, followed by a tangy glazed lemon tart with fresh raspberries.

Times: 12–3/6–10.30, Closed
25 Dec, BHs, L Sat, D Sun
Prices: 3 Course Fixed D £22.50
–£25 Main £11.50–£19.50
Directions: Telephone for
directions

The Winter Garden

Modern British

Stunning atrium restaurant

Former headquarters of British Rail and one of the last great railway hotels, the building is over 100 years old. The Winter Garden is a stunning open-plan, naturally lit restaurant situated at the base of an eight-storey atrium complete with palm trees, which also features the sophisticated Mirror Bar. At night, the restaurant turns into a more intimate affair. A selection of modern British dishes is offered on a menu featuring fresh quality produce. Typical starters might include shellfish bisque with vodka crème fraîche, while a main course of pine nut-crusted rack of lamb is accompanied with basil mash, Provençal vegetables and shallot jus. Desserts might include rhubarb and vanilla baked Alaska with rhubarb compôte.

The Landmark London,
222 Marylebone Rd,
LONDON NW1 6JQ
Tel: 020 7631 8000
Email: restaurants.reservation@
thelandmark.co.uk
Website:
www.landmarklondon.co.uk
Chef: Gary Klaner
Owners: Jatuporn Sihanatkathakul

Times: 11.30–3/6–11.30
Prices: Main £15–£40
Directions: M25 turn on to the A40 and continue 16m following signs for West End. Continue along Marylebone Rd for 300 mtrs. Restaurant on left
Parking: 75

The County Hall Restaurant

Modern British

Stunning Thames-side setting in Westminster

Formerly the members' reading room of County Hall, the restaurant here is a high-ceilinged, oak-panelled room facing the Palace of Westminster and Big Ben, looking out across the River Thames. It's a wonderful setting by day or by night and the formal feel is reflected in high levels of staffing and classical, but friendly and informative, service. The dishes on the fixed-price menu and carte are modern British with European influences. Main courses might include fillets of John Dory with brown shrimp risotto, broad beans and basil sauce, or pumpkin gnocchi, wilted spinach, goat's cheese and walnut sauce.

London Marriott Hotel,
Westminster Bridge Road,
LONDON SE1 7PB
Tel: 020 7902 8000
Website: www.marriotthotels.
com/marriott/lonch
Chef: Craig Carew-Wootton
Owners: Marriott International

Times: 12–2.30/6–10.30, Closed D 26 Dec
Prices: 3 Course Fixed D £23–£25 Main £16–£25.50
Directions: Situated next to Westminster Bridge on the South Bank. Opposite Houses of Parliament

London Eye

Roast

British   🍷 NOTABLE WINE LIST

Airy modern restaurant above Borough Market

The Floral Hall, Borough Market,
Stoney Street,
LONDON SE1 1TL
Tel: 020 7940 1300
Email: info@roast-restaurant.com
Website:
www.roast-restaurant.com
Chef: Lawrence Keogh
Owners: Iqbal Wahhab

Borough Market provides the atmospheric setting for this first-floor establishment, with views of the hubbub below from the bar and over to St Paul's Cathedral from its glass-fronted dining room. The floral portico featured in the dining room was bought from Covent Garden for £1 by Borough Market trustees. Menus make good use of quality produce in classic British dishes. Think roast Banham chicken with bread sauce and Ayshire bacon, Inverawe smoked Loch Etive trout with watercress and lemon, or roast Welsh black sirloin. Breakfast and afternoon tea are served, and there's a superb cocktail list.

Times: 12–3/5.30–11,
Closed D Sun
Prices: Main £12.95–£25
Directions: Please telephone for directions

Franklins

British

Smart restaurant and popular pub operation

157 Lordship Lane,
LONDON SE22 8HX
Tel: 020 8299 9598
Email:
info@franklinsrestaurant.com
Website:
www.franklinsrestaurant.com
Chef: Tim Sheehan
Owners:
Tim Sheehan & Rodney Franklin

A traditional pub on the outside, Franklins opens off Lordship Lane into a well-frequented locals' bar where the open-all-day policy attracts a posse of regulars. A few paces beyond this atmospheric space can be found the bright bistro-style restaurant where diners glimpse the kitchen operation through a wide hatch. Seasonal produce from in and around the UK dominates the carte, with its daily-changing set lunch menu offering excellent value for money. Traditional English favourites like Old Spot belly with fennel and black pudding, Glamorgan sausages, and mutton faggots with pease pudding will be found alongside guinea fowl with butter beans and chorizo.

Times: 12/12, Closed 25-26,
31 Dec, 1 Jan
Prices: Main £10.50–£18
Directions: Please telephone
for directions

The Palmerston

Modern British

Popular gastro-pub close to Dulwich village

91 Lordship Lane, East Dulwich,
LONDON SE22 8EP
Tel: 020 8693 1629
Email: thepalmerston@tiscali.co.uk
Website:
www.thepalmerston.co.uk
Chef: Jamie Younger
Owners: Jamie Younger,
Paul Rigby & Remi Olajoyegbe

There are pubs aplenty down trendy Lordship Lane, but few have reinvented themselves as successfully as this one. Behind the pastel-painted exterior, the long bar and separate dining area – each warmed by a real fire in winter – are wood-panelled, brightly coloured and welcoming. But the real delight is the food, a homage to fresh, carefully sourced ingredients deftly handled without a hint of artifice. Expect to find potted beef with pickled beetroot, grilled veal chop with celeriac remoulade and sauce charcuterie, and perhaps a homely rhubarb and custard tart with rhubarb compôte to finish. The set lunch is a real bargain.

Times: 12–2.30/7–midnight,
Closed 25-26 Dec, 1 Jan
Prices: Main £11–£16.50
Directions: 2m from Clapham,
0.5m from Dulwich Village, 10min
walk from East Dulwich station

Boisdale of Belgravia

British

Traditional, clubby but fun Scottish restaurant

15 Eccleston Street,
LONDON SW1W 9LX
Tel: 020 7730 6922
Email: info@boisdale.co.uk
Website: www.boisdale.co.uk
Chef: Colin Wint
Owners: Mr R Macdonald

A determinedly Scottish experience is delivered at this Belgravia restaurant-cum-whisky and cigar bar, with its deep reds and greens, tartan, dark floorboards and panelled, picture-laden walls. There is an endearingly clubby atmosphere to its labyrinth of dining areas and bars, and live jazz adds to the atmosphere in the evenings. The Caledonian menu supports the theme with Dunkeld oak-smoked salmon, ravioli of Western Isles king scallops, a daily game dish, and 28-day matured Scottish beef served with a wide choice of sauces and accompaniments. Desserts tempt with the likes of warm pear and fig tart served with prune and Armagnac ice cream, or hot chocolate cake with Banyuls syrup.

Times: 12–2.30/7–11.15, Closed
Xmas, New Year, Easter, BHs, Sun,
L Sat
Prices: 2 Course Fixed D £17.80
Main £14.50–£28.50
Directions: Turn left along
Buckingham Palace Rd heading W,
Eccleston St is 1st on right

Boxwood Café

British **v** 🍷 NOTABLE WINE LIST

Upmarket brasserie in high-class hotel

From the Gordon Ramsay stable, this upmarket interpretation of a New York-style café predictably oozes class, located on one corner of The Berkeley Hotel with its own street entrance on Knightsbridge. The elegant dining room is a stylish, split-level basement affair, with a bar and smart table settings. Natural earthy tones parade alongside golds and bronzes and lashings of darkwood and leather, while service is youthful, slick but relaxed, and there's a vibrant metropolitan buzz. The accomplished kitchen's upmarket brasserie repertoire hits the spot, utilising high-quality seasonal ingredients with the emphasis on flavour, innovative combination and stylish presentation; think braised fillet of wild halibut served with baked potato gnocchi, peas, broad beans and courgette flower.

The Berkeley Hotel, Wilton Place, Knightsbridge, LONDON
SW1X 7RL
Tel: 020 7235 1010
Email: boxwoodcafe@
gordonramsay.com
Website: www.gordonramsay.com
Chef: Stuart Gillies
Owners: Gordon Ramsay
Holdings Ltd

Times: 12–3/6–11
Prices: Main £16–£28
Directions: Please telephone for directions

The Goring

Traditional British NOTABLE WINE LIST

Carefully prepared food in grand hotel setting

A sumptuous and elaborate hotel done out in the grand style, as befits a traditional property in its central London location just behind Buckingham Palace. This family-owned property may be traditional in style but it's anything but stuffy with staff providing friendly and efficient service. David Linley's redesign has created a lighter, modern touch to the grand Victorian dining room, with its sumptuous silks and contemporary centrepiece 'Blossom' chandeliers. Menus are a celebration of all things British, accomplished classics using prime-quality, fresh produce. Think Dover sole (grilled or pan fried) served with new potatoes and spinach, or perhaps steak and kidney pie with cream potatoes, while there are British cheeses from the trolley and puddings like a classic custard tart.

Beeston Place, LONDON
SW1W 0JW
Tel: 020 7396 9000
Email:
reception@goringhotel.co.uk
Website: www.goringhotel.co.uk
Chef: Derek Quelch
Owners: Goring Family

Times: 12.30–2.30/6–10,
Closed L Sat
Prices: 3 Course Fixed D £44
Directions: From Victoria St turn left into Grosvenor Gdns, cross Buckingham Palace Rd, 75yds turn right into Beeston Place
Parking: 5

Just St James

Modern British

Dining in high style in old St James's

The lavish, impressive, Edwardian Baroque interior with its marble columns, arched windows and corniced ceilings has been cleverly softened with contemporary styling (think suede banquette seating, modern artwork and a glass lift to a mezzanine gallery) to provide a striking setting for some accomplished modern dining. It used to be a private bank, so don't be shocked at some of the St James's prices, but then the menu comes dotted with luxury. The cooking is self-assured and stylishly presented, so open your account with a ballotine of foie gras, duck salad and toasted brioche, and perhaps baked wild halibut with a herb crust, boulangère potatoes and green beans to follow. A large, glass-topped bar and leather seating completes a class act.

12 St James's Street,
LONDON SW1A 1ER
Tel: 020 7976 2222
Email: bookings@juststjames.com
Website: www.juststjames.com
Chef: Peter Gladwin
Owners: Peter Gladwin

Times: 12–3/6–11, Closed 25-26 Dec, 1 Jan, Sun, L Sat
Directions: Turn right on Piccadilly towards Piccadilly Circus, then right into St James's St. Restaurant on corner of St James's St & King St

---

The Rib Room

British v

Robust British cooking in the heart of Knightsbridge

Housed on the ground floor of the towering Jumeirah Carlton Tower Hotel, this buzzy restaurant has a sophisticated and moody club-like atmosphere, and comes richly furnished with acres of wood panelling, awesome floral displays, seductive lighting, artwork by Feliks Topolski and crisp napery. The service gently balances British etiquette with friendliness. Tantalising aromas waft from the large open 'theatre' kitchen, its repertoire pure British gastronomy driven by the best home-reared produce and the successful blend of traditional and more contemporary style. Enjoy classic signature dishes like calves' liver with spring onion mash and fricassée of lentils, bacon and mushrooms, hard to resist Aberdeen Angus rib of beef with Yorkshire pudding or Rib Room seafood platter. A pianist entertains in the evenings.

Jumeirah Carlton Tower Hotel,
Cadogan Place, LONDON
SW1X 9PY
Tel: 020 7858 7250
Email: JCTinfo@jumeirah.com
Website: www.jumeirah.com
Chef: Simon Young

Times: 12.30–2.45/7–10.45
Prices: Main £24–£64
Directions: From major roads follow signs for City Centre, towards Knightsbridge/Hyde Park/Sloane Sq, then into Sloane St/Cadogan Place
Parking: 70

St James's Park

The Stafford

British 🍷 NOTABLE WINE LIST

Luxurious hotel dining in an exclusive location

16-18 St James's Place, LONDON SW1A 1NJ
Tel: 020 7493 0111
Email: information@ thestaffordhotel.co.uk
Website: www.thestaffordhotel.co.uk
Chef: Mark Budd
Owners: Shire Hotels

Tucked away behind Green Park, this genteel hotel has the feel of a luxurious country house in the heart of St James's. Public areas are comfortable with an understated opulence. The world-famous American bar, known for mixing a mean martini, displays an eccentric collection of club ties, sporting momentoes and signed celebrity photographs. A simpler menu is offered at lunchtime with a daily special from the trolley Sunday to Friday, generally a roast, and fish on Friday. Luxury ingredients are to the fore on the extensive carte: starters might include a soufflé of lobster and sole with caviar and champagne sauce, or steak tartare, while mains range from roast wild duck with apple and foie gras, to Chateaubriand.

Times: 12.30–2.30/6–10.30, Closed L Sat
Prices: Main £14.50–£35
Directions: 5 mins St James's Palace

Lamberts

Modern British

Relaxed, modern fine dining with impressive cooking

2 Station Parade, Balham High Road, LONDON SW12 9AZ
Tel: 0208 675 2233
Email: bookings@ lambertsrestaurant.com
Website: www.lambertsrestaurant.com
Chef: Chas Tapaneyasastr
Owners: Mr Joe Lambert

Balham's Lamberts is a cool, minimalist-vogue, modern venue and, whilst styling itself as a fine-dining restaurant, offers a relaxed and comfortable atmosphere. It is a deservedly popular venue, with a growing reputation, where the food is fresh and vibrant. No surprise then that the kitchen prides itself on using the freshest seasonal British ingredients, including organic produce, with the majority of meat sourced direct from farms while fish comes straight from day boats. The impressive, well-presented cooking takes a modern approach that suits the surroundings, with old favourites sitting comfortably alongside contemporary interpretations of classics; think Farmer Sharp's Herdwick mutton, wether and lamb, and don't miss the blueberry cheesecake and white chocolate ganache.

Times: 12/7–10.30, Closed 25 Dec, 1 Jan, Mon, L Tues, Wed, Thurs, Fri
Prices: 3 Course Fixed D £20–£25 Main £14–£18
Directions: Just S of Balham station on Balham High Rd

The Athenaeum, Damask

Traditional British

A relaxed space at this famous hotel

116 Piccadilly, LONDON W1J 7BJ
Tel. 020 7499 3464
Email: info@athenaeumhotel.com
Website:
www.athenaeumhotel.com
Chef: David Marshall
Owners: Ralph Trustees Ltd

The sumptuous Athenaeum is discreet in every way but the interior of the building, despite limited space, oozes contemporary style after a designer make-over. It's all change with the food options too, by way of the introduction of 'The Elevenses' menu offered from 11am to 11pm (flexible all-day dining with something for everyone) to complement the set lunch and dinner menus and the retro-chic daily-changing carving trolley. The new Damask Restaurant is a glamorous yet relaxed space, where the likes of risotto of New Forest mushrooms and truffles, grilled new season Dorset lamb with buttered spinach and glazed onions followed by a double-baked chocolate pudding might tempt the palate. Service is of the highest level, superbly hosted and supervised and smartly attired.

Times: 12.30–2.30/5.30–10.30
Prices: 3 Course Fixed D £25
Main £15–£28.50
Directions: Telephone for
directions

Brian Turner Mayfair

Modern British

Back-to-basics British cooking in upmarket hotel

Millennium Hotel, 44 Grosvenor
Square,Mayfair, LONDON
W1K 2HN
Tel: 020 7596 3444
Email: annie.mckale@mill-cop.com
Website: www.brianturneronline.
co.uk/mayfair.asp
Chef: Brian Turner & Paul Bates
Owners: Millennium Hotels

In contrast to the other smart eateries in this swanky Mayfair hotel, Brian Turner's split-level restaurant – which makes the most of the views across Grosvenor Square – boasts understated retro-chic, decked out in contemporary shades and natural materials. Famed for his interest in traditional British comfort food, cooking is based on simple, wholesome and satisfying British classics, yet dishes are given a light and modern touch. Think spit-roast duck on butternut purée with crisp potato, broad beans and bacon, or Finnebrogue venison loin with potato and parsnip terrine, while a soft-centred chocolate pudding with Jaffa Cake ice cream might catch the eye at dessert.

Times: 12.30–2.30/6.30–10.30,
Closed BHs, Sun, L Sat
Prices: Main £15–£42
Directions: Close to Oxford St,
Bond St and Park Ln

Butler's

Traditional British

Traditional dining in an elegant Mayfair retreat

Step through the door of this exclusive hotel and you'll find a luxurious Georgian interior appropriate to its prestigious Mayfair address. A clubby feel pervades the public spaces thanks to high quality antiques, leather chairs, and heavy fabrics, and the elegance continues into Butler's restaurant, a sumptuous room with a strong red and brown décor and a subtle African theme. Dine here or in the light and airy Conservatory, where a traditional British menu offers a good range of straightforward dishes based on high-quality ingredients. Kick things off with a pear, gorgonzola and pecan salad, before tucking into the likes of rump of lamb with herb mash and red wine and bay leaf sauce, or choose from the carving trolley, followed by Eton Mess or sticky toffee pudding.

Chesterfield Mayfair Hotel,
35 Charles Street, Mayfair,
LONDON W1J 5EB
Tel: 020 7491 2622
Email: fandbch@rchmail.com
Website:
www.chesterfieldmayfair.com
Chef: Andrew Fraser
Owners: Red Carnation Hotels

Times: 12.30–2.30/5.30–10.30
Prices: 3 Course Fixed D £26
Main £17.50–£23
Directions: From N side exit tube station turn left and then first left into Berkeley St. Continue down to Berkeley Sq and then left heading towards Charles S

The Grill (Dorchester Hotel)

Modern British

Splendid food in opulent surroundings

Now redecorated, this grand, world-renowned hotel's The Grill
Room has a whimsical, flamboyantly Scottish feel, while formal
settings and a luxurious ambience make this a wonderful venue
to sample some equally striking cooking. The menu may still
feature a few classic grills, such as roast beef from the trolley or
perhaps grilled Dover sole, but the main thrust takes a modern
British approach in the hands of young head chef, Aiden Byrne – a
protégé of Tom Aikens, and previously at Danesfield House Hotel in
Marlow. Highly accomplished dishes are multi-faceted but deliver
well-balanced combinations, driven by top quality ingredients and
fresh, clean flavours that are presented with real panache. Think
roasted scallops with white chocolate and truffle risotto, pan-fried
John Dory served with celeriac, apple and horseradish, or squab
pigeon with pickled cabbage and a sweet garlic-butter sauce.

The Dorchester, Park Lane,
LONDON W1K 1QA
Tel: 020 7629 8888
Email:
restaurants@thedorchester.com
Website: www.thedorchester.com
Chef: Aiden Byrne
Owners: The Dorchester Collection

Times: 12.30–2.30/6–11
Prices: Main £19.50–£30
Directions: On Park Ln,
overlooking Hyde Park

Scott's Restaurant

British v

Fashionable, glamorous seafood bar and restaurant

This legendary fish restaurant – relaunched by Caprice Holdings (the people behind The Ivy, Le Caprice and J. Sheekey) – sees it return to its past glories in great style. The contemporary, fashionable remix of this classic oak-panelled restaurant comes inspired by its heyday, with rich burgundy-leather seating, an exquisite chandelier, specially commissioned modern art and a central crustacea bar in the style of a turn-of-the-century cruise liner. There's a doorman to greet, while table service is slick, attentive and polished. The kitchen uses top-notch ingredients in well-presented dishes, with the likes of oysters, caviar, crustacea, smoked fish, whole fish and meat on the bone finding a place. Think classics like Dover sole (grilled or meunière), lobster (américaine, grilled or thermidor), or maybe pan-fried skate with periwinkles, nut-brown butter and capers.

20 Mount Street, LONDON
W1K 2HE
Tel: 020 7495 7309
Website:
www.scotts-restaurant.com
Chef: Kevin Gratton
Owners: ICD Ltd

Times: 12–3/5.30–11, Closed Xmas, Jan 1, Aug BH
Prices: Main £18.50–£26.50
Directions: Just off Grosvenor Sq, between Berkeley Sq and Park Ln

---

Island Restaurant & Bar

Modern British

Designer hotel restaurant with seasonal fare

Royal Lancaster Hotel, Lancaster Terrace, LONDON W2 2TY
Tel: 020 7551 6070
Email: eat@islandrestaurant.co.uk
Website:
www.islandrestaurant.co.uk
Owners: Lancaster Hotel Co Ltd

Enter this contemporary hotel restaurant via the salubrious reception area or directly from the street. Huge plate glass windows overlook the park opposite and there is a sleek bar (with great cocktails) and open-plan kitchen in the split-level dining area. In the evening, crisp white tablecloths and dramatic lighting bring an extra touch of glamour. Quality ingredients are handled with skill to produce a daily-changing choice of dishes, presented in a pleasingly minimalist style. Sourcing from British suppliers, popular dishes sit alongside more sophisticated fare – potted crab and brown shrimps with shellfish mayonnaise, and roast rump of lamb with creamed garlic mash and rosemary jus.

Times: 12/10.30, Closed Xmas, BHs, between Xmas and New Year
Prices: Main £9.95–£28
Parking: 50

Kensington Place

Modern British

Busy brasserie-style restaurant with vibrant colour

Watch the world go by at this prominently located and ever-popular Notting Hill haunt. Passers-by also get a good look in through the long plate-glass fascia, while a revolving door leads into a bustling, energetic bar, and the main restaurant decorated with a striking mural depicting nearby Kensington Gardens. Closely-set tables and colourful wooden chairs are reminiscent of the schoolroom. Well-executed brasserie food, simple and precise, uses top-quality seasonal produce, with old favourites offered alongside more imaginative creations. Fish is a speciality, with dishes like red mullet, potato and olive pancake, followed by steamed sea bass with cauliflower and skate tempura, and chocolate and mascarpone torte served with coffee sauce to finish. The restaurant has its own elegant fish shop next door to cater for your every need, and includes goodies from the restaurant.

201-9 Kensington Church Street,
LONDON W8 7LX
Tel: 020 7727 3184
Email: kpparty@egami.co.uk
Website: www.egami.co.uk
Chef: Sam Mahoney
Owners: Place Restaurants Ltd

Times: 12–3.30/6.30–11.15,
Closed 24-26 Dec, 1 Jan
Prices: 3 Course Fixed D £24.50
(Mon–Fri) Main £17–£30
Directions: Telephone for directions

The Montague on the Gardens

Modern British

Stylish hotel restaurant with modern cuisine

15 Montague Street, Bloomsbury,
LONDON WC1B 5BJ
Tel: 020 7637 1001
Email: bookmt@rchmail.com
Website:
www.montaguehotel.com
Chef: Neil Ramsey
Owners: Red Carnation Hotels

A swish boutique hotel in the heart of Bloomsbury, the Montague has two dining options – the Blue Door bistro or the fine-dining restaurant, the Chef's Table. The latter is a light, airy space with panoramic views over London on three sides and an outside terrace for alfresco dining and summer barbecues. Attentive staff are on hand to make guests feel at ease and the cooking is modern British with some French influences. Expect dishes such as lobster risotto with mascarpone and parmesan crisp, followed by pan-fried sea bream with confit tomato and caviar beurre blanc.

Times: 12.30–2.30/5.30–10.30
Prices: 3 Course Fixed D £25–£50
Main £13.95–£24.50
Directions: 10 minutes from Covent Garden, adjacent to the British Museum

Llynnau Mymbyr, Conwy

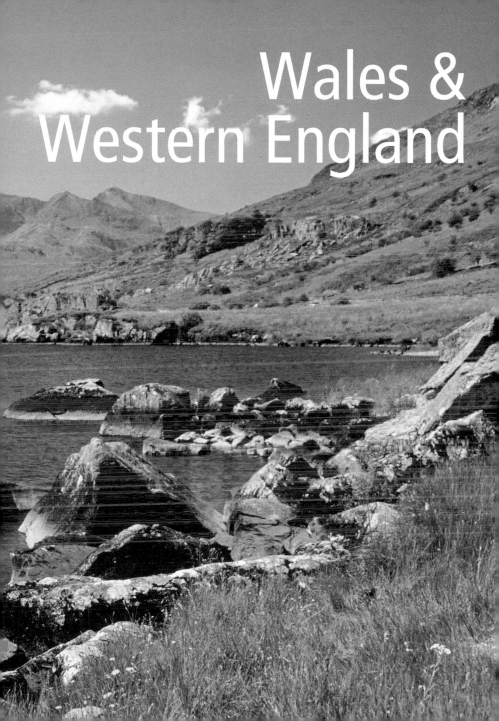

Wales &
Western England

Ye Olde Bulls Head Inn

Modern British

Historic place with punchy food

Charles Dickens and Samuel Johnson were both regular visitors to this historic coaching inn. Originally built in the late 1400s, there are still exposed beams and antique weaponry linking it to its heritage, although the rest of the décor is smart and contemporary, particularly the Loft restaurant, the more formal of the two dining options. The food is confident, progressive and demonstrates creativity – ravioli of girolle mushrooms, aged parmesan, white truffle and wild mushroom ragout to start, then a main of line-caught sea bass with purple broccoli, crab risotto, champagne and sorrel cream, and oyster tempura. To finish, Valrhona dark chocolate tart with roasted pistachio ice cream and chocolate sauce.

Castle Street, BEAUMARIS,
Isle of Anglesey LL58 8AP
Tel: 01248 810329
Email: info@bullsheadinn.co.uk
Website: www.bullsheadinn.co.uk
Chef: Keith Rothwell &
Craig Yardley
Owners: D Robertson & K Rothwell

Times: 7–9.30, Closed 25-26 Dec,
1 Jan, Sun, L Mon–Sat
Prices: 3 Course Fixed D
£37–£38.50
Directions: Town centre,
main street
Parking: 10

The Laguna Kitchen & Bar

Modern British

Enjoyable dining in contemporary surroundings

Laguna is far from your typical hotel restaurant, a large contemporary space in a new-build hotel, with wooden floors, low lighting, unclothed tables, an open-plan kitchen at one end and huge windows affording river views. The extensive menu lists simple snacks alongside skilfully-prepared dishes, but quality ingredients bring out vibrant flavours throughout. Choose small or large plates of dishes like brown shrimp and sweet chilli risotto, or pappardelle, Parma ham and wild mushrooms, and mains like slow-roasted Welsh lamb shank with bubble-and-squeak, or fish with hand-cut chips and mushy peas.

Park Plaza Cardiff, Greyfriars Road,
CARDIFF, CF10 3AL
Tel: 029 2011 1103
Email:
ppcres@parkplazahotels.co.uk
Website:
www.parkplazacardiff.com
Chef: Mark Freeman
Owners: Martin Morris

Times: 12–2.30/5.30–10.30
Prices: Main £8–£19.50
Directions: City centre, next to
New Theatre

The Angel Salem

British

Hearty food in a delightful rural location

Salem, LLANDEILO,
Carmarthenshire SA19 7LY
Tel: 01558 823394
Chef: Rod Peterson
Owners: Rod Peterson & Liz Smith

It's well worth a trip into the Carmarthenshire countryside to find this welcoming inn, with its big comfy sofas and an interesting mixture of modern and antique furniture. People come for the pleasant surroundings and friendly service, but above all for the carefully prepared food made from quality produce. Contemporary dishes with classical influences are offered from lunchtime blackboard specials and a regularly-changing carte. Recommendations are the soufflé of Welsh goat's cheese and walnut to start, a main course of cumin braised shoulder of Welsh lamb with onion and raisin jus and minted yogurt, and dessert of white chocolate and raspberry trifle. Everything is home made including the excellent breads.

Times: 12–3/7–9, Closed 2 wks in Jan, Sun-Mon (ex BHs), L Tue
Prices: Main £15–£19
Directions: Please telephone for directions
Parking: 25

Ty Mawr Mansion

Modern British

Country-house dining showcasing quality local produce

Cilcennin, ABERAERON,
Ceredigion SA48 8DB
Tel: 01570 470033
Email: info@tymawmavision.co.uk
Website:
www.tymawmavision.co.uk
Chef: Paul Owens
Owners: Martin & Catherine McAlpine

Set in 12 acres of countryside grounds, this recently refurbished, Grade II listed mansion offers a true country-house experience where peace and tranquility are key. There's a choice of three lounges for aperitifs, each with its own theme, while the restaurant comes smartly decked out in polished-oak flooring and bold blue colours that coordinate with furnishings, pictures and prints. Service is relaxed and friendly, while the kitchen deals in fresh, locally-sourced, seasonal produce, including herbs from the mansion's garden. The cooking style has a classical theme but with a contemporary Welsh twist; take a fillet of Welsh beef served with horseradish pomme purée, creamed leeks, oxtail ravioli and foie gras espuma, or loin of venison with caramelised cauliflower, braised red cabbage and chestnut and rowanberry jus.

Times: 7–9, Closed 26 Dec-7 Jan, Sun-Mon, L all week
Prices: 3 Course Fixed D £32–£42
Directions: 4m from Aberaeron on A482 to Lampeter Rd
Parking: 20

Ynyshir Hall

Modern British v

Adventurous and stunning country-house cuisine

Set at the end of an impressive tree-lined drive, in 14 acres of glorious gardens that are ablaze with azaleas and rhododendrons in spring, this white-painted Tudor manor-house is boldly decorated using vibrant colours and its walls are adorned with bright canvasses. The restaurant here is the epitome of a country-house dining room, small and decked out with crisp linen and comfortable high-backed chairs, while offering views over the stunning garden. Head chef Shane Hughes' cooking oozes pedigree, his modern approach underpinned by classical technique and driven by high-quality Welsh produce, including herbs and vegetables from Ynyshir's walled garden. His innovative, creative, sharp cooking might deliver beef fillet and mushroom ravioli with celery, parsnip and black pepper, or perhaps monkfish and squid teamed with fennel risotto, cherry tomatoes and kohlrabi.

EGLWYSFACH, Machynlleth, Ceredigion SY20 8TA
Tel: 01654 781209
Email: ynyshir@relaischateaux.com
Website: www.ynyshir-hall.co.uk
Chef: Shane Hughes
Owners: Rob & Joan Reen

Times: 12.30–1.30/7–8.45, Closed Jan
Prices: 4 Course Fixed D £65
Directions: On A487, 6m S of Machynlleth
Parking: 15

Tan-y-Foel Country House

Modern British

Gourmet sanctuary in Snowdonia

Perched in the hills above the pretty village of Betws-y-Coed, this family-run hotel and restaurant offers stunning views of the Conwy valley. The cosy restaurant seats only a dozen diners at a time. Daughter Kelly and husband Peter serve, while mum Janet (Pitman) delivers some of the finest cuisine in Wales, with mains such as a fillet of Welsh Black beef, perhaps served with pomme rösti, sautéed shiitake and oyster mushrooms, butter beans and a rich oxtail jus. The compact fixed-price menu changes daily and features a choice of two dishes at each course, with accompanying wine recommendations. Start with seared scallops with a liquorice sauce and crisp-fried greens, maybe take the wild turbot main course, teamed with fennel purée, sautéed potatoes, celeriac fritter and a red wine cream sauce, and maybe finish with pannacotta with roasted plum and almond purée and Anglesey biscuit.

Capel Garmon, BETWS-Y-COED, Conwy LL26 0RE
Tel: 01690 710507
Email: enquiries@tyfhotel.co.uk
Website: www.tyfhotel.co.uk
Chef: Janet Pitman
Owners: Mr & Mrs P Pitman

Times: 7.30–8.15,
Closed Dec/Jan, Mon, L all week
Prices: 3 Course Fixed D £39–£42
Directions: A5 onto A470; 2m N towards Llanrwst, then turning for Capel Garmon. Country House on left 1m before village
Parking: 14

Llugwy Restaurant

Modern British, Welsh

Upmarket Welsh cooking in a popular hotel

Royal Oak Hotel, Holyhead Road,
BETWS-Y-COED, LL24 0AY
Tel: 01690 710219
Email:
royaloakmail@btopenworld.com
Website: www.royaloakhotel.net
Chef: Dylan Edwards
Owners: The Royal Oak Hotel

This former coaching inn situated in the pretty village of Betws-y-Coed was once home to a 19th-century artists' colony, whose members included JMW Turner. These days The Royal Oak caters to a wider clientele as hotel guests breakfast alongside mountain trekkers in the modern bistro. Through the comfortable bar with its antique furniture, there's a Victorian dining room with ornate plaster ceiling and linen-clothed tables. Helpful staff serve carefully prepared starters of home-cured gravad lax with coarse grain mustard and crème fraîche dressing, followed by noisettes of Welsh venison on wilted spinach with damson and red wine jus.

Times: 12–3/6.30–9,
Closed 25, 26 Dec, Mon–Tue,
L Wed Sat, D Sun
Prices: Main £12.95–£18.95
Directions: Situated on A5
trunk road
Parking: 100

Castle Hotel Conwy

Modern British

An ideal venue for special occasions

High Street, CONWY, LL32 8DB
Tel: 01492 582800
Email: mail@castlewales.co.uk
Website: www.castlewales.co.uk
Chef: Graham Tinsley
Owners: Lavin Family &
Graham Tinsley

This family-run coaching inn – set in the Unesco World Heritage town with its imposing 13th-century castle – is itself one of Conwy's most distinguished buildings. A popular modern bar offers light meals, but Shakespeare's is the main event, a fine-dining restaurant that takes its name from a set of theatrical scenes painted for the hotel by the distinguished Victorian artist John Dawson-Watson in exchange for his supper. The lengthy carte of modern British dishes features the likes of chargrilled fillet of Welsh beef with steamed oxtail pudding, creamed vanilla shallots, parsley and horseradish mash, and a rich shallot sauce, with perhaps a bread-and-butter pudding to finish, served with crème Chantilly and a sticky apricot compôte.

Times: 12.30–2/7–9.30,
Closed L Sat
Prices: Main £17–£20
Directions: From A55 junct 18
towards town centre. Follow signs
for town centre and continue on
one-way system. Hotel halfway up
High St
Parking: 36

St Tudno Hotel and Restaurant

Modern British

Accomplished cuisine in elegant surroundings

The Promenade, LLANDUDNO,
Conwy LL30 2LP
Tel: 01492 874411
Email:
sttudnohotel@btinternet.com
Website: www.st-tudno.co.uk
Chef: Stephen Duffy
Owners: Mr Bland

Perched on the seafront opposite the Victorian pier, this elegant establishment caters to a genteel clientele, offering classical cuisine and a magnificent afternoon tea. Ornate columns and arches provide glimpses of Lake Como – in mural form sadly, prettily complemented by imposing Italian chandeliers and a working fountain. Quality ingredients are brought together in intriguing combinations to form an appealing modern seasonal carte, plus a list of daily specials. Expect line-caught sea bass to be served with Asian greens, lemongrass and a coconut velouté, or perhaps a rump of Welsh lamb teamed with tomato couscous, tried courgettes and a minted butter sauce, while an orange yogurt pannacotta with orange sherbet and candied kumquat might catch the eye at dessert.

Times: 12.30–1.45/7–9.30
Prices: 3 Course Fixed D £38.50
Directions: Town centre, on Promenade opposite the pier entrance (near the Great Orme)
Parking: 9

Conwy

Tyddyn Llan

Tyddyn Llan

Modern British v 🍷 NOTABLE WINE LIST

Relaxed and stylish North Wales dining destination

This stylish restaurant with rooms is situated in a quiet corner of North Wales in an elegant Georgian house that was once a shooting lodge for the Duke of Westminster. Comfortable, thoughtfully furnished bedrooms and lounges provide every excuse to stay over. The dining room has particularly attractive views over the surrounding gardens (perfect for a post-meal stroll or summer alfresco dining on the terrace), while service is informal and efficient. The emphasis is on quality local produce with the chef-proprietor offering a daily-changing repertoire to reflect availability, with a tasting option bolstering the choice. Expect the likes of a loin of local lamb with tapenade and braised peppers, or a fillet of aged Welsh Black beef au poivre, while an impressive wine list rounds things off in fine style.

LLANDRILLO, Corwen,
Denbighshire LL21 0ST
Tel: 01490 440264
Email:
tyddynllan@compuserve.com
Website: www.tyddynllan.co.uk
Chef: Bryan Webb
Owners: Bryan & Susan Webb

Times: 12.30–2.30/7–9.30, Closed
3 wks Jan/Feb, L Mon–Thurs
Prices: 3 Course Fixed D £45
Directions: Take B4401 from
Corwen to Llandrillo. Restaurant
on right leaving village.
Parking: 20

Seiont Manor Hotel

Traditional British v

Culinary hideaway near Snowdonia

Imaginatively developed from the old farmstead of a Georgian manor house, this friendly hotel extends a warm welcome that makes you feel instantly at home. Contemporary fabrics and pastel colours are teamed with original features such as stone slabs and exposed brickwork in the public areas, while the beamed dining room is traditionally appointed with crisp linen cloths, fresh flowers and sparkling glassware. Simple cooking and effective presentation allow local produce to really shine: start with home-made haddock and leek fishcakes, with a tarragon and lemon mayonnaise, before moving on to succulent duck, pan seared and served on a bed of garlic rösti, with spaghetti vegetables and sautéed wild mushrooms. After dinner, relax in the cosy bar or library.

Llanrug, CAERNARFON,
Gwynedd LL55 2AQ
Tel: 01286 673366
Email:
seiontmanor@handpicked.co.uk
Website: www.handpicked.co.uk
Chef: Martin Williams
Owners: Hand Picked Hotels

Times: 12–2/7–9.30
Prices: 3 Course Fixed D £29.50
Directions: From Bangor follow signs for Caernarfon. Leave Caernarfon on A4086. Hotel 3m on left
Parking: 40

Plas Bodegroes

Modern British

Destination restaurant on the Llyn Peninsula

Once a Georgian residence, this sympathetically converted restaurant with rooms occupies a secluded corner of the beautiful Llyn Peninsula. There's a covered terrace, a walled garden and a ha-ha. The elegant, contemporary dining room doubles as a showcase for paintings by famous local artists. Service is personable and efficient. Modern British dishes are cooked with care and flavours are deftly balanced using the best of North Welsh produce. Start perhaps with seared Cardigan Bay scallops with caramelised chicory and vanilla sauce before griddled sirloin of Welsh Black beef with glazed shallots and a steak-and-kidney pudding. Finish with a cinnamon biscuit of rhubarb and apple with elderflower custard.

Nefyn Road, PWLLHELI,
Gwynedd LL53 5TH
Tel: 01758 612363
Email: gunna@bodegroes.co.uk
Website: www.bodegroes.co.uk
Chef: Chris Chown
Owners: Mrs G Chown
& Chris Chown

Times: 12–2.30/7–9, Closed Dec-Feb, Mon, L Tues-Sat, D Sun
Prices: 4 Course Fixed D £40
Directions: On A497, 1m W of Pwllheli
Parking: 30

Llansantffraed Court Hotel

Modern British ♦NOTABLE WINE LIST

Stylish country-house hotel with winning menus

Llanvihangel Gobion, Llytha,
ABERGAVENNY, Monmouthshire
NP7 9BA
Tel: 01873 840678
Email: reception@llch.co.uk
Website: www.llch.co.uk
Chef: Simon King
Owners: Mike Morgan

A Grade II listed former manor house set in 20 acres of landscaped gardens, this country-house hotel has lovely views, sumptuous lounges and roaring fires. There's a comfortable bar and a beamed dining room with country-style furniture and pretty floral prints. Attentive but friendly service, crisp linen and candles make this a romantic affair, and there's a south-facing terrace for summer alfresco dining. The menu comprises stylish classical dishes with unfussy modern presentation based on quality local and home-grown produce. Think Welsh Black beef fillet served with rich oxtail ravioli, or Old Spot pork in apple juice with a gratin mustard and chive sauce, and then banana tarte Tatin with rum-and-raisin ice cream.

Times: 12–2/7–8.45
Prices: 3 Course Fixed D £29.50 –£42.50 Main £13.50–£21
Directions: From junction of A40 & A465 at Abergavenny, take B4598 signed to Usk. Hotel 4.50m on left (with white gates). 0.50m along drive
Parking: 250

The Bell at Skenfrith

British ♦NOTABLE WINE LIST

Restaurant with rooms and all-round appeal

SKENFRITH, Monmouthshire
NP7 8UH
Tel: 01600 750235
Email: enquiries@skenfrith.co.uk
Website: www.skenfrith.co.uk
Chef: David Hill
Owners: Mr & Mrs W Hutchings

Standing beside the River Monnow in a lovely village setting, this stylishly refurbished former coaching inn still retains much charm and character. Beams, flagstone floor and big fires blend with plain walls and simple wooden tables that contribute to the understated elegance, backed by relaxed, friendly and efficient service. The menu follows a modern British approach, with keen attention to seasonality and the use of quality local produce – with the herbs used in the kitchen's well-presented dishes grown in The Bell's own garden. Think a fillet of Brecon beef with fondant potato, creamed leeks and spinach, green beans and a pancetta, mushroom and shallot tortellini served in a red wine jus, while to finish, a fig sticky toffee pudding with caramelised banana and coconut ice cream. The award-winning wine list shows great enthusiasm with well-written notes.

Times: 12–2.30/7–9.30, Closed Last wk Jan 1st wk Feb, Mon (Nov–Mar)
Prices: Main £14.25–£18.50
Directions: N of Monmouth on A466 for 4m. Left on B4521 towards Abergavenny, 3m on left
Parking: 35

Morgan's

Modern British

Family-run restaurant serving fresh local fare

20 Nun Street, ST DAVID'S,
Pembrokeshire SA62 6NT
Tel: 01437 720508
Email:
eat@morgans-restaurant.co.uk
Website: www.morgans-restaurant.co.uk
Chef: Tara Pitman

A schoolhouse, dentist and laundrette in its time, this 19th-century building now serves the inhabitants of Britain's smallest city as a chic little eatery. Husband-and-wife team Tara and David run the show, offering a modern British menu that makes the most of fresh local ingredients. Twice-baked Caerfai cheese soufflé gets things started, followed by Gressingham duck with a Seville orange and Grand Marnier sauce, or Welsh beef with Madeira jus, parsley cream and truffled potato boulangère. Save room for the likes of banana and butterscotch crumble with honey ice cream and raspberry sauce, or lemon tart with lemon curd milkshake.

Owners: David & Tara Pitman
Times: 12–2.30/6.30–11.30,
Closed Jan, Tue, L all week (May–Aug), Mon–Thu (Sept–Apr), D Tue (Apr–Aug), Tue–Wed (Sep–Mar)
Prices: Main £12.50–£20
Directions: Haverfordwest 16m.
On A487 to Fishguard, just off main square, 100m from Cathedral

---

Milebrook House Hotel

Modern, Traditional British 🌸 NOTABLE WINE LIST

Family-run hotel with contemporary food

Milebrook, KNIGHTON,
Powys LD7 1LT
Tel: 01547 528632
Email:
hotel@milebrook.kc3ltd.co.uk
Website:
www.milebrookhouse.co.uk
Chef: Christopher Marsden, Robert Henshaw
Owners: Mr & Mrs R T Marsden

The former home of the explorer Sir Wilfred Thesiger, this charming 18th-century dower house is set amidst typical wooded, rolling Marches landscape and was once visited by Emperor Haile Selassie. His imperial majesty would no doubt have enjoyed the exquisite formal gardens with its remarkable variety of indigenous and exotic trees and plants, and may even have partaken of a game of croquet before dinner. Nowadays the country-house hotel's kitchen garden provides virtually all the vegetables, herbs and fruits served in the elegant, traditional restaurant, complementing the local produce that makes its way on to the kitchen's imaginative modern British menus. Food is presented with real flair and panache; take an excellent salad of pan-fried chicken livers with crispy pancetta, followed perhaps by a succulent rack of Welsh lamb served with dauphinoise potatoes and butternut squash purée in a rosemary jus.

Times: 12–2/7–9, ClosedL Mon, D Sun/Mon (open for residents)
Prices: 3 Course Fixed D £30.95
Directions: 2m E of Knighton on A4113 (Ludlow)
Parking: 24

Seeds

Modern British

Good honest cooking in Grade II listed building

5 Penybryn Cottage, High Street,
LLANFYLLIN, Powys SY22 5AP
Tel: 01691 648604
Chef: Mark Seager
Owners: Felicity Seager &
Mark Seager

In a property built in 1580, Seeds is a low-ceilinged parlour with an intimate dinner-party atmosphere. Original beams and slate flooring combine with curios, maps, books and original works of art to provide a truly intriguing setting. Jazz music plays in the background and friendly staff provide relaxed service. The menu offers up unfussy modern British fare. Try grilled sardine fillets with basil butter and lemon, or Welsh fillet steak with brandy and green peppercorn sauce. Comforting puddings include bread-and-butter pudding with butterscotch sauce and crème brûlée.

Times: 11–2.15/7–8.30, Closed
1 wk Oct, 1 wk Mar, 1 wk Jun,
25 Dec, Mon-Wed, D Sun
Prices: 3 Course Fixed D £25.25
–£27.20 Main £10.95–£14.95
Directions: Village centre, on
A490, 15 mins from Welshpool,
follow signs to Llanfyllin

Lake Vyrnwy Hotel

Modern British

Stunning views and cooking presented to perfection

Lake Vyrnwy, LLANWDDYN,
Powys SY10 0LY
Tel: 01691 870692
Email: res@lakevyrnwy.com
Website: www.lakevyrnwy.com
Chef: David Thompson
Owners: The Bisiker family

Set in 24,000 acres of woodland and moors, this fine country-house hotel stands above Lake Vyrnwy. The accommodation makes the most of the views, not least the conservatory restaurant where the yield of local farms, the lake and game shoots is given pride of place on the menu. Faultless presentations whet the appetite, with options like venison Wellington and roast rack of Lake Vyrnwy lamb following roast breast of pigeon on a salad of Jerusalem artichokes, or pork and hazelnut terrine with tomato chutney. Look out for the malted milk chocolate gâteau.

Times: 12–2/7–9.15, Closed
23-27 Dec & 30 Dec-2 Jan
Prices: 5 Course Fixed D £33.50
Directions: Follow Tourist signs
on A495/B4393, 200 yds past dam
at Lake Vyrnwy.
Parking: 80

Lake Vyrnwy, Powys

The Village Pub

Modern British

An inn for all seasons

As the name might suggest, you can still expect a warm welcome, flagstones and floorboards, beams and open winter fires at this revamped, weathered-stone Cotswold inn. But this is no average village pub. Here five interconnecting dining areas radiate round a central bar, decked out with eclectic wooden furniture and contemporary décor. There's a garden patio for summer eating, too. Modern thinking shows its hand in the cooking, with dishes intelligently not overcomplicated and showing a strong reliance on quality local produce. Take roast duck breast served with Savoy cabbage and parsnips, perhaps roast pollack with mussels, clams, aubergine and coriander, or crowd-pleasing beer-battered fish and chips with tartare sauce. Desserts follow the theme, from a chocolate St Emilion and crème fraîche, to warm beer cake with thick cream.

BARNSLEY, Cirencester,
Gloucestershire GL7 5EF
Tel: 01285 740421
Email: info@thevillagepub.co.uk
Website: www.thevillagepub.co.uk
Chef: Rory Duncan
Owners: Tim Haigh
& Rupert Penered

Times: 11–2.30/7–9.30
Prices: Main £10.50–£15.50
Directions: 4m from Cirencester, on B4425 to Bibury
Parking: 40

Bibury Court

British v

Comfortable, relaxing formal dining in Tudor manor

Grand country mansion tucked away behind a beautiful Cotswold village in a picture-postcard spot with six acres of grounds on the River Coln. Dating back to 1633, it offers an oasis of calm in gracious rooms that ooze historic charm and character, with traditional wood-panelling, log fires, comfy sofas and antique furniture, but the atmosphere is warm, relaxed and informal. For such a grand and elegant setting the cooking is refreshingly unfussy, unpretentious and understated. A confident kitchen uses fine, seasonal ingredients to create quality, modern dishes with a classical base; take a breast of free-range Cotswold guinea fowl served with truffled mash, braised leek and morels. Dine in the more informal conservatory at lunch and the formal, newly refurbished restaurant over dinner.

BIBURY, Cirencester,
Gloucestershire GL7 5NT
Tel: 01285 740337
Email: info@biburycourt.com
Website: www.biburycourt.com
Chef: Antony Ely
Owners: Robert Johnston

Times: 12–2/7–9
Prices: 3 Course Fixed D £35–£39
Directions: On B4425 between Cirencester & Burford; hotel behind church
Parking: 100

Cotswold House

Modern British v 🍷 NOTABLE WINE LIST

Vibrant and stylish cooking and interior design

An amazing staircase and bold, design-led decorative style cuts a contemporary edge to the inside of restaurant set in a Regency wool merchant's house, the artwork and design as exciting as the food on the plate. But this is contemporary elegance without pomposity, the service professional but relaxed. The kitchen's modern approach comes underpinned by a classical theme on enticing and intelligently compact fixed-price menus that bring skill, flair and clear flavours to top-notch produce. Think tian of Cornish crab with tomato fondue, fennel and cress salad, or perhaps Buccleuch beef fillet with foie gras, and, heading up dessert, maybe a caramelised fig gratin with spiced port wine sorbet. An extensive wine list, decent range of cheeses and ancillaries like excellent breads and petits fours all hold form through to the end.

The Square, CHIPPING CAMPDEN, Gloucestershire GL55 6AN
Tel: 01386 840330
Email:
reception@cotswoldhouse.com
Website: www.cotswoldhouse.com
Chef: Jamie Forman
Owners: Christa & Ian Taylor

Times: 12–2.30/7–10, Closed
L Mon–Sat
Prices: 3 Course Fixed D
£49.50–£55
Directions: 1m N of A44 between
Moreton-in-Marsh & Broadway
on B4081
Parking: 25

115

Hicks' Brasserie and Bar

British

Relaxed, modern brasserie-style dining

The more relaxed dining option at this contemporarily designed hotel hits all the right notes. The décor's typically stylish and modern like everything else here, with its warm colours and modern furnishings, artwork and lighting. Think marble-topped bar, ivory or burgundy-coloured walls, banquettes or cool chairs and polished-wood tables, all colour-coordinated and suitably fashionable. The youthful service is unstuffy and friendly, while the kitchen's modern approach to brasserie fare takes a straightforward but highly accomplished line, playing to the gallery by offering something for everyone. Expect braised pork belly served with seared scallops and herb lasagne, and a passionfruit brûlée with pistachio biscotti finish.

The Cotswold House Hotel,
The Square, CHIPPING CAMPDEN,
Gloucestershire GL55 6AN
Tel: 01386 840330
Email: reception@cotswold.com
Website: www.cotswoldhouse.com
Chef: Alan Dann

Times: 12–3/5–9.30
Directions: Please telephone for directions

Three Ways House

Modern British

Cotswold home of the famous Pudding Club

A Cotswold country-house hotel offering traditional comforts, though the restaurant is more contemporary in style, with a light and simple décor, and plenty of fresh flowers. This is the home of the famous Pudding Club, founded in 1985 to promote the great British dessert, where you will also find pudding-themed bedrooms. The menu offers contemporary to traditional British fare using quality, local seasonal produce. Try braised Gloucestershire Old Spot pork belly with an English mustard jus, and finish with one of those scrumptious custard-enhanced English puddings; rhubarb crumble, syrup sponge or sticky toffee.

Mickleton, CHIPPING CAMPDEN,
Gloucestershire GL55 6SB
Tel: 01386 438429
Email:
reception@puddingclub.com
Website: www.puddingclub.com
Chef: Mark Rowlandson
Owners: Simon Coombe &
Peter Henderson

Times: 12–2.30/7–9.30,
Closed L Mon–Sat
Prices: 3 Course Fixed D £34–£40
Directions: On B4632, in village centre
Parking: 37

Tudor Farmhouse Hotel

Traditional British

Hearty fare at romantic converted farm

CLEARWELL, Gloucestershire
GL16 8JS
Tel: 01594 833046
Email:
info@tudorfarmhousehotel.co.uk
Website:
www.tudorfarmhousehotel.co.uk
Chef: Peter Teague
Owners: Owen & Eirwen Evans

Situated within walking distance of Clearwell Castle in the heart of the Forest of Dean, Tudor Farmhouse is an ideal place to stay over. The architectural style is heavily hinted at in the name: this 13th-century, Grade II listed converted farm has the requisite oak beams, exposed stone and, more unusually, wooden spiral staircases. With a growing reputation in the area, the cooking is accomplished and demonstrates clear technical ability. Seasonality and local ingredients are duly celebrated in modern British dishes such as a duo of beef fillet and oxtail suet pudding served with puréed root vegetables and thyme fondants, or perhaps wild sea bass with wilted sea spinach, olive oil mash and a herb beurre blanc. Portions are generous and full-flavoured.

Times: 12–5.30/7–9, Closed
24-27 Dec
Prices: 3 Course Fixed D
£27.50–£30
Directions: Leave Monmouth
to Chepstow road at Redbrook,
follow signs Clearwell, turn left
at village cross. Hotel on left
Parking: 24

The White Horse

Modern British

Colourful foodie pub

Cirencester Road, FRAMPTON
MANSELL, Gloucestershire
GL6 8HZ
Tel: 01285 760960
Email: emmawhitehorse@aol.com
Website: www.
cotswoldwhitehorse.com
Chef: Howard Matthews
Owners: Emma & Shaun Davis

This outwardly unassuming roadside pub on the A419 has a remodelled interior and relaxed dining-pub vibe. Pastel-coloured walls, seagrass carpeting, high-backed chairs and colourful artwork create that restaurant edge, while a large bow window overlooks the garden with its alfresco dining opportunities – there's a separate bar area too. The modern British menu makes sound use of quality produce presented in a simple, unpretentious style. Take pan-fried calves' liver served with roasted pears, chestnuts and bacon jus, or perhaps grilled sea bass with lemon and thyme risotto and a watercress sauce. Crowd-pleasing desserts – like steamed marmalade pudding and crème anglaise – provide the finale.

Times: 11–3/6–11, Closed 24-26
Dec, 1 Jan, D Sun
Prices: 3 Course Fixed D £16.95
(Mon–Thur) Main £10.95–£15.95
Directions: 6m from Cirencester
on the A419 towards Stroud
Parking: 30

The Puesdown Inn

Modern British

Quality local produce cooked with skill and flair

This traditional Cotswold coaching inn, said to date back to 1236, has been lovingly and stylishly refurbished by its hands-on owners. The warm colours, cosy sofas and log fires create a welcoming, relaxed atmosphere, while chic Italian chairs and a personal collection of paintings and photographs add additional style. The daily-changing menu reflects market and seasonal variations, with quality produce carefully sourced from local producers. While wife Maggie is found front of house, chef-proprietor John Armstrong – with a classical training starting out at The Savoy – is passionate about attention to detail. Typical dishes might include a supreme of duck with beetroot risotto, honey soused vegetables and a green peppercorn sauce, and perhaps a bread-and-butter pudding finish, served with marmalade ice cream.

Compton Abdale, NORTHLEACH, Gloucestershire GL54 4DN
Tel: 01451 860262
Email: inn4food@btopenworld.com
Website: www.puesdown. cotswoldinns.com
Chef: John Armstrong
Owners: John & Maggie Armstrong

Times: 11–3/6.30–11, Closed 1-2 wks Jan, D Sun
Prices: 3 Course Fixed D £19.95–£35
Directions: On A40 (Cheltenham-Oxford), 7m from Cheltenham, 3m from Northleach
Parking: 80

Churchill Arms

Modern British

Confident cooking in charming Cotswold pub

PAXFORD, Nr Chipping Campden, Gloucestershire GL55 6XH
Tel: 01386 594000
Email: mail@thechurchillarms.com
Website: www.thechurchillarms.com
Chef: D Toon & S Brooke-Little
Owners: Sonya & Leo Brooke-Little

An inglenook fireplace, beams, flagstones and oak flooring are what you might expect to find at this endearingly unpretentious, mellow Cotswold stone pub. However, the Churchill's clean-cut, modern-focused cooking will surprise all but the well informed. And, though the space may have been opened up, it still retains bags of rustic charm and informality, from the assortment of wood furniture to yellow walls hung with prints and wine and menu chalkboards. Food is ordered at the bar in the traditional fashion. Think attractively presented, light, modern dishes with a nod to quality and seasonality, perhaps steamed fillet of brill with grapes and white wine or a lamb pasty with onion gravy.

Times: 12–2/7–9, Closed 25 Dec
Prices: Main £9–£18
Directions: Situated 2m E of Chipping Campden

Calcot Manor

Modern British

Perfect Cotswold retreat with enjoyable dining

Built in the 14th century by Cistercian monks, this sprawling farmhouse-hotel-restaurant nevertheless has a very 21st century feel with beautifully designed bedrooms, a stunning health spa and outstanding facilities for children. The light and airy Conservatory Restaurant, with its understated elegance, makes a delightful dinner venue with white linen-clad tables and good-quality settings; it's a classy venue in an area with some really good dining establishments. Service is both professional and friendly. Modern British dishes include liberal splashes of the Mediterranean as in starters like slow-braised rabbit with sage and black olive pappardelle followed by honey-roasted Gloucester Old Spot pork belly with chestnut gnocchi and seared scallops, or wood-roasted rump of organic Highgrove beef. Desserts are similarly adventurous – how about liquorice crème brûlée with blackberry sorbet?

Calcot, TETBURY,
Gloucestershire GI8 8YJ
Tel: 01666 890391
Email:
reception@calcotmanor.co.uk
Website: www.calcotmanor.co.uk
Chef: Michael Croft
Owners: Richard Ball (MD)

Times: 12–2/7–9.30
Prices: Main £16.95–£19.25
Directions: M4 junct 18, take A46 towards Stroud and at x-roads with A4135 turn right and then 1st left
Parking: 150

Thornbury Castle

Modern British

Modern cuisine in a fairytale castle setting

A grand Tudor castle that combines atmosphere and history with modern comforts. Baronial public rooms are impressive, featuring magnificent fireplaces, high mullioned windows, tapestries, grand portraits and suits of armour. Elegant, wood-panelled dining rooms are candlelit at night and make a memorable setting for a leisurely meal. Sensibly compact and straightforward British based menus are enhanced with international influences. A competent kitchen demonstrates good technical skills and makes good use of quality seasonal ingredients, including home-grown herbs and vegetables. Choices include the likes of seared scallops with cauliflower purée and squid ink beurre blanc, John Dory with braised ox cheeks and sautéed girolles, and hot coconut soufflé with tropical fruit salsa.

Castle Street, THORNBURY,
Gloucestershire BS35 1HH
Tel: 01454 281182
Email: info@thornburycastle.co.uk
Website:
www.thornburycastle.co.uk
Chef: Paul Mottram
Owners: von Essen

Times: 12–2/7–9.30
Directions: M5 junct 16. N on A38. Continue for 4m to lights and turn left. Following brown Historic Castle signs
Parking: 50

Lords of the Manor

Lords of the Manor

Modern British v

Relaxed and welcoming country-house dining

A 17th-century former rectory of mellow Cotswold stone, this welcoming hotel and restaurant enjoys a picture-postcard setting. The dining room is smart with comfortable high-backed chairs and service is discreet and informed. The kitchen's modern approach comes underpinned by a classical theme and uses well-sourced, high-quality local ingredients. Attention to detail and consistency characterise the style, with skill and passion parading alongside some innovative elements on a repertoire of crisply scripted, fixed-price menus that includes a tasting option. Think pan-fried foie gras with tamarind ice cream and aged balsamic vinegar to start, perhaps followed by roast Old Spot tenderloin of pork served with pasta garganelli, crosnes and vanilla, and to finish, perhaps a warm carrot cake with orange pannacotta and buttermilk sorbet. Alfresco summer dining completes the accomplished package.

UPPER SLAUGHTER, Cheltenham, Gloucestershire GL54 2JD
Tel: 01451 820243
Email:
enquiries@lordsofthemanor.com
Website:
www.lordsofthemanor.com
Chef: Les Rennie
Owners: Empire Ventures

Times: 12–2.30/7–8
Prices: 3 Course Fixed D £40–£49
Directions: Follow signs towards
The Slaughters 2m W of A429.
Hotel on right in centre of Upper
Slaughter
Parking: 40

Castle House

Castle House

Modern British

Adventurous cooking in contemporary luxury

Tucked away in a residential street, this Grade II listed property is now a modern, stylish and elegant Georgian town-house hotel. The chic Castle House Restaurant has a topiary theme and extends out on to the terrace, with views over the old castle moat and gardens. Tables are clothed in their best whites with good-quality settings of silver and crystal. Staff are impeccably trained, well informed and knowledgeable. The kitchen's fresh, contemporary interpretations – underpinned by classical roots – are driven by well-sourced, top ingredients and come delivered on a repertoire that includes a seven-course tasting option. Expect pan-fried fillet of halibut with spring onion polenta, truffled peas and an oyster beignet, or perhaps a fillet of Herefordshire beef served with creamed greens, a tian of liver and morel jus, while a rhubarb and vanilla soufflé might catch the eye at dessert.

Castle Street, HEREFORD,
Herefordshire HR1 2NW
Tel: 01432 356321
Email: info@castlehse.co.uk
Website: www.castlehse.co.uk
Chef: Claire Nicholls
Owners: David Watkins

Times: 12.30–2/7–10
Prices: 3 Course D from £25
Directions: City centre, follow
signs to Castle House Hotel
Parking: 12

The Stagg Inn and Restaurant

Modern British

Friendly, quality-driven gastro-pub

Titley, KINGTON,
Herefordshire HR5 3RL
Tel: 01544 230221
Email:
reservations@thestagg.co.uk
Website: www.thestagg.co.uk
Chef: S Reynolds, G Powell &
M Handley
Owners: Steve & Nicola Reynolds

The Stagg provides a country restaurant with a pub atmosphere, including large farmhouse tables and open fires. There are three dining rooms on different levels, the largest in a medieval barn. All the dining rooms connect to the bar where the locals enjoy a drink and a chat. The kitchen's classy but unpretentious modern approach makes admirable use of quality seasonal and local produce. Recommended dishes include seared scallops on parsnip purée to start, followed by a main course of Herefordshire beef fillet served with horseradish cream, and for dessert three crème brûlées of vanilla, elderflower and lime, or maybe bread-and-butter-pudding with vanilla custard. An extensive range of regional cheeses bolsters the repertoire.

Times: 12–3/6.30–9.30, Closed
1st wk Nov, 25-26 Dec, 1 Jan,
1 wk Feb, BHs, Mon, D Sun
Prices: Main £13.90–£18
Directions: Between Kington
and Presteigne on B4335
Parking: 22

Feathers Hotel

Modern British

Popular and well-established inn serving modern food

High Street, LEDBURY,
Herefordshire HR8 1DS
Tel: 01531 635266
Email:
mary@feathers-ledbury.co.uk
Website:
www.feathers-ledbury.co.uk
Chef: Steve Rimmer
Owners: David Elliston

This impressive black and white coaching inn has dominated historic Ledbury's main street since Elizabethan times. Oozing charm and character, it combines all the characteristics of a town-centre hostelry with the comforts of a modern hotel. Dinner is served in the elegant Quills Restaurant or the bustling Fuggles brasserie with adjoining bar. The cooking style is modern British and features local beef and lamb, and a good range of fresh fish dishes. For starters, take chicken liver parfait with home-made chutney, followed by a main course of fillet of Herefordshire beef with fondant potato.

Times: 12–2/7–9.30
Prices: Main £11.50–£17.50
Directions: M50 junct 2, Ledbury
is on A449/A438/A417, hotel is on
main street
Parking: 30

Saracens at Hadnall

Modern British

Skilful cooking at an elegant restaurant with rooms

A Grade II listed building, the Saracens was originally a Georgian farmhouse, later a pub and today a smart restaurant with rooms. There are two dining rooms, the Georgian-style front room, with its polished-wood floor, panelled walls and stone fireplace, or the conservatory, which features a capped well. The kitchen deals in skilfully prepared fare, with the emphasis on quality, locally-sourced ingredients. Think pan-fried fillet of Welsh Black beef, with root vegetable mash, sautéed oyster mushrooms and a bacon and horseradish reduction, or pan-fried loin of Attingham Park venison, while an oven-baked apple with pecan and orange crumble and sweet sabayon might tempt at dessert. Children under 12 years not allowed at dinner Fridays and Saturdays.

Shrewsbury Road, HADNALL, Shropshire SY4 4AG
Tel: 01939 210877
Email: reception@saracensathadnall.co.uk
Website: www.saracensathadnall.co.uk
Owners: Ben & Allison M Christie

Times: 11.30–2.30/6.30–9.30, Closed Mon, L Tue, D Sun
Prices: Main £12.95–£17.95
Directions: On A49 5m N of Shrewsbury
Parking: 20

The Clive Bar & Restaurant

British

Bright, modern restaurant in former farmhouse

Once the home of Clive of India, this recently refurbished roadside farmstead has a relaxed and comfortable ambience, with large windows, mirrors, stylish contemporary seating, quality glassware and fresh flowers all adding to the atmosphere. The cooking style is modern British with some Mediterranean influences, using locally-sourced produce wherever possible. Organic locally-smoked salmon with smoked olive oil dressing might be followed by the likes of sirloin of Shropshire beef served with Yorkshire pudding, horseradish sauce and seasonal vegetables, while an appropriate finale might be ginger and pistachio parfait, with hot berry and apple filos, or an excellent 'tulip' of dark chocolate mousse with green tea ice cream. On Sundays, a separate lunchtime menu is available to include a roast of the day.

Dromfield, LUDLOW, Shropshire SY8 2JR
Tel: 01584 856565
Email: info@theclive.co.uk
Website: www.theclive.co.uk
Chef: Adam Ashley
Owners: Paul & Barbara Brooks

Times: 12–3/7–9.30, Closed 25-26 Dec
Prices: Main £6.95–£15.95
Directions: 2m N of Ludlow on A49, near Ludlow Golf Club, racecourse and adjacent to Ludlow food centre
Parking: 80

Goldstone Hall

Modern British

Modern cooking amidst period charm

Goldstone, MARKET DRAYTON,
Shropshire TF9 2NA
Tel: 01630 661202
Email:
enquiries@goldstonehall.com
Website: www.goldstonehall.com
Chef: Andrew Keeling
Owners: Mr J Cushing &
Mrs H Ward

Set in impressive gardens and woodland, Goldstone Hall is a relaxed, comfortable Georgian manor house. Beams, exposed timbers and open fires abound and many rooms, including the elegant dining room, have original panelled walls. The carefully evolving menus are based on seasonal and local produce, notably home-grown herbs and vegetables from the well-stocked walled garden. Fixed-price dinner menus and the light 'Upper Crust' supper choice list simple, contemporary British dishes – wild duck and apricot terrine with damson preserve and toasted brioche, and butterfly fillet of gilt head bream on a warm salad of chick peas, leeks and sweet potato show the style. Service is relaxed but attentive.

Times: 12–2.30/7.30–11
Prices: 3 Course Fixed D £22.50
Main £18
Directions: From A529, 4m S
of Market Drayton, follow signs
for Goldstone Hall Hotel
Parking: 40

Mytton & Mermaid Hotel

Modern British v

Historic riverside inn serving contemporary cuisine

Atcham, SHREWSBURY,
Shropshire SY5 6QG
Tel: 01743 761220
Email: admin@
myttonandmermaid.co.uk
Website: www.
myttonandmermaid.co.uk
Chef: Adrian Badland
Owners: Mr & Mrs Ditella

Dating from 1735, this Grade II listed, ivy-clad hotel is within easy reach of Shrewsbury and enjoys spectacular views over the River Severn. During the 1930s it was owned by architect Sir Clough Williams-Ellis, of Portmeirion fame. The restaurant strives for excellence in food and service while maintaining a comfortable, friendly environment, and is furnished with oak floors and antique oak tables adorned with candles and fresh flowers. Local seasonal produce is used wherever possible in dishes such as Attingham Park venison served with fennel mash, creamed leeks, carrot purée and a red wine and juniper jus, and to finish, perhaps a Calvados brûlée with apple tuile, mango compôte and Granny Smiths apple sorbet. There's also a convivial bar with separate menu.

Times: 11.30–2.30/6.30–10,
Closed 25 Dec, D 26 Dec
Prices: Main £13.95–£18.50
Directions: Just outside
Shrewsbury on the B4380 (old A5).
Opposite Attingham Park
Parking: 80

Old Vicarage Hotel

Modern British

Quality cooking in a one-time vicarage

An Edwardian former vicarage provides an elegant setting for this small family-run hotel, which has its own two acres of grounds in a peaceful village location. The interior features fresh flowers and polished wood floors and tables, and the relaxing lounge is perfect for pre-dinner drinks or afternoon tea. Lovely views of Shropshire countryside are afforded from the Orangery Restaurant, and service is as friendly and unobtrusive as the atmosphere. The highly accomplished, modern-focused kitchen is firmly driven by flavour and intelligent simplicity, which is entirely appropriate to the surroundings. This refreshing approach allows high-quality produce to shine. The light lunch menu is a useful introduction to the Old Vicarage experience but, for the full effect, try house specialities from the dinner menu, such as a starter of roast chicken and foie gras terrine with golden raisin purée, Muscat jelly and toasted country bread, and a main course of roast Gloucester Old Spot pork fillet with truffled haricot beans, chestnut-spiked potato cake and port sauce. Finish your meal with a dessert of apple and brioche fritter with a sorbet and pannacotta of green apple, a tasting plate of Old Vicarage mini desserts or artisan cheeses from the trolley. An excellent tasting menu and separate Sunday lunch menu is also available.

WORFIELD, Bridgnorth,
Shropshire WV15 5JZ
Tel: 01746 716497
Email: admin@the-old-vicarage.
demon.co.uk
Website:
www.oldvicarageworfield.com
Chef: Simon Diprose
Owners: Mr & Mrs D Blakstad

Times: 12–2/7–9, L Mon,
Tue & Sat (by reservation only),
D 24–26 Dec
Prices: 3 Course Fixed D £39.50
Directions: From Wolverhampton
take A454 (Bridgnorth road), from
M54 junct 4 take A442 towards
Kidderminster
Parking: 30

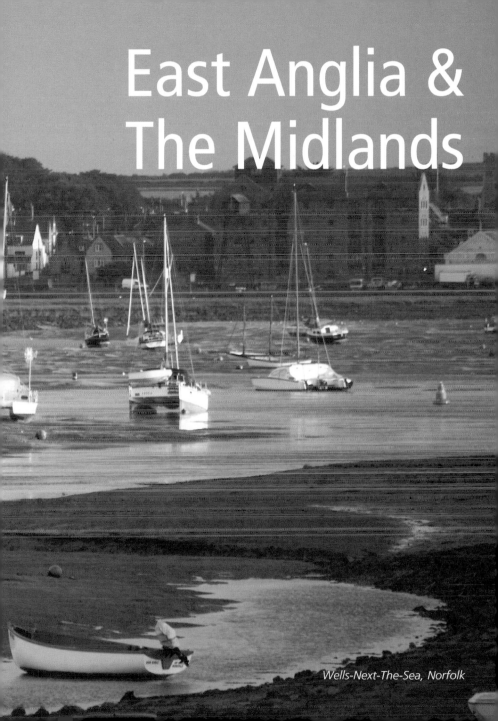

East Anglia &
The Midlands

Wells-Next-The-Sea, Norfolk

The George Inn

Modern British

Coaching inn offering an exciting range of dishes

High Street, BABRAHAM,
Cambridgeshire CB22 3AG
Tel: 01223 833800
Email: george@inter-mead.com
Website: www.
georgeinnbabraham.co.uk
Chef: Mark Edgeley
Owners: G A Wortley

This smart gastro-pub is full of character. A coaching inn since 1774, following a fire in 2004 the inn has been beautifully restored, retaining original features alongside contemporary furnishings. There is also a new barn-style restaurant. Service in the two dining rooms is relaxed and professional with black-clad staff sporting long aprons. The lunch menu offers ciabattas and a range of main courses like dressed Cromer crab. The evening menu has some exotic starters like tempura-fried salmon nori roll with ginger mirin and coriander dressing, while main courses might include tandoori-marinated chicken breast with lime and coriander wild rice. There is a beautiful terrace for alfresco dining.

Times: 11.30–3/5.30–11,
Closed D Sun in Winter
Prices: Main £14.95–£22.95
Directions: At junct of A11 & A1307 take A1307 towards Cambridge. Turn left after 200mtrs
Parking: 40

---

22 Chesterton Road

Modern British

Accomplished cooking and intimate dining

22 Chesterton Road, CAMBRIDGE,
Cambridgeshire CB4 3AX
Tel: 01223 351880
Email:
davidcarter@restaurant22.co.uk
Website: www.restaurant22.co.uk
Chef: Martin Cullum & Seb Mansfield
Owners: Mr D Carter

A relaxed, candlelit Victorian dining room with tables cosily close together and the atmosphere of a private house, which is precisely what this once was. Academics, families and business people are equally at home here. The kitchen's monthly-changing fixed-price modern British menu with French influences takes a modern approach, and is short but versatile, with an optional fish and cheese course. Sound skills and an emphasis on quality, fresh local ingredients and flavour ensure consistent results; think a roast loin of venison served with braised red cabbage, pommes Parmentier and celeriac, and perhaps a rum pannacotta with poached pear and ginger shortbread to finish.

Times: 7–9.45, Closed 25 Dec & New Year, Sun-Mon, L all week
Prices: 3 Course Fixed D £26.50
Directions: Telephone for directions

Graffiti at Hotel Felix

Modern British

Enjoyable brasserie dining in stylish hotel

Whitehouse Lane, CAMBRIDGE,
Cambridgeshire CB3 0LX
Tel: 01223 277977
Email: help@hotelfelix.co.uk
Website: www.hotelfelix.co.uk
Chef: Ian Morgan
Owners: Jeremy Cassel

Originally built for a local surgeon, this beautifully refurbished Victorian mansion is set in 3 acres of landscaped gardens. It retains many original features and the décor throughout is simple and contemporary in style. The Graffiti restaurant is a stylish dining venue, decked out with raspberry coloured chairs and modern art. Expect a brasserie-style menu comprising mainly Mediterranean-inspired fare with a smattering of British dishes given a modern twist. Take Cornish spider crab spring rolls with coriander, spring onion and coconut shavings, followed by medallions of slow-roasted rump beef with oxtail ravioli, creamed potatoes and honey-roast vegetables. Mandarin parfait with toasted marshmallows, fromage frais sorbet and a citrus filo might prove an interesting finale.

Times: 12–2/6.30–10.30
Prices: Main £13.50–£18.50
Directions: M11 junct 12. From A1 N take A14 turning onto A1307. At City of Cambridge sign turn left into Whitehouse Lane
Parking: 90

The George Hotel & Brasserie

Modern British

Stylish, busy brasserie in former coaching inn

High Street, Buckden, ST NEOTS,
Cambridgeshire PE19 5XA
Tel: 01480 812300
Email:
mail@thegeorgebuckden.com
Website:
www.thegeorgebuckden.com
Chef: Haydn Laidlow
Owners: Richard & Anne Furbank

This venerable coaching inn may date to the 17th century, but it has had a stylish refurbishment to bring it right up to date. Each of its chic bedrooms is individually designed in homage to a famous George, from Washington to Best, while its ground-floor brasserie is a bustling modern affair that caters to casual diners throughout the day. Brown leather stools perch at the long metal bar, while polished wooden tables gleam beneath sparkling glassware; it's a convivial setting, perfectly complemented by a menu of modern British cuisine. Braised venison arrives with parsnip mash, black pudding and sauce bordelaise, while sea bass is served with squid, risotto nero, chilli and rocket.

Times: 12–2.30/7–9.30
Prices: Main £12.50–£21.50
Directions: Off A1, S of junct with A14
Parking: 25

The Prospect

Modern British

Town-centre restaurant with a good atmosphere

Theme Court, Bridge Street,
BAKEWELL, Derbyshire DE45 1DS
Tel: 01629 810077
Email:
theprospect@btinternet.com
Chef: Darren Goodwin
Owners: Darren Williams

Reclaimed antique oak panelling mixes well with polished tabletops and modern place settings at this former forge, and a brand new bar and lounge area create the perfect setting for pre- or post-dinner drinks. The kitchen's no-nonsense approach uses the freshest local ingredients, delivering dishes that are modern in style with Mediterranean and Asian influences, yet firmly rooted in the British tradition. You might start with smoked mackerel, salmon and sorrel fishcakes with aïoli and lemon dressing, and then follow with Elton estate venison Wellington with sweet potato purée, braised red cabbage and Cumberland sauce, with a delicious bread-and-butter pudding and apricot coulis to finish.

Times: 12–2.30/6.30–12, Closed 25-26 Dec, 1 Jan, Easter Sun, Mon
Prices: 3 Course Fixed D £17.50 Main £13.50–£20
Directions: From A6 (Matlock to Buxton road), follow signs for Baslow. Theme Court is opposite The Queens Arms pub

---

Rutland Arms Hotel

Traditional, British

Enjoyable dining in welcoming, traditional hotel

The Square, BAKEWELL,
Derbyshire DE45 1BT
Tel: 01629 812812
Email:
rutland@bakewell.demon.co.uk
Website:
www.bakewell.demon.co.uk
Chef: Brian Lee
Owners: David Donegan

This imposing 19th-century stone-built hotel – in whose kitchens the Bakewell pudding was invented – is a local landmark at the heart of town. Its Four Seasons restaurant is classically traditional in style, with polished granite fireplace, lofty ceilings, chandeliers and several clocks, evoking an endearing air of a bygone era. By contrast, the accomplished cooking is up-to-date, showcasing Peak District fare – smoked salmon tian with crème fraîche, followed by rack of lamb with buttered leeks and redcurrant and orange jus and, of course, traditional Bakewell pudding to finish, served with clotted cream and fresh berry compôte.

Times: 12–2/7–9
Prices: 3 Course Fixed D £28.50 –£34 Main £8–£18
Directions: On A6 in Bakewell centre opposite war memorial. Parking opposite side entrance
Parking: 30

Darleys Restaurant

Modern British v

Accomplished cuisine delivered in a former mill

Located in part of an old cotton mill overlooking the River Derwent, this sophisticated restaurant is contemporary in style with an open-plan layout and neutral tones of leather, suede and silk, quality table settings and polished glassware. Additional seating is available outside on the decked terrace overlooking the weir, where afternoon tea is also served. Deftly prepared modern dishes are created from top-quality local ingredients, such as roast quail salad with pomegranate dressing, followed perhaps by peppered loin of venison with juniper sauce, or fillet of turbot with squid ink linguine and saffron and mussel chowder. For an unusual finish try rice pudding 'fritter' with roast pineapple and rum syrup.

Darley Abbey Mill, DARLEY ABBEY, Derby, Derbyshire DE22 1DZ
Tel: 01332 364987
Email: info@darleys.com
Website: www.darleys.com
Chef: Jonathan Hobson
Owners: Jonathan & Kathryn Hobson

Times: 12–2/7–10, Closed BHs, 1st 2 wks Jan, D Sun
Prices: Main £17.25–£19.50
Directions: A6 N from Derby (Duffield Rd). After 1m turn right into Mileash Lane, down to Old Lane, turn right and follow road over bridge. Restaurant on right
Parking: 12

Masa Restaurant and Wine Bar

Modern British v

Contemporary wine bar-restaurant

The sensitive and stylish refurbishment of this one-time Wesleyan chapel in the town centre – which saw its last service in 2002 – deserves high praise indeed, retaining many original features and bags of character alongside contemporary good looks. The ground floor comes decked out as a spacious bar, while the galleried restaurant has well-spaced tables on different levels. The skilled kitchen shows obvious pedigree (chef Kevin Stone previously worked at Darleys Restaurant at Darley Abbey), with its intelligent handling of quality produce in slick, clean-flavoured, balanced and well-presented dishes. Take a roasted fillet and braised belly of pork served with black pudding, Savoy cabbage and mustard cream, and perhaps a brioche summer pudding finale.

The Old Chapel, Brook Street DERBY, Derbyshire DE1 3PF
Tel: 01332 203345
Email: enquiries@masarestaurantwinebar.com
Website: www.masarestaurantwinebar.com
Chef: Kevin Stone
Owners: Didar & Paula Dalkic

Times: 12–2.30/6–9.30
Prices: 3 Course Fixed D £21
Main £12.50–£19.50
Directions: 8m from M1 junct 25. Brook St off inner ring road near BBC Radio Derby

The Old Vicarage

Modern British

Memorable dining in striking house and gardens

The welcome at The Old Vicarage is warm and friendly, the décor pleasingly unfussy country-house and cosy lounges with open fires are perfect for enjoying aperitifs and canapés. There is a comfortable main dining room and the conservatory dining area opens out onto the terrace and lovely views – perfect for summer outdoor dining. The kitchen's modern focus is admirably inspired by top-quality, seasonal produce from local and specialist suppliers, as well as the kitchen garden itself. Expect some unusual blends of flavours, but the precision cooking is not tied to fashion or gimmicks. Sound combinations, accomplished skills and clear flavours abound in dishes like roasted fillet of Whitby cod with sevruga caviar, steamed mussels and thyme crispy polenta cake, or perhaps roast fillet of Aberdeen Angus beef on cinnamon-braised shin with Seville orange and fondant potato.

Ridgeway Moor, RIDGEWAY,
Derbyshire S12 3XW
Tel: 0114 247 5814
Email: eat@theoldvicarage.co.uk
Website:
www.theoldvicarage.co.uk
Chef: T Bramley, N Smith
Owners: Tessa Bramley

Times: 12.30–2/6.30–9.30,
Closed 10 days Xmas/New Year,
2 wks Aug & BHs, Sun & Mon,
L Sat
Prices: 3 Course Fixed D £55
Directions: Please telephone
for directions
Parking: 18

The Peacock at Rowsley

Modern British v

Ambitious cooking at a chic hotel

Once again under the ownership of the Haddon Hall estate, this chic little establishment (the former dower house) has undergone a contemporary makeover – a clever fusion of ancient manor with ultra-modern boutique-hotel styling. The mix is easy on the eye, its cool interiors enriched with original features and period furnishings. The dining room follows the theme, backed by well-drilled, hospitable service and garden views. Highly accomplished, flavourful dishes come dressed to thrill and testify to the kitchen's ambition and technical skill. The enticing repertoire takes a modern approach, and making a decision can be tricky; perhaps scallops with confit potatoes, seaweed and fish sauce, or beef fillet with horseradish croquette, broad beans and delicious chips.

Bakewell Road, ROWSLEY, Derbyshire DE4 2EB
Tel: 01629 733518
Email: reception@ thepeacockatrowsley.com
Website: www. thepeacockatrowsley.com
Chef: Mathew Rushton
Owners: Rutland Hotels

Times: 12–2/7–9, Closed D 24–26 Dec
Prices: Main £22.50–£27.50
Directions: M1 junct 29 (Chesterfield), 20 mins to Rowsley
Parking: 25

The Blakeney Hotel

Traditional British

Quayside hotel with a wide-ranging menu

The Quay, BLAKENEY,
Norfolk NR25 7NE
Tel: 01263 740797
Email:
reception@blakeney-hotel.co.uk
Website:
www.blakeney-hotel.co.uk
Chef: Martin Sewell
Owners: Michael Stannard

Situated on the quayside, this attractive brick-and-flint hotel offers panoramic views across the estuary and salt marshes to Blakeney Point. It has two comfortable lounges for pre-dinner drinks, one with a log fire for the winter months and the other a sun room that makes the most of the beauty of the north Norfolk coast. The elegant restaurant offers a lengthy menu firmly rooted in British cuisine, and features old favourites (home-made local fish pie topped with mashed potato and cheese), as well as more sophisticated fare such as a marinated saddle of venison with fondant potato, spiced plum compôte and port sauce.

Times: 12–2/6.30–8.45,
Closed 24-27 Dec , D 31 Dec
Prices: 3 Course Fixed D
£25–£34.50
Directions: From the A148
between Fakenham and Holt, take
the B1156 to Langham & Blakeney
Parking: 60

The Moorings

Modern British

Small, relaxed predominantly fish-based bistro

High Street, BLAKENEY, Norfolk
NR25 7NA
Tel: 01263 740054
Email: reservations@blakeney-
moorings.co.uk
Website:
www.blakeney-moorings.co.uk
Chef: Richard & Angela Long
Owners: Richard & Angela Long

Aptly named, relaxed, seaside-style bistro, situated on a busy side road adjacent to the quayside. Yellow walls, oiled wooden boards, closely-packed clothed tables and relaxed service all hit the mark. Unsurprisingly, the menu comes awash with the fruits of the sea, with fish (much of it sourced locally) dominating the fixed-price menu. Cooking is straightforward and accurate, with simple dishes and presentation that don't stint on flavour. Think grilled halibut fillet with wilted spinach and a rich fennel purée, or perhaps roast local partridge with honey and thyme roasted root vegetables and a port jus. Homely puddings, like treacle sponge and custard, provide the finish.

Times: 10.30–5/7–9.30, Closed
2 wks Jan, Mon-Thu (Nov-Mar),
D Sun
Prices: Main £10.95–£17.50
Directions: Off A149 where High
St runs N to the quay

The Lavender House

Modern British v

Thatched cottage offering a gourmet experience

This thatched cottage with heavy oak beams dates from around 1540. Sympathetically restored and extended, it now offers a light modern interior. There are comfortable sofas in the bar and high-backed wicker dining chairs and crisp white table settings in the restaurant areas. The modern British cooking takes advantage of products from artisan local suppliers. An appetiser to start and taster dishes between courses give you a chance to try an enormous selection of wonderful delicacies. Starters like sea-salt grilled mackerel with blinis, tomato, broad bean and olive might be followed by local skate wing with a fricassée of mussels, lettuce and peas, with Calvados-poached apple served with butter cake and candied apple ice cream to finish. The selection of English farmhouse cheeses is extensive.

39 The Street, BRUNDALL,
Norfolk NR13 5AA
Tel: 01603 712215
Website:
www.thelavenderhouse.co.uk
Chef: Richard Hughes &
Richard Knights
Owners: Richard Hughes

Times: 6.30–12, Closed 24 Dec
–30 Dec, Sun & Mon, L all week
Prices: 6 Course Fixed D £38
Directions: 4m from Norwich
city centre
Parking: 16

Rushmore's

British

Assured cooking of traditional British food

14 High Street, HEACHAM,
Norfolk PE31 7ER
Tel: 01485 579393
Website:
www.heacham.fsnet.co.uk
Chef: Colin Rushmore
Owners: P Barrett & D Askew

Good honest service with a smile is offered at this traditional restaurant, with its proper tablecloths and linen napkins. The eponymous chef hails from Norfolk and his monthly menu is drawn from seasonal local ingredients, including shellfish from the coast and game from Sandringham. Utterly British in style, this is simple, effective cooking with a classic feel. Recommended dishes are William pear with vanilla dressing and stilton mousse, or local pork with apricot stuffing and Fenland leeks. Steamed treacle pudding is just one of the great home-made sweets.

Times: 12–2/6.30–9.30,
Closed Mon, L Tue & Sat, D Sun
Prices: 3 Course Fixed D £19.95
Directions: A149 towards
Hunstanton. At Heacham, turn
left at Lavender Fields. Follow into
village, take 1st left into High St
Parking: 25

Arlington Grill & Brasserie

Modern British v

Enjoyable dining at historic city-centre venue

The George Hotel, 10 Arlington Lane, Newmarket Road, NORWICH, Norfolk NR2 2DA
Tel: 01603 617841
Email: reservations@georgehotel.co.uk
Website: www.arlingtonhotelgroup.co.uk
Chef: Paul Branford
Owners: David Easter/Kingsley Place Hotels Ltd

Behind the frosted glass frontage of this city-centre hotel brasserie lies a contemporary dining room with leather banquette seating, darkwood panelling and mirrors which give a bright but intimate atmosphere – the open-plan grill adds a touch of theatre. Expect formal service from friendly, uniformed staff. Simply cooked dishes make good use of fresh seasonal produce such as starters of warm pigeon breast, bacon lardons and cherry tomatoes, and main courses of marinated lamb loin with rosemary-roasted potatoes, root vegetables and red wine jus. Desserts include sticky toffee pudding with caramel sauce.

Times: 12–2/6–10
Prices: 3 Course Fixed D £19.95 Main £9.95–£16.95
Directions: 1m from Norwich city centre, 1m from Norwich city station, 1m from A140
Parking: 40

De Vere Dunston Hall

Modern British

Accomplished cuisine in grand hotel

Ipswich Road, NORWICH, Norfolk NR14 8PQ
Tel: 01508 470444
Email: dhreception@devere-hotels.com
Website: www.devereonline.co.uk
Chef: Paul Murfitt
Owners: De Vere Hotels

An imposing Grade II listed building set in 170 acres of landscaped grounds, just a short drive from the city centre. The newly refurbished brasserie restaurant offers an extensive carte showcasing modern interpretations of French classics that utilise quality ingredients, so expect soundly cooked dishes and good flavours. Try a starter of ham hock terrine with dressed leaves and piccalilli, followed perhaps by tender crispy belly pork, served with leek and parmesan risotto and roasted root vegetables. Vegetarians are well catered for. Typical desserts include a trio of chocolate – fondant, tart and sorbet.

Times: 7–10, Closed Sun, L Mon–Sat
Prices: 3 Course Fixed D £26.50 –£36.50, Main £16.50–£23.50
Directions: On A140 between Norwich & Ipswich
Parking: 300

The Old Rectory

Modern British

A Georgian haven in the heart of Norwich

This Georgian house sits in pretty grounds overlooking the River Yare just a few minutes drive from the centre of Norwich. Deep sofas and comfortable armchairs beckon in the lounge – enjoy a pre-dinner drink, and then move through to the restaurant, a period room lit by candles, with a sensibly concise, set-price menu that changes daily. Dishes are mostly modern British in style, with a winning emphasis on flavour and good-quality local seasonal ingredients. Think marinated roast Gressingham duck breast served with Savoy cabbage, spring onion mash and a roasted young beetroot sauce, and perhaps a baked pressed dark chocolate soufflé cake with crème fraîche and whisky-soaked jumbo sultanas and raisins to finish. Service is attentive and thoughtfully paced.

103 Yarmouth Road, Thorpe
St Andrew, NORWICH, Norfolk
NR7 0HF
Tel: 01603 700772
Email: enquiries@
oldrectorynorwich.com
Website:
www.oldrectorynorwich.com
Chef: James Perry
Owners: Chris & Sally Entwistle

Times: 7–10.30, Closed Xmas
& New Year, Sun, Mon, L all week
Prices: 3 Course Fixed D £25–£28
Directions: From A47 take A1042
to Thorpe, then A1242. Hotel right
after 1st lights
Parking: 16

---

1 Up

Modern British

Contemporary restaurant above a popular pub

Aptly named, '1 Up' is upstairs from this trendy, bustling gastro-pub and provides its fine-dining arm at dinner only (plus Sunday lunch). The recently refurbished, elegant, chic look offers a twist on the classical – where modern wallpaper rubs shoulders with chandeliers and luxurious velvet curtains. The atmosphere is intimate, sophisticated and unpretentious and comes backed by appropriately professional yet relaxed service. The food fits the bill, too, the accomplished cooking is big on clear flavours and balance, and committed to the use of high-quality seasonal ingredients from the abundant local larder. Take a loin of Norfolk venison with duck-fat potatoes, creamed Savoy cabbage, baby onions and a bitter chocolate sauce, or perhaps a free-standing cinnamon crème brûlée with grilled figs and plum ice cream to finish. (In addition, a substantial bar menu is offered downstairs.)

The Mad Moose Arms & 1Up,
21, Warwick Street, NORWICH,
Norfolk NR2 3LD
Tel: 01603 627687
Email: madmoose@animalinns
.co.uk
Chef: Eden Derrick
Owners: Mr Henry Watt

Times: 12–3/7–9.30, Closed
25-26 Dec, 1 Jan, L Mon–Sat,
D Sun
Prices: 3 Course Fixed D £22.50
Main £10.50–£14.50
Directions: A11 onto A140. Turn
right at lights onto Unthank Rd,
then left onto Dover/Warwick St

Rose & Crown

Modern British

Bustling local with culinary verve

Old Church Road, SNETTISHAM,
Kings Lynn, Norfolk PE31 7LX
Tel: 01485 541382
Email: info@
roseandcrownsnettisham.co.uk
Website: www.
roseandcrownsnettisham.co.uk
Chef: Andrew Bruce
Owners: Anthony &
Jeanette Goodrich

Behind the rose-covered façade of this 14th-century inn lies a cosy warren of nooks and crannies, uneven floors and log fires. Colourful contemporary décor extends throughout the range of dining areas, which include a garden room opening on to a walled garden with a children's play area. The menu offers pub favourites prepared to a high standard with quality, locally-sourced ingredients. Try a starter of sautéed chicken livers with pancetta, baby spinach and sherry vinegar dressing, followed by a main course of salmon and butterfish brochettes with chilli vegetables, or prime Holkham beef burger with relish and fries.

Times: 12–2/6.30–9
Prices: Main £7.50–£15
Directions: From King's Lynn take A149 N towards Hunstanton. After 10m into Snettisham to village, then into Old Church Rd towards church. Hotel is 100yds on left

---

Number Twenty Four Restaurant

Modern British

Sound cooking in listed townhouse

24 Middleton Street,
WYMONDHAM, Norfolk
NR18 0AD
Tel: 01953 607750
Website: www.number24.co.uk
Chef: Jonathan Griffin
Owners: Jonathan Griffin

There's nothing pretentious or stuffy about this relaxed, friendly, family-run restaurant located in a row of listed terraced cottages. Low-key style, pale cream walls and well-spaced, neatly clothed tables hit just the right note. The compact menu takes a modern approach, with a nod to international influences. Changing daily to reflect quality market choice, the selection includes a vegetarian option. The cooking is straightforward with clear flavours. Look out for grilled fillet of smoked haddock on parsnip purée with saffron vanilla sauce and watercress, followed by seared loin of venison on bubble and squeak with sautéed winter vegetables and port wine gravy. Finish with white chocolate and lemon mousse Pavlova.

Times: 12–2/7–9, Closed 26 Dec, 1 Jan, Mon, L Tue, D Sun
Prices: 3 Course Fixed D £23.95
Directions: Town centre opposite war memorial

Horsey, Norfolk

The Tresham Restaurant

Traditional British

Accomplished cooking in magnificent surroundings

The epitome of elegant country-house hotels, the imposing Rushton – dating back to 1438 – is set in acres of parkland surrounded by beautiful countryside. The interior is kitted out in the grand style, from its large, heavy-timbered entrance doors to huge stone and timber fireplaces, ornate plasterwork and stained glass, plus there's a varied array of deep, comfortable lounge seating. The impressive oak, linenfold panelled dining room continues the theme, its modern British approach – underpinned by classical influences – delivering highly accomplished cuisine with fine depth of flavour, utilising high-quality well-sourced produce. Take John Dory and langoustines served with oxtail cannelloni and roast fish sauce, and to finish, perhaps a passionfruit soufflé with mango sorbet.

Rushton Hall, Rushton,
KETTERING, Northamptonshire
NN14 1RR
Tel: 01536 713001
Email: enquiries@rushtonhall.com
Website: www.rushtonhall.com
Chef: Alan Coulthard
Owners: Tom & Valerie Hazelton

Times: 12–2.30/7–9.30
Prices: Main £15.95–£26
Directions: A14 junct 7. A43 to Corby, A6003 to Rushton, turn off after bridge
Parking: 140

Roade House Restaurant

Modern British

Popular village restaurant

An 18th-century, stone-built pub has been sympathetically extended to provide a large, comfortable lounge bar and restaurant. Menus are seasonally based and ingredients are sourced from all over the country, including Scottish beef, Cornish lamb and local game. A starter of cured venison with fig marmalade and fresh pear could be followed by grilled fillet of halibut with pan-fried new potatoes, fine beans and a warm salad of scallops. Set menus are good value at lunch and dinner, and special dining evenings are held throughout the year.

16 High Street, ROADE,
Northamptonshire NN7 2NW
Tel: 01604 863372
Email:
info@roadehousehotel.co.uk
Website:
www.roadehousehotel.co.uk
Chef: Chris Kewley
Owners: Mr & Mrs C M Kewley

Times: 12–2/7–9.30, Closed 1 wk Xmas, Sun, L Sat
Prices: 3 Course Fixed D £35
Directions: M1 junct 15 (A508 Milton Keynes) to Roade, left at mini rdbt, 500yds on left
Parking: 20

Vine House Hotel & Restaurant

Modern British

Fresh local ingredients in a friendly atmosphere

100 High St, Paulerspury,
TOWCESTER, Northamptonshire
NN12 7NA
Tel: 01327 811267
Email: info@vinehousehotel.com
Website:
www.vinehousehotel.com
Chef: Marcus Springett
Owners: Mr M & Mrs J Springett

Two 300-year-old limestone cottages were converted to create this homely restaurant with rooms, run by husband-and-wife team Marcus and Julie Springett. The emphasis is on relaxed, informal dining in a friendly atmosphere. Original features have been preserved and guests are made to feel really welcome in the cosy dining room. Outside there's a carefully tended cottage garden. Food is rustic and full bodied, offered from a daily-changing menu using as much local produce as possible. Prime examples are home-smoked organic salmon with roasted black pudding and curry oil, or local belly of Tamworth pork with sage and onion, with rhubarb and honey crumble served with clotted cream to finish.

Times: 12–2/6–10, L Closed
L Sun–Mon
Prices: 3 Course Fixed D £29.95
Directions: 2m S of Towcester,
just off A5
Parking: 20

The Four Seasons Restaurant

Modern British

Stunning mansion and impressive cuisine.

Swinfen Hall Hotel, Swinfen
LICHFIELD, Staffordshire WS14 9RE
Tel: 01543 481494
Email:
info@swinfenhallhotel.co.uk
Website:
www.swinfenhallhotel.co.uk
Chef: Neil Peers
Owners: Helen & Vic Wiser

Set in 100 acres of parkland including a deer park, diners might gasp when they arrive at the stunning entrance hall to the beautiful 18th-century Swinfen Hall country-house hotel, but there is more to come. The lavishly decorated public rooms, including carved ceilings and impressive oil paintings, soon exhaust all superlatives. Despite the high style, the place is welcoming and comfortable. A three-course fixed-price menu showcases the kitchen's modern approach – underpinned by a classical French theme – in the oak-panelled Four Seasons Restaurant, with quality, fresh locally-sourced, often luxury, ingredients taking pride of place. Expect roast loin of venison served with braised red cabbage, celeriac, chestnut foam and a bitter chocolate sauce, or perhaps a fillet of sea bass with boulangère potatoes, roasted salsify and a red wine sauce.

Times: 12.30–2.30/7–9.30,
Closed L Sat, D Sun
Prices: 3 Course Fixed D £39.50
Directions: 2m S of Lichfield on
A38 between Weeford rdbt and
Swinfen rdbt. Follow A38 to
Lichfield, hotel is 0.50m on right
Parking: 80

The Plum Pudding

Modern British

Innovative cooking, canal-side location

Rugeley Road, Armitage,
RUGELEY, Staffordshire WS15 4AZ
Tel: 01543 490330
Email:
enquiries@theplumpudding.co.uk
Website:
www.theplumpudding.co.uk
Chef: Carl Jones
Owners: Mr & Mrs J Takhar

'Plum Pudding' was once a popular name for canal-side pubs but this is the only one left in the UK. With a large terrace alongside the canal, the atmosphere in this gastro-pub is relaxed and intimate, with friendly and attentive service. Fresh, locally sourced produce, from organic meats through to local cheeses, is found throughout a modern British menu that might include a starter of seared tuna with creamed and roasted corn. Main courses might feature a braised Packington pork shoulder with roasted stuffed fillet, broad bean and tomato risotto, while creative desserts are characterised by the likes of mandarin and cinnamon crème brûlée.

Times: 12–3.30/6–11.30, Closed 1 Jan
Prices: Main £9.95–£15.95
Directions: M6 junct 11 follow signs for Cannock to Rugeley. Situated on A513 through Rugeley to Lichfield
Parking: 50

The Moat House

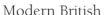

Modern British

Cutting-edge menu meets conservatory dining

Lower Penkridge Road, Acton Trussell, STAFFORD, Staffordshire ST17 0RJ
Tel: 01785 712217
Email: info@moathouse.co.uk
Website: www.moathouse.co.uk
Chef: Matthew Davies
Owners: The Lewis Partnership

Aptly named, this well restored hotel occupies a moated former manor house – with a striking canal-side setting. The main building is full of oak panelling and exposed beams, while the spacious and stylish conservatory restaurant is a modern, luxurious affair with high-backed seating and generous-sized tables, set to a backdrop of barges plying the canal. The enticing menu is dotted with luxury items, promoting an agony of choice on a classically-based, modern-focused repertoire. Fresh, high-quality seasonal ingredients combine with a sense of flair to deliver skilfully crafted, flavour-driven dishes that show the kitchen's pedigree. Take a main course of pan-fried turbot with seared scallops, salsify, garlic confit and Sauternes sauce, or perhaps a rosette of Staffordshire beef with oxtail bon-bon, wilted spinach, girolles, baby onions and red wine and truffle jus.

Times: 12–2/7–9.30, Closed 25 Dec, 1-2 Jan
Directions: M6 junct 13 towards Stafford, 1st right to Acton Trussell, hotel by church
Parking: 200

142

Restaurant Gilmore

Modern British

Friendly, family-run farmhouse restaurant

The building is a converted three-storey farmhouse set in acres of open grounds (including cottage gardens, herb and vegetable plots), making it a popular venue for weddings. It's the second incarnation of Restaurant Gilmore, the first was in Birmingham a few years back. This farmhouse version occupies three separate dining rooms, each with its own character. The kitchen takes its role seriously, sourcing the finest produce from all markets, and the cooking incorporates traditional techniques and a modern approach. There's an emphasis on flavours throughout the regularly-changing menu, with dishes like pan-fried fillet of wild sea bass served with piquillo peppers, mange-tout and a bouillabaisse sauce, or Valrhona milk chocolate brûlée, bitter chocolate sorbet and white chocolate foam.

Strine's Farm, Beamhurst,
UTTOXETER, Staffordshire ST14 5DZ
Tel: 01889 507100
Email: paul@restaurantgilmore.com
Website:
www.restaurantgilmore.com
Chef: Paul Gilmore
Owners: Paul & Dee Gilmore

Times: 12.30–2/7.30–9, Closed
1 wk Jan, 1 wk Etr, 1 wk Jul, 1
wk Oct, Mon & Tue, L Sat & Wed,
D Sun
Prices: 3 Course Fixed D £35
Directions: 1.50m N of Uttoxeter
on A522 to Cheadle. Set 400yds
back from the road along a fenced
farm track
Parking: 12

Foresters At Yoxall

Modern British

Informal dining with simple flair

The Foresters is a modern-styled pub-restaurant, set in rural surroundings – as the name indicates – on the main road north of the village. Spread over three rooms – with one decked out with some comfy sofas – with a mix of wooden and carpeted floors. Tables are plain wood as are chairs, all helping to cultivate a relaxed, informal atmosphere, as does the polite and helpful service. The kitchen shows confident form, with simply prepared, clean-flavoured dishes from quality produce; take lamb fillet with a red wine jus or Barbary duck breast with sweet and sour mango, and a blueberry tart to close.

62 Wood Lane, YOXALL, Nr Burton
on Trent, Staffordshire DE13 8PH
Tel: 01283 575939
Email: theforesters@hotmail.com
Website:
www.forestersatyoxall.co.uk
Chef: Jeff Thomas & Mark Hadfield
Owners: Jeff & Lillan Thomas

Times: 11.30–3/6.30–11.30,
Closed 25-28 Dec, Mon, D Sun
Prices: 3 Course Fixed D £20–
£22.95 Main £12.95–£19.50
Directions: On A515 Litchfield
to Ashbourne road, 1m outside
village of Yoxall
Parking: 30

Wentworth Hotel

Modern British

Traditional values with modern twists in seaside hotel

Overlooking the beach at the quiet end of town, this reassuringly traditional hotel is popular with returning guests and diners, and boasts staff who create a friendly and informal ambience. In this family-friendly atmosphere, the smart dining room, elegantly decorated in Etruscan red, is a beacon of excellence locally, with its mixture of firm favourites and an upbeat modern approach. Seasonal changes and local suppliers keep the food fresh and interesting on daily-changing menus; think roast rump of Suffolk lamb served with rosemary mash and mint sauce, or baked whole sea bream with ratatouille vegetables and sun-dried tomato pesto, and for dessert, perhaps banoffee pie with a rich toffee sauce or a winter strudel with warm vanilla sauce.

Wentworth Road, ALDEBURGH, Suffolk IP15 5BD
Tel: 01728 452312
Email:
stay@wentworth-aldeburgh.co.uk
Website:
www.wentworth-aldeburgh.com
Chef: Graham Reid
Owners: Wentworth Hotel Ltd/ Michael Pritt

Times: 12–2/7–9
Prices: 3 Course Fixed D £16.50–£18.50
Directions: From A12 take A1094 to Aldeburgh. In Aldeburgh straight on at mini rdbt, turn left at x-roads into Wentworth Rd
Parking: 33

The Bildeston Crown

Modern British

Highly accomplished cooking in a stylish country inn

This charming 15th-century coaching inn has been skilfully renovated to provide comfortable, stylish, modern dining and accommodation. Beams, ancient brickwork, oak floors, leather chairs, imposing artwork and open fires all set the tone, while friendly, helpful staff move between elegantly set tables in the bar, dining room and, in summer, the terrace. Fresh, high-quality local produce, clear flavours and accomplished skills reign on an appealing, crowd-pleasing repertoire of modern and classic dishes. This is innovative, striking and ambitious cooking from a kitchen that really understands flavour. Halibut served with crab, artichoke, iceberg lettuce and a bay leaf foam or rabbit with tarragon gnocchi, Braeburn purée, caper berries and ceps might be on the menu. The popular Classics repertoire includes steak and kidney pudding and knickerbocker glory. One to watch.

104 High Street, BILDESTON,
Suffolk IP7 7EB
Tel: 01449 740510
Email:
hayley@thebildestoncrown.co.uk
Website:
www.thebildestoncrown.co.uk
Chef: Chris Lee
Owners: Mrs G Buckle &
Mr J K Buckle

Times: 12–7/3–10, Closed D
25 Dec, 1 Jan
Prices: 3 Course Fixed D £20
Main £10–£20
Directions: A12 junct 31. B1070
to Hadleigh, B1115 to Bildeston
Parking: 24

Angel Hotel - The Eaterie

Modern British **v**

Fine dining in an imposing coaching inn

Angel Hill, BURY ST EDMUNDS,
Suffolk IP33 1LT
Tel: 01284 714000
Email: sales@theangel.co.uk
Website: www.theangel.co.uk
Chef: Simon Barker
Owners: Robert Gough

Just a few minutes from the centre of Bury St Edmunds, this imposing coaching inn has a long history of hospitality and boasts Charles Dickens among former guests. It stands in a pretty square looking across to the cathedral, and has a cosy contemporary feel despite its heritage charms. Both the newly refurbished Angel eaterie, with its stunning artwork and stylish design, and the 12th-century stone Vaults restaurant below the ground floor are relaxed in style, and serve accomplished food along modern British lines. Starters might include pan-seared scallops with a pea and mint blini, with slow-roast pork belly a typical main, served with cabbage and an apple and sage jus. Save room for dessert: mango and lime pannacotta perhaps, or lemon tart with red berry coulis.

Times: 7am/10pm
Prices: Main £11.95–£21.50
Directions: Town centre, right from Northgate St traffic lights
Parking: 30

The Leaping Hare Restaurant

Modern British

Seasonal and local produce in a vineyard restaurant

Stanton, BURY ST EDMUNDS,
Suffolk IP31 2DW
Tel: 01359 250287
Email: info@wykenvineyards.co.uk
Website:
www.wykenvineyards.co.uk
Chef: Peter Harrison
Owners: Kenneth & Carla Carlisle

This is a vineyard restaurant, part of the Wyken Hall estate, set in a 400-year-old Suffolk barn with high ceilings, wooden flooring, old beams, wood-burning stoves and paintings and tapestries of leaping hares. (The barn is divided between a restaurant and café.) Modern simple cooking – with the emphasis on flavour – makes fine use of quality local produce (usually from within a 5-mile radius). Think braised Wyken hare served with potato gnocchi to start, and perhaps mains like Troston chicken breast with greens, parsley and garlic, or Bardwell Redpoll rib-eye steak with hand-cut chips and green salad. The wine list naturally features the estate-made Wyken wines amongst others, while the adjacent Country Store – and Saturday morning farmers' market – is well worth a visit too.

Times: 12–2.30/7–9, Closed 2 wks Xmas, D Sun–Thu
Prices: Main £11.95–£16.95
Directions: 8m NE of Bury St Edmunds, 1m off A143. Follow brown signs at Ixworth to Wyken Vineyards
Parking: 50

Fox & Goose Inn

Modern British

Pub turned restaurant in a pretty village setting

FRESSINGFIELD, Nr Diss,
Suffolk IP21 5PR
Tel: 01379 586247
Email: foxandgoose@uk2.net
Website: www.foxandgoose.net
Chef: P Yaxley, M Wyatt
Owners: Paul Yaxley

The Fox & Goose is a country inn next door to the church in a classic village location. All the comforting features are here – exposed timbers and open fires – with a handsome bar and two smart dining rooms set off by lovely fabrics, modern art and a background of light jazz. On offer are a good-value lunch, an evening seven-course tasting menu and a great choice from the carte. The modern British dishes – with French influences – read beautifully, their various elements blending harmoniously on the plate. Think a fillet of halibut served with cauliflower purée, dill gnocchi, buttered spinach and a mustard vinaigrette, and to finish, perhaps an apple tarte Tatin with fennel and caramelised almond ice cream.

Times: 12–2/7–9, Closed 27-30
Dec, 2nd wk Jan for 2 weeks, Mon
Prices: Main £11.95–£17.95
Directions: A140 & B1116
(Stradbroke) left after 6m - in village centre by church
Parking: 15

The Beehive

Modern British

Great gastro-pub dining in cottage-style surroundings

The Street, HORRINGER,
Suffolk IP29 5SN
Tel: 01284 735260
Chef: Dougie Lindsay
Owners: Gary & Di Kingshott

A traditional-looking brick and flint pub, converted from a Victorian cottage, and full of period features. Embracing the gastro-pub concept, you'll find antique wooden tables and a chalkboard menu, updated during service. Patio seating and a walled beer garden with picnic benches are a popular option in summer. Traditional pub food is given a modern twist, using excellent fresh ingredients. Try a starter like cream of spinach and crabmeat soup, or a main course like steak and kidney cooked in ale, served on a bed of creamy mashed potatoes with root vegetables.

Times: 12–2/7–9.30, Closed
25-26 Dec, D Sun
Prices: Main £9.95–£15.95
Directions: A149 (Bury St Edmunds to Haverhill road). Restaurant towards end of village
Parking: 30

Theobalds Restaurant

Modern British

Village restaurant that's stood the test of time

68 High Street, IXWORTH, Bury St
Edmunds, Suffolk IP31 2HJ
Tel: 01359 231707
Website: www.
theobaldsrestaurant.co.uk
Chef: Simon Theobald
Owners: Simon &
Geraldine Theobald

Simon and Geraldine Theobald turned this oak-beamed cottage
into a restaurant more than two decades ago and have built up
a loyal following over the years. It's simply decorated with fresh
flowers and paintings by local artists, and boasts a comfy lounge
with an inglenook fireplace for after-dinner coffee, plus a pretty
patio garden for drinks in summer. Expect flavourful cooking
conjured from quality ingredients: twice-baked cheddar cheese
soufflé is a typical starter, while mains might include lamb with
roast garlic and a Madeira and rosemary sauce, or sea bass with
spinach purée and a wholegrain mustard sauce.

Times: 12.15–1.30/7–9, Closed
10 days in Summer, Mon, Tue,
Thu, Sat, D Sun
Prices: 3 Course Fixed D £27
Main £14.95–£19.50
Directions: 7m from Bury St
Edmunds on A143 Bury/Diss road

The Angel

Modern British

Medieval inn with lip-smacking food

Market Place, LAVENHAM,
Suffolk CO10 9QZ
Tel: 01787 247388
Email: angellav@aol.com
Website: www.theangelhotel.com
Chef: Michael Pursell
Owners: Mr & Mrs R Whitworth
& Mr J Barry

First licensed in 1420, the Angel is at the centre of one of
England's finest medieval villages and is replete with traditional
period décor, including oak beams, inglenook fireplace and sturdy
wooden tables and chairs. The cooking style is simple, combining
modern British dishes with traditional pub favourites, with careful
preparation of quality ingredients. Expect good flavours and
well cooked dishes, like haddock, crab and chilli fishcakes with
spicy tomato sauce, grilled fillet of arctic char with braised leeks
and red pepper sauce, or chargrilled tuna with lemon and thyme
risotto. Finish with a classic pear and almond tart, or a comforting
steamed syrup pudding.

Times: 12–2.15/6.45–9.15,
Closed 25-26 Dec
Prices: Main £9.95–£19.95
Directions: Between Bury St
Edmunds and Sudbury on A1141.
In town centre, Market Place just
off High St
Parking: 5

The Crown

Modern British

Coaching inn offering modern city-style cuisine

An original early 19th-century coaching inn with a wonderful panelled, nautical-themed snug back bar, casual front bar and small restaurant. Service is relaxed and friendly throughout. The main front bar is lively with a cosmopolitan feel and offers a more informal dining option, while the restaurant delivers a quieter atmosphere. The same modern city-style cuisine is served throughout, using fresh locally-sourced ingredients. Roasted cod fillet on a crumble of celeriac, leek, potato and spinach, or perhaps seared Suffolk lamb's liver served with red cabbage marmalade and a sage and bacon bread-and-butter pudding show the style. And to finish, perhaps a rhubarb tart with stem ginger sorbet, or warm steamed treacle sponge pudding with custard and clotted cream ice cream.

90 High Street, SOUTHWOLD, Suffolk IP18 6DP
Tel: 01502 722275
Email: crown.reception@adnams.co.uk
Website: www.adnams.co.uk
Chef: Ian Howell
Owners: Adnams plc

Times: 12–2/6.30–9.30
Prices: Main £9.95–£19.95
Directions: Take A1095 from A12; hotel in the middle of the High Street
Parking: 15

The Shepherd and Dog

Modern British

Relaxed gastro-pub atmosphere with cooking to match

Forward Green, STOWMARKET, Suffolk IP14 5HN
Tel: 01449 711361
Email: marybruce@btinternet.com
Chef: Christopher Bruce & Daniela Bruce
Owners: Christopher & Mary Bruce

Pretty much in the gastro-pub mould, with its stripped-pine tables, plain walls and casually dressed staff, the Shepherd and Dog name seems rather appropriate -the proprietors (who once owned the town's Tot Hill House restaurant) having been guided back here after a sojourn in Wales. The place is split into two main areas, the bar (serving snacks) and the restaurant, where the kitchen's modern approach might deliver roast rump of lamb with sweet potato purée and white onion sauce, or a pear and ginger sponge finish, perhaps served with a rich chocolate sauce.

Times: 12–3/7–11, Closed mid Jan, Mon, D Sun
Prices: 3 Course Fixed D £19.50 –£21.50 Main £12.50–£18.50
Directions: On A1120 between A14 and A140
Parking: 25

149

The Westleton Crown

Modern British

Great British food in a great British setting

This traditional 12th-century coaching inn retains the rustic charm of its heritage with the comfort you'd expect of contemporary dining. Diners can choose between the cosy parlour, elegant dining room, or large airy conservatory. In fine weather, the pretty terrace also provides the perfect setting for alfresco dining. An extensive menu includes daily specials and offers classic dishes with a twist. Mains might include 7-hour slow-roast leg of lamb with its own shepherd's pie and beer gravy, or roast loin of venison with griottine cherries and roast vegetable creamed potatoes. For dessert, why not try pear tarte Tatin with blackberry ice cream, accompanied by a suggested dessert wine. And don't forget the excellent range of home-made breads.

The Street, WESTLETON, Nr Southwold, Suffolk IP17 3AD
Tel: 01728 648777
Email: reception@westletoncrown.co.uk
Website: www.westletoncrown.co.uk
Chef: Richard Bargewell
Owners: Agellus Hotels Ltd

Times: 12–2.30/7–9.30
Prices: Main £9.50–£22
Directions: From Ipswich head N on A12, turn right past Yoxford, follow tourist signs for 2m
Parking: 30

Simply Simpsons

Modern British **v**

Stylish bistro serving classically-based modern dishes

A contemporary bistro on the pretty town's main street. The fashionable affair has quarry-tiled floors, polished wooden tables, artwork and painted bricks. Its name says it all, sister restaurant to the fine-dining Simpsons in Edgbaston, but here you'll find simpler cooking with a good balance of flavours and friendly informal service. Fresh local produce and stylish presentation combine in accomplished dishes like a pavé of cod with curried yellow split peas, belly of pork with black pudding and apple sauce, or grilled calves' liver with onions and smoked bacon. For dessert, perhaps vanilla pannacotta with an exotic fruit brochette.

101-103 Warwick Road, KENILWORTH, Warwickshire CV8 1HL
Tel: 01926 864567
Email: info@simplysimpsons.com
Website: www.simplysimpsons.com
Chef: Iain Miller
Owners: Andreas & Alison Antona

Times: 12.30–2/6.30–10, Closed Last 2 wks of Aug, BHs, Sun, Mon
Prices: Main £13–£19
Directions: A452. In main street in Kenilworth centre
Parking: 15

Mallory Court Hotel

Mallory Court Hotel

Modern British v NOTABLE WINE LIST

Exquisitely prepared dishes in country-house splendour

The harmonious blend of country-house splendour and contemporary design at this Lutyens-style hotel creates a wonderful homely atmosphere. There are two dining options: the formal oak-panelled Dining Room, and the art deco-style Brasserie. In summer, guests can also dine in the charming walled garden. The accomplished modern British cooking is underpinned by classical French themes, blending top-class ingredients in sophisticated combinations. Flavours are clear, and presentation designed to impress; there's nothing quirky or over-stretched here, just fine quality produce treated with admirable technical skill. The fixed-price menu is intelligently compact and enticing; enjoy a bisque of shellfish with crab tortellini and Pernod cream to start, followed by venison loin with braised pork belly and a peppery port sauce, or best end of local lamb on braised shoulder with tapenade jus.

Harbury Lane, Bishop's Tachbrook,
ROYAL LEAMINGTON SPA,
Warwickshire CV33 9QB
Tel: 01926 330214
Email: reception@mallory.co.uk
Website: www.mallory.co.uk
Chef: Simon Haigh
Owners: Sir Peter Rigby

Times: 12–1.45/6.30–9
Prices: 3 Course Fixed D £39.50–£55
Directions: M40 junct 13 N-bound.
Turn left, and left again for Bishops
Tachbrook. Continue for 0.5m
and turn right/Harbury Ln. M40
junct 14 S-bound. Follow A452
for Leamington. At 2nd rdbt take
left/Harbury Ln
Parking: 50

Billesley Manor Hotel

Modern British

Modern food in a fine historic setting

Set in 11 acres of delightful grounds and parkland with a yew topiary garden and fountain, this impressive Elizabethan manor house is close to Stratford-upon-Avon and Shakespeare is believed to have written part of *As You Like It* here. The Stuart Restaurant is a splendid oak-panelled room with a huge stone fireplace, chandeliers and silver pheasants, enjoying pleasant views across the gardens. A modern approach is taken to food and ingredients are carefully sourced. You might start with crab and spring onion risotto with lemon vinaigrette, before moving on to a main course of braised blade of beef, with roasted root vegetables, horseradish rösti and thyme. Caramelised banana bavarois might proving a fitting finale.

Billesley, Alcester, STRATFORD-UPON-AVON, Warwickshire B49 6NF
Tel: 01789 279955
Email: enquiries@billesleymanor.co.uk
Website: www.billesleymanor.co.uk
Chef: Christopher Short
Owners: Paramount

Times: 12.30–2/7–9.30
Prices: 3 Course Fixed D £37.50 Main £11–£22
Directions: M40 junct 15, then take A46 S towards Stratford/Worcester. Follow the A46 E over three rdbts. Continue for 2m then take a right for Billesley
Parking: 100

Mercure Shakespeare

British

Modern cooking behind a Tudor-timbered façade

This 17th-century building is just what you would expect to see in Shakespeare's home town, with its Tudor-timbered façade. Inside it's just as authentic, with lots of original beams, and open fires lit in winter. The smart décor uses rich, deep fabrics, giving a traditional feel throughout. The cooking, however, is up to the minute using the best of fresh ingredients. Think olive oil poached sea bass accompanied by a roast butternut squash risotto, crab and tarragon, or perhaps a breast of guinea fowl with braised endive, fondant potato and pink peppercorns. Save room for glazed lemon tart with vanilla ice cream, or a chocolate fondant with banana and Muscovado ice cream to finish.

Chapel Street, STRATFORD-UPON-AVON, Warwickshire CV37 6ER
Tel: 0870 400 8182
Chef: Jon Wood

Times: 12–2/6–9.30, Closed L Mon–Sat (ex by arrangement)
Prices: 3 Course Fixed D £24.95 Main £15.50–£22.95
Directions: Follow signs to town centre. Round one-way system, into Bridge St. At rdbt turn left. Hotel 200yds on left
Parking: 35

Isobels Restaurant

Modern British

Friendly, popular modern restaurant

A smart, black-and-white half-timbered exterior hides the chic modern interior of this popular hotel and restaurant, within easy reach of the NEC and motorway. Privately-owned and family-run, the hotel prides itself on its levels of comfort and service. The modern British cuisine draws praise from regulars and visitors alike, offering some interesting combinations, and Sunday lunch is a big occasion with an extensive menu on offer. The seasonally-changing menu includes a good selection of vegetarian options. You might start with a tart of warm wild mushrooms, sun-blushed tomatoes and ricotta cheese, and move on to pan seared gnocchi with baby spinach and walnuts. A global wine list produces an interesting selection of fine wines and champagnes.

Haigs Hotel, Kenilworth Road, BALSALL COMMON, West Midlands CV7 7EL
Tel: 01676 533004
Email: info@haigshotel.co.uk
Website: www.haigshotel.co.uk
Chef: Jenny Goff
Owners: Bill & Diane Sumner

Times: 12.30–2.30/7–9.30, Closed L Mon–Sat, D Sun
Prices: Main £8.75–£15.50
Directions: On A452, 6m SE of NEC/airport, on left before village centre
Parking: 25

Jessica's

British v

Discreet suburban dining meets accomplished cooking

Jessica's pretty courtyard entrance is just off the busy Hagley Road in a leafy suburb, and offers unexpected privacy. The conservatory-style restaurant with views over the garden has a minimalist edge, decked out with pale-wood floors, white walls hung with modern art, and rich purple chairs contrasting with the white-clothed tables. The kitchen takes a modern approach to food, which is prepared with a high level of technical skill. Top-quality ingredients and innovative combinations are features of the menu, with dishes such as slow-cooked lamb shoulder in lavender honey, or sea bass with braised celery and pig's trotter ravioli. Finish with a dessert of lemon and lime posset, cardamom and tamarilo with tamarilo sorbet, or perhaps double chocolate mousse with apple and mint, apple sorbet and chocolate crisps.

1 Montague Road, Edgbaston, BIRMINGHAM, West Midlands B16 9HN
Tel: 0121 455 0999
Website: www.jessicasrestaurant.co.uk
Chef: Glynn Purnell
Owners: Mr K & Mrs D Stevenson, Glynn Purnell

Times: 12.30–2.30/7–10.30, Closed 1 wk Xmas, 1 wk Etr, last 2 wks Jul, Sun, L Sat & Mon
Prices: Fixed ALC £36.95

Opus Restaurant

Modern British

Chic modern eatery with crustacea counter

This spacious contemporary restaurant is close to the City Chambers in Birmingham city centre. Wood flooring, wine racks and a crustacea counter set the scene for an upbeat modern dining experience, while warm colours, a large window frontage and rear atrium flood the restaurant with light during the day. Service is friendly but professional, the atmosphere relaxed. Well-sourced, quality seasonal ingredients – including freshly caught wild fish delivered daily (shellfish is a speciality here) and commitment to free-range meats – drive the accomplished kitchen's modern approach. Start with the likes of Carlingford rock oysters, and maybe follow up with pan-fried scallops and belly pork with a spring onion mousseline and Puy lentil and leek sauce, or fillets of Cornish lamb served with brinjal potatoes and baby spinach.

54 Cornwall Street, BIRMINGHAM, West Midlands B3 2DE
Tel: 0121 200 2323
Email: restaurant@opusrestaurant.co.uk
Website: www.opusrestaurant.co.uk
Chef: Dean Cole, David Colcombe
Owners: Ann Tonks, Irene Allan, Dean Cole, David Colcombe

Times: 12–2.30/6–10, Closed between Xmas and New Year, Sun, L Sat
Prices: 3 Course Fixed D £17.50 Main £12.50–£19.50
Directions: Telephone for directions

Best Western Fairlawns Hotel

Modern British

Elegant hotel with robust modern cooking

Set in 9 acres of landscaped gardens, this popular family-run hotel is located in an extended Victorian building, complete with fitness centre and spa. The restaurant's contemporary elegance, with cream décor, comfortable seating and white-clothed tables, sets the scene for some accomplished cooking. International influences are evident on the essentially British menu, which makes the most of fresh, seasonal ingredients from local producers where possible. Simply prepared yet imaginative and well presented dishes are available on the two- and three-course dinner menus, and on the wide-ranging brasserie-style lunch menu available Monday to Friday. For mains, take pot-roast blade of local beef, with bubble-and-squeak and pepper and Cognac sauce, and finish with chocolate and orange bread-and-butter pudding with whisky anglaise, or iced pistachio soufflé with toffee sauce.

178 Little Aston Road, Aldridge, WALSALL, West Midlands WS9 0NU
Tel: 01922 455122
Email: reception@fairlawns.co.uk
Website: www.fairlawns.co.uk
Chef: Neil Atkins
Owners: John Pette

Times: 12–2/7–10, Closed 25-26 Dec, 1 Jan, Good Fri, Etr Mon, May Day, BH Mon, L Sat
Prices: 3 Course Fixed D £24.50–£32.50
Directions: Outskirts of Aldridge, 400 yds from junction of A452 (Chester Rd) & A454 (Little Aston Road)
Parking: 120

The Elms Hotel & Restaurant

Modern, Traditional British

Fine dining in elegant surroundings

Built in 1710 by Gilbert White (a pupil of Sir Christopher Wren), this stunning Queen Anne house overlooks beautifully manicured lawns to the countryside beyond. The lavish interiors are very much in keeping with the grandiose exteriors, with ornate plaster ceilings, carved fireplaces, antique furnishings and stained-glass windows evoking a sense of historical glamour. The kitchen shows a high level of technical skill and the accomplished modern British cooking aspires to greater heights through clear flavours and the imaginative use of first-class ingredients. You might expect a starter of seared scallops with sweet potato, pineapple and Asian spiced foam, followed perhaps by roast monkfish with pancetta, langoustine, lemongrass and ginger, with raspberry and Pol Roger champagne jelly accompanied by its own sorbet to finish.

Stockton Road, ABBERLEY,
Worcestershire WR6 6AT
Tel: 01299 896666
Email: info@theelmshotel.co.uk
Website: www.theelmshotel.co.uk
Chef: Daren Bale
Owners: von Essen Hotels

Times: 12–2.30/7–9.30
Prices: 3 Course Fixed D £35
Main from £22.50
Directions: Located on A443 near Abberley, 11m NW of Worcester
Parking: 40

Best Western Fairlawns Hotel

The Cottage in the Wood Hotel

British ♠ NOTABLE WINE LIST

Country retreat with imaginative food

A relaxing, family-run hotel in a glorious setting, with arguably the 'best view in England', looking out over the Severn Plain from high on the steep wooded slopes of the Malvern Hills. The Cottage is a cluster of three white-painted buildings, with the classically decorated restaurant located in the heart of the elegant Georgian dower house. Views from window tables are stunning but the ambitious cooking does its best to distract, with a modern British menu that focuses on quality local seasonal produce. Take turbot with Bayonne ham, roast cherry tomatoes, Puy lentils and a tomato fondue, or perhaps pork loin served with rosemary poached apples, boudin noir and pommery mash potatoes. The thoughtfully compiled wine list is packed with interest, enthusiasm and a refreshing lack of pretension.

Holywell Road, Malvern Wells, MALVERN, Worcestershire WR14 4LG
Tel: 01684 575859
Email: proprietor@cottageinthewood.co.uk
Website: www.cottageinthewood.co.uk
Chef: Dominic Pattin
Owners: The Pattin Family

Times: 12.30–2/7–9.30
Prices: Main £9–£22
Directions: 3m S of Great Malvern off A449. From Great Malvern, take 3rd turning on right after Railway pub
Parking: 40

Whites @ the Clockhouse

Modern British

Modern, high-street bistro with cooking to match

A contemporary bistro, Whites sits on the town's pretty main street and delivers modern cooking with lashings of friendly service and warm, welcoming hospitality. In the corner of the ground-floor wine bar (serving a tapas menu), a spiral staircase leads up to the main light-and-airy, loft-style restaurant, with its wooden floors and polished-wood tables. Here high-quality fresh local produce, accomplished skills and stylish presentation combine in well-executed dishes of balanced combination and clean flavour. Take slow-cooked belly of pork served with black pudding and an apple, sage and cider sauce, or perhaps steamed fillet of halibut with a prawn and roasted pepper brochette, and to finish, maybe a ginger-scented pannacotta with rhubarb jelly.

14 Market Street, TENBURY WELLS, Worcestershire WR15 8BQ
Tel: 01584 811336
Email: whites@theclockhouse.net
Website: www.whites@theclockhouse.net
Chef: Jonathon Waters
Owners: Sarah MacDonald, Chris Whitehead

Times: 10.300am/11pm, Closed 2wks mid Jan, last wk Aug, 1st wk Sep, Mon, L Tue–Wed, D Sun
Prices: Main £12.50–£18.50
Directions: A456/A4112 into Tenbury Wells. Continue over the bridge and along the main street. Restaurant on right

White Lion Hotel

Modern British

Historic coaching inn with appealing food

21 High Street, UPTON UPON
SEVERN, Worcestershire WR8 0HJ
Tel: 01684 592551
Email: info@whitelionhotel.biz
Website: www.whitelionhotel.biz
Chef: Jon Lear, Richard Thompson
Owners: Mr & Mrs Lear

Famed for playing home to author Henry Fielding during the writing of *Tom Jones*, this coaching inn dates back to 1510 and has a colourful history. Period details – exposed timbers, lathe and plaster walls – have been sensitively incorporated into the modern décor which maintains a traditional feel. Slick presentation and quality ingredients lift its extensive restaurant menu out of the ordinary. Start with seared monkfish with crispy pancetta and a mango, paw paw and chilli salsa, and then tuck into hearty mains such as pan-fried calves' liver with white pudding, smoked bacon and mushrooms, or mustard and herb-crusted lamb with honey-glazed vegetables and rosemary jus.

Times: 12–2/7–9.15, Closed
31 Dec 1 Jan, L part Xmas season
Prices: Main £15.25–£19.25
Directions: From A422 take A38
towards Tewkesbury. After 8m
take B4104 for 1m, after bridge
turn left to hotel
Parking: 16

The Glasshouse

Modern British

Bustling town centre brasserie with cathedral views

55 Sidbury, WORCESTER,
Worcestershire WR1 2HU
Tel: 01905 611120
Email: eat@theglasshouse.co.uk
Website:
www.theglasshouse.co.uk
Chef: Shaun Hill &
Calum MacKimmon
Owners: Brandon Weston &
Shaun Hill

Shaun Hill's latest exciting venture occupies a renovated former antique shop in the centre of town. Immediately beyond the large plate-glass windows is a small bar leading through into the downstairs dining area with its striped banquette seating and light grey/blue leather chairs. The upstairs dining room, with views of the cathedral, is open to the ground floor and retains the great atmosphere. A Shaun Hill-designed menu is always going to be about good ingredients and simplicity of cooking and presentation. The choice is extensive – perfectly-timed calves' sweetbreads with potato and olive cake, or sautéed monkfish with mustard and cucumber sauce, are fine examples of what is on offer. Try the expertly made caramel and apple tart served with cinnamon ice cream for a grand finale.

Times: 12–2.30/5.30–10, Closed
D Sun
Prices: Main £11–£19
Directions: M5 junct 7 towards
Worcester. Continue straight over
2 rdbts, through 2 sets of lights.
At 3rd set of lights turn left into
car park, restaurant is opposite

North England

Buttermere, Lake District

Rowton Hall Country House Hotel

Traditional British

Magnificent Georgian country-house hotel

Whitchurch Road, Rowton,
CHESTER, Cheshire CH3 6AD
Tel: 01244 335262
Email: reception@
rowtonhallhotelandspa.co.uk
Website: www.rowtonhall.co.uk
Chef: Matthew Lloyd
Owners: Mr Wigginton

History buffs might be interested to know that this cosy country-house hotel stands on the site of a major battle in the English Civil War, but these days you're more likely to encounter a jogger in the award-winning gardens than a cavalier, thanks to Rowton's impressive health facilities which include a beauty suite, pool and gym. Inside, surviving period features include an impressive Robert Adams fireplace, extensive oak-panelling and a hand-carved, self-supporting fireplace. Take your seat in the Langdale restaurant and choose from an extensive selection of complex dishes, such as roasted monkfish in pancetta with burgundy risotto, calamari and a ginger beurre blanc, or seared organic salmon with creamed cauliflower, asparagus and a broad bean velouté.

Times: 12–2/7–9.30
Prices: 3 Course Fixed D
£13–£26.50 Main £13.50–£23
Directions: M56 junct 12 take A56
to Chester. At rdbt turn left on A41
to Whitchurch. Approx 1m and
follow signs for hotel
Parking: 170

Rookery Hall

Modern British

Classic cooking in a grand château setting

Main Road, Worleston,
NANTWICH, Cheshire CW5 6DQ
Tel: 01270 610016
Email:
rookeryhall@handpicked.co.uk
Website: www.handpicked.co.uk
Chef: Gordon Campbell
Owners: Hand Picked Hotels/
Julia Hands

This magnificent Georgian mansion, set in 38 acres of gardens, wooded parkland and meadows bordered by the River Weaver, bears more than a passing resemblance to a French château. With its mellow sandstone walls, polished mahogany panelling, ornamental ceilings, sumptuous leather sofas, rich brocades, and stained glass, the place oozes warmth and comfort. The impressive restaurant is the perfect setting for romantic candlelight dining. Modern British cooking with international influences delivers some originally themed dishes and interesting flavour combinations, as in grilled black pudding with creamed leeks and poached hen's egg, followed by a fillet of Cheshire beef with horseradish potato purée, and warm chocolate fondant with caramelised milk ice cream for dessert. Service is smooth, efficient and unobtrusive.

Times: 12–2/7–9.30
Prices: 3 Course Fixed D £32
Main £15.50–£25
Directions: On B5074 N of
Nantwich, 1.50m on right towards
Worleston
Parking: 100

The White House Restaurant

Modern British

Chic modern restaurant with a good track record

Housed in a former farmhouse, this chic restaurant, modishly littered with contemporary paintings, sculptures and etched glass screens, rubs shoulders with mullioned, leaded windows, stone fireplaces and limed oak beams. A straightforward menu is available in the bar, while the dining room offers more challenging fare; it's all served up courtesy of a long-serving chef who knows his stuff and consistently delivers quality modern cuisine. Take best end of Welsh lamb served with a cannellini bean and smoked sausage cassoulet, or perhaps pan-fried Cornish sea bass teamed with herb and lemon risotto and tempura anchovies. A bread-and-butter soufflé pudding or warm chocolate and pear tart with mascarpone ice cream might catch the eye to close.

PRESTBURY, Cheshire SK10 4DG
Tel: 01625 829336
Email: enquiries@
thewhitehouseinprestbury.com
Website: www.
thewhitehouseinprestbury.com
Chef: James Roberts
Owners: Shade Down Ltd

Times: 12–2/7–10, Closed
25 Dec-1 Jan, L Mon, D Sun
Prices: 3 Course Fixed D £15.95
–£19.95 Main £12.75–£22.50
Directions: Village centre on A538
N of Macclesfield
Parking: 11

The Highwayman

British

Traditional inn with modern approach

From the outside, The Highway Man looks like the stereotypical country inn, but inside it's a successful marriage of old-style pub and modern makeover. Here, character stone floors, open fires and low ceilings blend with leather sofas and, in the small dining room, wooden tables and leather chairs. Service takes a modern approach – attentive, knowledgeable and helpful – while the kitchen follows a traditional path with some interesting twists, driven by quality local produce and intelligent simplicity. Take Gloucestershire Old Spot pork belly served with black pudding, creamed cabbage and roasting juices, and perhaps glazed lemon curd tart with iced lemon parfait. (Lunch is a simpler affair.)

Whaley Bridge Road, RAINOW,
Macclesfield, Cheshire SK10 5UU
Tel: 01625 573245
Chef: Gareth Davies,
Matthew Wray & Luke Jackson
Owners: Thwaites

Times: 12–2.30/5–9
Prices: Main £9.25–£18.95
Directions: Main road between
Macclesfield & Whaley Bridge.
Situated between Rainow and
Kettleshulme
Parking: 22

Nunsmere Hall Country House

Modern British

Traditional fine dining in elegant surroundings

Dating back to 1900, this grand country-house hotel with 60-acre lake and extensive grounds was originally owned by the Brocklebank family, renowned for the Cunard-Brocklebank shipping line. The Crystal restaurant offers an elegant and intimate dining experience, overlooking the south-facing terrace and sunken garden. Modern British and European-style cooking is accomplished and makes fine use of quality fresh ingredients. A tasting menu is available for the whole table to sample, or expect carte dishes like thyme-roasted turbot with pomme Anna, braised celery and rioja jus, or perhaps a loin of venison with celeriac rösti, chestnut purée and sauce Robert, and to finish, maybe citrus fruit and camomile pannacotta with warm poppy seed cake and citrus sorbet.

Tarporley Road, SANDIWAY,
Northwich, Cheshire CW8 2ES
Tel: 01606 889100
Email:
reservations@nunsmere.co.uk
Website: www.nunsmere.co.uk
Chef: Paul Robertson
Owners: Mr & Mrs M S McHardy

Times: 12–2/7–10
Prices: Main £17.50–£28
Directions: From M6 junct 19 take A56 for 9 miles. Turn left onto A49 towards Tarporley. Hotel is 1m on left
Parking: 80

Stanneylands Hotel

Modern British

Country-house hotel with an engaging cooking style

Within easy reach of Manchester airport and the city centre, this traditional country-house hotel is set in 4 acres of beautifully maintained grounds. Tastefully refurbished, the elegant panelled restaurant has well-appointed tables, and is a popular venue for locals and visitors alike. Relax over a drink in one of the modern lounges before tucking into a starter of baked sage gnocchi with purées of root vegetable and parmesan tuile. Follow with a main course of lightly smoked potato-crusted fillet of sea bass with roasted sweet onions and fennel marmalade, or vegetarians may opt for cannelloni of leek with honey and cumin roasted butternut squash and stilton fondue. Desserts include some unusual choices, as in baked beetroot and olive oil cake with feta cheese sorbet and lemon jelly.

Stanneylands Road,
WILMSLOW, Cheshire SK9 4EY
Tel: 01625 525225
Email: enquiries@
stanneylandshotel.co.uk
Website:
www.stanneylandshotel.co.uk
Chef: Ernst Van Zyl
Owners: Mr L Walshe

Times: 12.30–2.30/7–9.30,
Closed D Sun
Prices: 4 Course Fixed D £27.50
Main £14.50–£22.95
Directions: From M56 junct 5, signs for Cheadle. At lights turn right, through Styal, left at Handforth sign, follow into Stanneylands Rd
Parking: 110

Drunken Duck Inn

Modern British 🍾 NOTABLE WINE LIST

Great local produce in a fantastic Lakeland setting

Barngates, AMBLESIDE,
Cumbria LA22 0NG
Tel: 015394 36347
Email: info@drunkenduckinn.co.uk
Website:
www.drunkenduckinn.co.uk
Chef: Nick McCue
Owners: Stephanie Barton

It may be a 400-year-old coaching inn, but this stylish place has become an institution with a reputation for great food, ales and comfortable rooms. The restaurant is relaxed and informal with two traditional areas and one more modern. The emphasis is on top quality local produce with all suppliers listed. Barngates Brewery at the Duck brews up to six beers using its own water supply from the nearby fells. In the restaurant, modern and traditional British cuisine sees starters like pressed pork belly, poached quail's eggs and pickled chanterelles. For a main course, try braised leg of Kendal lamb with pomme purée, French green beans and Cabernet Sauvignon jus, or loin of wild deer with rosehip, chocolate and stout.

Times: 12–2.30/6–9.30
Prices: Main £12.95–£24.95
Directions: Take A592 from Kendal, follow signs for Hawkshead (from Ambleside), in 2.50m sign for inn on right, 1m up hill
Parking: 40

Rothay Manor

Traditional British

Fine dining in the Lakes

Rothay Bridge, AMBLESIDE,
Cumbria LA22 0EH
Tel: 015394 33605
Email: hotel@rothaymanor.co.uk
Website:
www.rothaymanor.co.uk/aa
Chef: Jane Binns
Owners: Nigel & Stephen Nixon

Built as a summer residence for a prosperous Liverpool merchant in 1825, this elegant country-house hotel has a Grade II listed Regency façade and has been in the current owners' family for 40 years. The interior retains many original features and is furnished in sedate style with antiques and floral displays, while outside a revolving summer house is a feature of the pretty garden. The friendly, family-run concern offers a mainly traditional English menu, taking in the likes of local Cartmel Valley oak-smoked salmon, Cumbrian fell-bred lamb and elderflower and damson gin jelly, or grilled fillet of sea bass with prawns and saffron sauce, with perhaps apple tarte Tatin for dessert. A separate children's menu is available.

Times: 12.30–1.45/7.15–9,
Closed 3-25 Jan
Prices: 3 Course Fixed D £36
Main £7.50–£10.50
Directions: From Ambleside, follow signs for Coniston (A593). Hotel is 0.25 mile SW from the centre of Ambleside opposite the rugby club
Parking: 35

Borrowdale Gates Country House

Modern British v

Ambitious cuisine in a peaceful Cumbrian setting

BORROWDALE, Keswick,
Cumbria CA12 5UQ
Tel: 017687 77204
Email:
hotel@borrowdale-gates.co.uk
Website:
www.borrowdale-gates.com
Chef: Mike Wilkinson
Owners: Green Symbol Ltd

Tucked away in an idyllic location in the heart of the Borrowdale Valley, this welcoming hotel maintains a genuine country-house atmosphere. Its elegant restaurant boasts magnificent views of the dramatic Lakeland scenery, so book ahead for a window table. Utilising the best local produce, the combination of traditional British fare with a modern French twist creates an excellent balance of flavours in dishes such as twice-baked cheese soufflé with a saffron-poached pear and walnut salad, followed by a pavé of Harryman-reared sirloin of beef wrapped in smoked butter, and Cumbrian air-dried ham with crispy celeriac and butterbean purée. Finish with a decadent marbled dark chocolate and peppermint soufflé with chocolate crisps.

Times: 12–2/6.30–8.45, Closed L (open on request)
Prices: 3 Course Fixed D £28–£35
Main £21–£26
Directions: B5289 from Keswick, after 4m turn right over bridge to Grange. Hotel 400yds on right
Parking: 25

Purdeys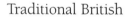

Traditional British

Enjoyable dining in old mill styled restaurant

Langdale Hotel & Country Club,
ELTERWATER, Cumbria LA22 9JD
Tel: 015394 37302
Email: purdeys@langdale.co.uk
Website: www.langdale.co.uk
Chef: Matt Hockney
Owners: Langdale Leisure

Founded on the site of an abandoned 19th-century gunpowder works, this modern hotel is set in 35 acres of woodland and waterways. Extensive public areas include an elegant bar with an interesting selection of snuff. But the main restaurant, Purdeys, is where the real action takes place, designed in the style of an old mill with oak floors, local stone and water features creating an interesting and unique atmosphere. The kitchen deals mainly in traditional British fare, cooked and presented with care and utilising fresh, local produce; take roasted Lakeland rump of lamb with spring greens, rosti potato and redcurrant jus or locally sourced loin of pork with braised potato, sage and apple tart and sautéed leeks.

Times: 6.30–9.30, Closed L (Group L booking essential)
Prices: 3 Course Fixed D £27.50
Parking: 50

Lakeside Hotel

Modern British **v**

Fine dining in picturesque Lakeland shore setting

Set on the peaceful southern shore of Lake Windermere, next to the steamer dock, this is an impressive, family-run hotel where guests and diners can expect high standards of service. Dinner is served in the elegant, oak-panelled Lakeview restaurant, with its fresh flowers, floor-length tablecloths and sparkling glassware, but more informal meals can be enjoyed in the contemporary John Ruskin's brasserie. Cooking is accomplished, with traditional British and European dishes prepared and presented with flair and expertise – classical dishes with a modern twist. Take a fillet of John Dory served with peas à la Français, braised gem, fondant potatoes and crispy pancetta, and to finish, perhaps a pistachio soufflé with dark chocolate truffle mousse. Staff are professional and highly skilled.

Lakeside, Lake Windermere,
NEWBY BRIDGE, Ulverston,
Cumbria LA12 8AT
Tel: 015395 30001
Email: sales@lakesidehotel.co.uk
Website: www.lakesidehotel.co.uk
Chef: Duncan Collinge
Owners: Mr N Talbot

Times: 12.30–2.30/6.15–9.30,
Closed 23 Dec–10 Jan
Prices: 6 Course Fixed D £45
Directions: M6 junct 36 follow
A590 to Newby Bridge, straight
over rdbt, right over bridge. Hotel
within 1m
Parking: 200

The Martindale Restaurant

Traditional British

Fine ingredients at modern hunting lodge-style hotel

North Lakes Hotel & Spa,
Ullswater Road, PENRITH,
Cumbria CA11 8QT
Tel: 01768 868111
Email: nlakes@shirehotels.com
Website: www.shirehotels.com
Chef: Mr Mike Haddow
Owners: Shire Hotels Ltd

Striking interior design, featuring timber beams, traditional Lakeland stone, wooden floors and impressive fireplaces, catches the eye at this contemporary hunting lodge-styled hotel with excellent leisure facilities. The Martindale Restaurant is where the main dining action takes place, the accomplished kitchen's straightforward, ingredient-led approach making fine use of quality local produce. The Cumbrian starter table (buffet selection of hors d'oeuvre) proves a highlight, while mains might feature slow-cooked Stainton belly pork and confit of duck, with Bramley apple mash, Savoy cabbage and cider sauce, and traditional-style desserts could include the ubiquitous sticky toffee pudding.

Times: 12.15–1.45/7–9.15,
Closed L Sat, Sun
Prices: Main £14.25–£23
Directions: M6 just off junct 40
Parking: 120

Temple Sowerby House Hotel

Modern British

Intimate setting for ambitious cooking

Dating back to 1727, this Grade II listed country-house hotel is complete with open fire, smartly dressed tables and candles, the charming oak-beamed restaurant is the perfect setting in which to enjoy some adventurous dishes that showcase the kitchen's innovative techniques and bold mix of contemporary and British cooking styles. There's a firm emphasis on seasonal, local and home-grown produce. Take butter-roasted haunch of venison with redcurrant samosa, pommes dauphine and a rosemary and Madeira sauce, or pan-fried fillet of sea bream on crushed ratte potatoes with fennel salad and bacon foam. Desserts tempt with the likes of rum pannacotta with gingerbread and caramelised garden pears, or perhaps hot chocolate and hazelnut fondant with toffee sauce and malted milk ice cream. In fine weather, the terrace is a splendid spot for pre-dinner drinks.

TEMPLE SOWERBY, Penrith, Cumbria CA10 1RZ
Tel: 017683 61578
Email: stay@templesowerby.com
Website:
www.templesowerby.com
Chef: Ashley Whittaker
Owners: Paul & Julie Evans

Times: 7–9, Closed 8 days Xmas, L all week
Prices: Main £15–£21
Directions: On A66, 7m E of Penrith in village centre
Parking: 20

Fayrer Garden Hotel

Modern British, Traditional

Country-house dining overlooking Lake Windermere

This former Edwardian gentleman's residence is set in 5 acres of beautiful gardens and has spectacular views over the lake. The interior is decorated in the country-house style, and the Terrace restaurant has sumptuous fabrics and drapes, crisp linen on the tables and formal settings. Generously priced, five-course, daily-changing menus use local seasonal ingredients that keep locals and visitors returning. The traditional British approach comes with a few modern twists; take a suprême of guinea fowl with a wild mushroom tart, baby vegetables and a thyme and Madeira sauce, or skate wing served with ratatouille, a quenelle of tapenade mash, crisp air-dried ham and a tomato coulis. Finish with a Bramley apple cheesecake.

Lyth Valley Road, Bowness on Windermere, WINDERMERE, Cumbria LA23 3JP
Tel: 015394 88195
Email:
lakescene@fayrergarden.com
Website: www.fayrergarden.com
Chef: Edward Wilkinson
Owners: Mr & Mrs Wildsmith

Times: 7–8.30, Closed 1st 2wks Jan, L all week
Prices: 4 Course Fixed D £25–£35
Directions: M6 junct 36, onto A591. Past Kendal, at rdbt turn left onto B5284 and continue for 8m, then turn left onto A5074 for 400yds
Parking: 40

Holbeck Ghyll Country House

Holbeck Ghyll Country House

Modern British **V**

Classical cuisine in former hunting lodge

The breathtaking views over the Lake and the Langdale Fells are just two of the many attractions of this sumptuous hotel and restaurant with its brace of classically-styled dining rooms. The professionalism and attentiveness of the staff are exemplary, and the kitchen's modern approach is underpinned by a classical theme, delivering a repertoire of fixed-price, compact menus (bolstered by a gourmet option – Fridays and Saturdays) that aren't short on appeal or imagination. An intelligent simplicity allows the high-quality produce to shine in well-presented, clear-flavoured dishes – think roasted turbot served with creamed leeks, crisp ham and a red wine sauce – while elaborate desserts might be headed-up by an assiette of lemon, though the chocolate plate might catch the eye, too. An extensive wine list, with a good range of half bottles, and a fine selection of cheeses make this a class act.

Holbeck Lane, WINDERMERE,
Cumbria LA23 1LU
Tel: 015394 32375
Email: stay@holbeckghyll.com
Website: www.holbeckghyll.com
Chef: David McLaughlin
Owners: David & Patricia Nicholson

Times: 12.30–2/7–9.30
Prices: 3 Course Fixed D £49.50
Directions: 3m N of Windermere on A591. Past Brockhole Visitor Centre. Turn right into Holbeck Lane. Hotel is 0.5m on left
Parking: 25

Jerichos

Modern British

Warm and intimate restaurant serving creative food

Birch Street, WINDERMERE,
Cumbria LA23 1EG
Tel: 015394 42522
Email: enquiries@jerichos.co.uk
Website: www.jerichos.co.uk
Chef: Chris Blaydes, Tim Dalzell
Owners: Mr & Mrs C Blaydes

Friendly and unpretentious with a great atmosphere, Jerichos is a modern restaurant off the main street in the centre of town. A warm, rich décor, linen tablecloths, tall chairs, an open-to-view kitchen and walls lined with prints of jazz players create an upbeat vibe. The accomplished, innovative cooking sings to an equally modern tune, with an emphasis on simplicity and flavour; take pan-fried organic corn-fed chicken breast with chorizo and thyme-roasted provençale vegetables, spiced orange couscous and a port wine sauce, and perhaps a white chocolate pannacotta finish, served with a summer fruit coulis, shortbread sablé and peach sorbet. Wine recommendations appear on menus, while the wine list comes helpfully grouped by food type rather than by country.

Times: 6.45–10, Closed 2 wk end Nov-1st wk Dec, Xmas, 1 Jan, Mon (Apr-Dec), Sun (Jan-Mar), L Tue–Sun
Prices: Main £14.50–£19
Directions: M6 junct 36, then A591.

Lindeth Howe Country House

Modern British

Accomplished fare in a famous author's former home

Lindeth Drive, Longtail Hill,
WINDERMERE, Cumbria LA23 3JF
Tel: 015394 45759
Email: hotel@lindeth-howe.co.uk
Website: www.lindeth-howe.co.uk
Chef: Graham Gelder
Owners: Lakeinvest Ltd

The former family home of Beatrix Potter is now a charming country-house hotel set on a hill overlooking the valley, Lake Windermere and distant fells. The bright, conservatory-style restaurant overlooks the secluded gardens and provides an elegant setting in which to enjoy well-presented modern cooking. Take canapés and aperitifs in the lounge or on the terrace while perusing the daily-changing four-course dinner menu, perhaps showcasing a baked loin of Cumbrian lamb with herb crust served with basil-flavoured mash potato, aubergine caviar and a redcurrant jus. A glazed lemon tart, with pineapple and Malibu compote, might provide the finish.

Times: 12–2.30/7–9
Prices: 3 Course Fixed D £30–£35
Directions: 1m S of Bowness onto B5284, signed Kendal and Lancaster. Hotel 2nd driveway on right
Parking: 50

Linthwaite House Hotel

Linthwaite House Hotel

Modern British v

Fine tuned cooking and stunning views

Enviable views from the restaurant look out over Lake Windermere to the fells beyond, and a new conservatory ensures that diners soak up the scenery whatever the weather. The décor is a refined combination of period chic with a modern colour scheme and plenty of natural light. Sourcing the best of local produce, chef Simon Bolsover's kitchen shows high aspirations, with menus full of ambitious dishes that consistently hit their target. There's no over-complication though, with clean flavours and good technical precision. Expect the likes of pan-roasted cod teamed with wild boar pancetta, pod peas and braised baby gem lettuce, or perhaps salt marsh lamb rump served with marjoram-crushed peas, roasted baby carrots 'Jacqueline' and chargrilled sweetbreads. While a deep-fried jam sandwich with pear sorbet and pistachio glacé for dessert might catch the eye.

Crook Road, WINDERMERE, Cumbria LA23 3JA
Tel: 015394 88600
Email: stay@linthwaite.com
Website: www.linthwaite.com
Chef: Simon Bolsover
Owners: Mike Bevans

Times: 12.30–2/7–9.30, Closed Xmas (non-residents)
Prices: 4 Course Fixed D £47
Directions: Take 1st left off A591 at rdbt NW of Kendal (B5284). Follow for 6m, hotel is 1m after Windermere Golf Club on left
Parking: 40

The Millstone at Mellor

Modern British

Cosy and traditional restaurant

The Millstone has a traditional bar and an elegant, refurbished restaurant, both immaculately presented. The restaurant is wood-panelled with a beamed ceiling, grandfather clock and framed prints of countryside images. These set the scene for tables clothed in white linen adorned with fresh flowers and laid with quality glassware. A flexible approach is taken to food, with the bar and restaurant menu available in either venue. Simple, straightforward classic dishes are offered, cooked from the best local, seasonal ingredients. Think braised and glazed Pendle lamb shank served with spring onion champ, buttered green beans and rosemary jus, or perhaps a fresh fillet of haddock in Bomber beer batter with mushy peas, thick-cut chips and tartare sauce. Equally crowd-pleasing desserts follow the egg custard tart, baked ginger parking and sticky toffee pudding route.

Church Lane, Mellor, BLACKBURN, Lancashire BB2 7JR
Tel: 01254 813333
Email: info@millstonehotel.co.uk
Website: www.shirehotels.com
Chef: Anson Bolton
Owners: Shire Hotels Ltd

Times: 12–2.15/6.30–9.30
Prices: 3 Course Fixed D £28.95
Main £14.50–£21.50
Directions: 4m from M6 junct 31 follow signs for Blackburn. Mellor is on right 1m after 1st set of lights
Parking: 45

Essence

Modern British

Modern bistro-style cuisine in relaxed surroundings

A Victorian terraced house with shop-window style frontage, giving way to high-ceilinged rooms with original cornicing and an open-plan kitchen. Contemporary furnishings and neutral brown and cream décor give a warm, stylish feel, enhanced by mood lighting and jazz music. The menu offers an impressive range of dishes based on local produce, like salt marsh lamb, venison and local cheeses. A few more unusual ingredients appear, like purple Moroccan potatoes, while extras like truffle essence and saffron oil add a touch of luxury. Desserts might feature fig and frangipane tart with honey ice cream.

2 Scotland Road, CARNFORTH, Lancashire LA5 9JY
Tel: 01524 735093
Email: info@essence-dining.co.uk
Website: www.essence-dining.co.uk
Chef: John Adler-Connor
Owners: John & Donna Adler-Connor

Times: 11.30–2/7–, Closed 24-27 Dec, Sun-Mon, L Tue–Wed
Prices: Main £13.95–£18.95
Directions: From M6 follow Carnforth signs (A6). On main crossroads in town centre, on left

Blackpool

Northcote Manor

Northcote Manor

Modern British v NOTABLE WINE LIST

A powerhouse of regional British gastronomy

A gastronomic haven, Northcote and chef-patron Nigel Haworth celebrated their 21st year in business back in 2005. The restaurant itself is a spacious affair with contemporary styling and eye-catching local modern art. Crisp white linen, a wine list of some 450 bins and service with a formal air of professionalism all play their part at this foodie destination. Nigel creates an enticing repertoire (carte, seasonal lunch, tasting and gourmet options), which have their roots firmly in Lancashire, making the most of the North West's abundant local larder to create dishes of true terroir. The cooking is intelligently simple, with an emphasis on freshness and the quality of prime seasonal ingredients, and exudes high technique. Think fillet of Bowland beef with smoked foie gras and crispy black pudding, or perhaps a melting ginger pudding with Simpson's iced double cream and caramel custard.

Northcote Road, LANGHO, Blackburn, Lancashire BB6 8BE
Tel: 01254 240555
Email: sales@northcotemanor.com
Website:
www.northcotemanor.com
Chef: Nigel Haworth & Lisa Allen
Owners: Nigel Haworth & Craig Bancroft

Times: 12–2/7–9.30, Closed 25 Dec, 1-2 Jan
Prices: Main £21.50–£27.50
Directions: M6 junct 31 take A59, follow signs for Clitheroe. Left at 1st traffic light, onto Skipton/Clitheroe Rd for 9m. Left into Northcote Rd, hotel on right
Parking: 60

The Longridge Restaurant

Modern British v

Chic contemporary setting for first-rate British cuisine

This chic eatery started life as a series of working men's cottages, and moonlighted as a pub, a cyclists' café and an Indian restaurant before assuming its current incarnation as the flagship of Paul Heathcote's culinary empire. A lounge – with comfortable sofas and brown leather chairs – leads the way to the interconnected dining areas, with their suede seating, lightwood floors and elegantly clothed tables, while upstairs discreet windows on to the kitchen let diners in on all the culinary action. Its brigade consistently impresses, handling high-quality ingredients with confident simplicity to deliver an appealing, seasonal-influenced, bistro-style carte   complemented by daily specials – of straightforward modern British fare. Take terrine foie gras and black pudding with toasted spiced bread to start. Mains might include roast fillet of Bowland beef and braised cheek served with crushed Jersey Royals, baby carrots, garden peas and tarragon, or pan-fried skate wing with a herb salad, capers, lemon pickle and new potatoes, while a classic Heathcote bread-and-butter pudding (with clotted cream and apricots), or more adventurous iced-almond parfait with honey-roasted white peach, marzipan and fresh raspberries might catch the eye at dessert. Service is relaxed yet professional. Treat yourself to the seven-course tasting menu to really do the place justice, or a day course at the cookery school, many of which are hosted by Paul Heathcote himself.

104-106 Higher Road,
LONGRIDGE, Preston,
Lancashire PR3 3SY
Tel: 01772 784969
Email:
longridge@heathcotes.co.uk
Website: www.heathcotes.co.uk/
collection/longridge/index.php
Chef: James Holah, Paul Heathcote
Owners: Paul Heathcote

Times: 12–2.30/6–10, Closed
1-5 Jan, Mon, L Sat
Prices: 3 Course Fixed D £35–£45
Main £20
Directions: Follow signs for Golf
Club & Jeffrey Hill. Higher Rd is
beside White Bull Pub in Longridge
Parking: 10

Greens Bistro

Modern British

Imaginative cooking in an intimate atmosphere

3-9 St Andrews Road South,
St Annes On Sea, LYTHAM ST
ANNES, Lancashire FY8 1SX
Tel: 01253 789990
Email: info@greensbistro.co.uk
Website: www.greensbistro.co.uk
Chef: Paul Webster
Owners: Paul Webster

Hidden among the shops and residences in the heart of town, the stairs down to this romantic cellar restaurant create an immediate sense of expectation, even, perhaps, a little theatre. Inside, the subtle décor and lighting – with tables discreetly hidden in nooks and crannies and smart uniformed staff – all conspire to create an ideal atmosphere for a special night out. The food is modern British and punches above its weight with great ingredients ticking the requisite local and seasonal boxes. Expect roast tenderloin of pork with a Brussels sprout bubble-and-squeak, Bury black pudding and sage and onion gravy, and perhaps a warm Bakewell tart served with Amaretto ice cream to finish.

Times: 6–10, Closed 25 Dec, BHs, 2 wks Jan, 1 wk summer, Sun-Mon, L all week
Prices: 3 Course Fixed D £15.95
Main £12.95–£15.95
Directions: Just off St Annes Sq

The West Beach Restaurant

Modern British v

Stylish hotel restaurant offering fine dining

Clifton Arms Hotel, West Beach,
LYTHAM ST ANNES, Lancs FY8 5QJ
Tel: 01253 739898
Email:
welcome@cliftonarms-lytham.com
Website:
www.cliftonarms-lytham.com
Chef: Jamie Sankey
Owners: Paul Caddy

Times: 12–2.30/7–9.30
Prices: 3 Course Fixed D £25–£30
Main £9.95–£22
Directions: M55 junct 4, first l onto A583 (Preston), take r-hand lane. At lights r onto Peel Rd. Turn r at t-junct into Ballam Rd. Continue onto Lytham town centre. Turn r, then l into Queen St

The Clifton Arms Hotel is an impressive, modern seafront hotel overlooking Lytham Green and the Ribble estuary, and the elegant West Beach Restaurant offers a unique setting and an intimate ambience. Enjoy candlelit dining from an imaginative menu, complemented by fine wines. Modern British cuisine is exemplified by dishes like pan-seared sea bass with tomato vinaigrette, or roast leg of lamb with rosemary and berry jus. No surprise then to find sticky toffee pudding on the menu, with a lovely butterscotch sauce, or vanilla pannacotta with red fruit coulis.

Pines Hotel

Traditional British

Traditional fare in comfortable surroundings

570 Preston Road, Clayton le-Woods, PRESTON, Lancashire PR6 7ED
Tel: 01772 338551
Email: mail@thepineshotel.co.uk
Website: www.thepineshotel.co.uk
Chef: Michael Slater, Ryan Greene & Sarah Love
Owners: Betty Duffin

Originally a cotton mill owner's house, set in 4 acres of mature grounds, the hotel has been extended over the years and the function suite is a renowned cabaret venue. Haworths Bar and Grill serves quality local produce in traditional style, on a seasonally-changing menu. Kick off with a starter of home-made soup or classic Caesar salad. For mains, traditional British dishes such as roast beef and Yorkshire pudding, or pot-roast English lamb, sit alongside king scallops with Bury black pudding, or perhaps Chateaubriand to share. Finish with baked rice pudding and raspberry jam, or marmalade glazed bread-and-butter pudding.

Times: 12–2.30/6–9.30
Prices: Main £10.25–£21
Directions: M6 junct 29 heading S 1m towards Chorley. M6 junct 29 heading N 1m towards Blackburn
Parking: 150

Twelve Restaurant

Modern British

Modern food in an intriguing architectural setting

Marsh Mill Village, Marsh Mill-in-Wyre, THORNTON, Lancs FY5 4JZ
Tel: 01253 821212
Email: info@twelve-restaurant.co.uk
Website: www.twelve-restaurant.co.uk
Chef: Paul Moss
Owners: Paul Moss & Caroline Upton

Twelve is a converted dance studio with the stylish new addition of a lounge bar; the bar's glazed roof and wall offering stunning views of the 60-ft Marsh Mill windmill that stands just feet away. The restaurant is contemporary in design with a sculptural feel and an industrial theme: exposed brickwork, steel girders and aluminium fencing on the mezzanine floor. Local ingredients shine in dishes of potted Southport shrimps with seared scallops and peppered gazpacho, or best end of Bowland Forest lamb with baby vegetables, creamed potatoes and parsnip crisps.

Times: 12–3/6.30–12, Closed 1st 2wks Jan, Mon, L Tue–Sat
Prices: Fixed D £18.95–£23.50 Main £14.50–£24
Directions: A585 follow signs for Marsh Mill Complex. Turn right into Victoria Rd East, entrance 0.5m on left
Parking: 150

The Mulberry Tree

Modern British v

Ambitious cooking in Lancashire village gastro-pub

Wrightington Bar,
WRIGHTINGTON, Nr Wigan,
Lancashire WN6 9SE
Tel: 01257 451400
Chef: Mark Prescott
Owners: Mr M Prescott &
Mr J Moore

Just two miles off the M6, this family-run gastro-pub in a tranquil Lancashire village setting is popular with the locals for its generously-sized, imaginative dishes in a bright, modern setting. Simple table settings and personable service make this a favoured venue, with its bar and restaurant menu for more refined items. Cooking is accomplished modern British with European influences, so expect the likes of pan-fried sea bass served with an aubergine and smoked mackerel potato cake, lobster and crayfish bisque, griddled Mediterranean vegetables and garlic-buttered tiger shrimps, or perhaps a fillet of beef teamed with Anna potatoes, creamy mushroom Stroganoff and a red wine and sun-blushed tomato jus.

Times: 12–2.30/6–9.30, Closed 26 Dec, 1 Jan
Prices: Fixed D £17.95–£36 Main £7.50–£19.95
Directions: 4m from Wigan. From M6 junct 27 towards Parbold, right after motorway exit, by BP garage into Mossy Lea Rd. On right after 2m
Parking: 80

---

60 Hope Street Restaurant

British v

Minimalist setting for smart modern dining

60 Hope Street, LIVERPOOL,
Merseyside L1 9BZ
Tel: 0151 707 6060
Email: info@60hopestreet.com
Website: www.60hopestreet.com
Chef: Sarah Kershaw
Owners: Colin & Gary Manning

At the heart of the creative quarter, 60 Hope Street is a Grade II listed building in an avenue between Liverpool's two cathedrals. The townhouse comprises the main restaurant, a basement bistro and a private dining room for special occasions. Simple interior design provides the ideal gallery space for regular art shows. The diverse menu with influences from around the world might include a starter of Garstang blue cheese and pear tart, followed by grilled fillet of Welsh black beef, and a signature dessert of deep-fried jam sandwich with Carnation milk ice cream.

Times: 12–2.30/6–10.30, Closed BHs, Sun, L Sat
Prices: Main £10.50–£40
Directions: From M62 follow city centre signs, then brown tourist signs for cathedral. Hope St near cathedral

Simply Heathcotes

Modern British

Modern eatery with extensive brasserie menu

Paul Heathcote's culinary outposts market themselves as laid-back destinations for a quick lunch, classic Sunday roast, or lazy dinner on nights when even making a ready meal feels like hard work. The Liverpool branch is a contemporary concoction of granite, glass, cherry wood and Philippe Starck bucket chairs with a modern British menu to suit – think roast cutlet of lamb and navarin of mutton with haricot beans and rosemary, or roasted haddock fillet with celeriac purée, smoked bacon, baby onions, mushrooms and red wine. Ingredients are fresh and seasonal, and come courtesy of the local area wherever possible, and the result is accomplished brasserie fare that should keep you popping in for more. Children's menu available.

Beetham Plaza, 25 The Strand,
LIVERPOOL, Merseyside L2 0XL
Tel: 0151 236 3536
Email: liverpool@heathcotes.co.uk
Website: www.heathcotes.co.uk
Chef: Steven Urquhart
Owners: Heathcotes Restaurants

Times: 12–2.30/6–10,
Closed Xmas, BHs
Prices: 2 Course Fixed D £15
Main £15.50
Directions: Opposite pier head,
located on The Strand, near Princes
Dock

The Italian Room Restaurant

Modern British

Sound British cooking at a charming country hotel

The Italian Room at this Victorian former manor house is so named because of its magnificent Italian leather ceiling, hand-tooled and inlaid with mother of pearl. In all other respects it's a traditional country house-style restaurant, with crisp linen and sparkling tableware, overlooking the stunning gardens. Modern British cooking is produced from the freshest ingredients sourced from local suppliers. Try pressed goat's cheese, with aubergine caviar and basil crème fraîche, followed by braised shin of beef with carrot purée and buttery mash, or perhaps roast wild sea bass with parsnip purée, pain d'épice and apple.

Thornton Hall Hotel, Neston Road,
THORNTON HOUGH, Wirral,
Merseyside CH63 1JF
Tel: 0151 336 3938
Email: reservations@
thorntonhallhotel.com
Website:
www.thorntonhallhotel.com
Chef: Brian Heron
Owners: The Thompson Family

Times: 12–2/7–9.30, Closed
1 Jan, L Sat
Prices: 3 Course Fixed D £29
Main £10–£20
Directions: M53 junct 4 onto
B5151 & B5136 and follow brown
tourist signs (approx 2.50m)
Parking: 250

Blackfriars Restaurant

Modern British

Modern dining in ancient surroundings

Friars Street, NEWCASTLE UPON TYNE, Tyne & Wear NE1 4XN
Tel: 0191 261 5945
Email:
info@blackfriarsrestaurant.co.uk
Website:
www.blackfriarsrestaurant.co.uk
Chef: Simon Brown
Owners: Andy & Sam Hook

Once the refectory of an early 13th-century priory, this informal eatery (café, bar and restaurant) may have the oldest dining room in the country. Massive stone walls, ancient beams, wooden floors and inglenooks lit by huge flickering candles set a Gothic tone. But you can escape to the peaceful courtyard for summer dining. Friendly, efficient staff serve modern British dishes based on fresh local ingredients, interesting flavours and simple, contemporary presentation. Take Tamworth pork loin served with mead-roasted apple stuffed with walnuts and a rosemary jus. (Afternoon tea and summer picnic menus are also available.)

Times: 12–2.30/6–12, Closed BHs except Good Fri, D Sun
Prices: 3 Course Fixed D £15 Main £10.50–£22
Directions: Take the only small cobbled road off Stowel St (China Town). Blackfriars 100yds on left

---

Jesmond Dene House

Modern British

Fashionable hotel restaurant with contemporary food

Jesmond Dene Road, NEWCASTLE UPON TYNE, Tyne & Wear NE2 2EY
Tel: 0191 212 3000
Email:
info@jesmonddenehouse.co.uk
Website: www.
jesmonddenehouse.co.uk
Chef: Terry Laybourne, Andrew Richardson
Owners: Terry Laybourne, Peter Candler

Built in the early 1820s, this Georgian house overlooking the wooded valley of Jesmond Dene has plenty of rural charm yet is only 5 minutes from the centre of town. Recently converted into a trendy contemporary hotel, the décor throughout looks pristine, with comfortable wood-panelled lounges and a restaurant split into two dining areas – a former music room with a dramatic colour scheme and the oak-floored garden room. The cooking is generous and skilful, with a seasonally-inspired menu concentrating on well-matched flavours with dashes of thoughtful innovation. Think sea bass served with a nage of Lindisfarne mussels, root vegetables, Yukon Gold potato gnocchi and fresh herbs, or perhaps suckling pig with Chantenay carrots and parsnips, Bramley apple purée and a sage pork jus.

Times: 12–2.30/7–10.30
Prices: Main £15–£28
Directions: From city centre follow A167 to junct with A184. Turn right towards Matthew Bank. Turn right into Jesmond Dene Rd
Parking: 64

Tickton Grange Hotel

Modern British

Georgian country-house retreat with exciting dining

This charming Georgian country-house hotel dates from the 1820s and has four acres of grounds and attractive gardens. Its elegantly modern dining room has bay windows and hill views, and staff here are both efficient and friendly, while suppliers of the kitchen's local produce get a prominent listing on menus. These carefully selected, fresh seasonal ingredients are skilfully transformed into light modern British dishes notable for imaginative combinations, clear flavours and attractive presentation. Expect Kelleythorpe beef fillet with cottage pie, red onion marmalade and a Wold Top ale jus, and to finish, perhaps a white chocolate and mint marquise with bitter chocolate sorbet and cinnamon brûlée, plus there are wonderful Tickton truffles to enjoy over coffee. For a special occasion, there's the Taittinger champagne dinner.

Tickton, BEVERLEY, East Riding of Yorkshire HU17 9SH
Tel: 01964 543666
Email: info@ticktongrange.co.uk
Website:
www.ticktongrange.co.uk
Chef: David Nowell,
John MacDonald
Owners: Mr & Mrs Whymant

Times: 12–2/5–9.30, Closed 26 Dec
Prices: 4 Course Fixed D £36.50
Main £16.95–£21.95
Directions: From Beverley take A1035 towards Bridlington. After 3m hotel on left, just past Tickton
Parking: 75

Boars Nest

Traditional British

Accomplished cooking in a one-time butcher's shop

Once an old butcher's shop, complete with ceramic wall-and-floor tiles, the Boars Nest sits in a rejuvenated area of fashionable boutiques, artisan and ethnic food shops and popular eateries. The old front 'shop' is filled with smaller tables, while the former drawing room at the back acts as an intimate dining area and upstairs parades as a sumptuous aperitif and coffee lounge. The kitchen shows pedigree and skill via a lengthy, flavour-driven British repertoire. Take Goosnargh corn-fed breast of duck, parsnip and goat's cheese glazed cottage pie and perhaps a hot chocolate pudding with clotted cream finish.

22 Princes Avenue, KINGSTON UPON HULL, East Riding of Yorkshire HU5 3QA
Tel: 01482 445577
Email:
boarsnest@boarsnest.karoo.co.uk
Website:
www.theboarsnesthull.com
Chef: Simon Rogers,
Andrew Young & Richard Bryan
Owners: Simon Rogers & Dina Hanchett

Times: 12–2/6.30–10, Closed 26 Dec
Prices: Main £10–£17.95
Directions: 1m from Hull city centre

Great Fryupdale, North Yorkshire

The Cook's Room

Modern British

Confident cuisine at popular, stylish restaurant

Overlooking the village green and appropriately looking down on the statue of Captain Cook, this popular village restaurant is accessed off the high street and up a flight of stairs. The décor is modern with splashes of colour coming from artwork, while pale wood, white fittings and paintwork (which change tone in different lights) cut a relaxed, stylish atmosphere. From the unclothed tables you might catch a glimpse of chef-patron Neal Bullock at the kitchen counter adding the finishing touches to his accomplished, classically-inspired, modern British with international influences cooking. Quality local seasonal produce is prepared with skill and enthusiasm; think pan-seared duck breast with roasted peach and cinnamon compôte served with a red onion tarte Tatin and foie gras sauce.

113a High Street, GREAT AYTON,
North Yorkshire TS9 6BW
Tel: 01642 724204
Email:
thecooksroom@yahoo.co.uk
Chef: Neal Bullock
Owners: Neal & Fiona Bullock

Times: 12–3/6.30–10, Closed
1st wk Jan, Mon, Tue, L Sat, Wed,
D Sun
Prices: 3 Course Fixed D £27.95
Main £8.95–£15.95
Directions: Take A172 from
Middlesbrough signed to
Stokesley, take B1292 to
Great Ayton

The Star Inn

Traditional British ♦NOTABLE WINE LIST

Creative cuisine at a popular village inn

Run by a committed family team, this pretty thatched inn is a gastronomic haven that's always busy with an appreciative crowd of locals and foodies alike. It's a cosy haunt, full of candlelit nooks, ancient beams and open fires, and recent expansions have seen the opening of a shop, selling their dishes and local produce. If the restaurant is full you can eat in the small bar area, furnished with Robert Thompson 'Mouseman' furniture, while for private dining there's the Loft with its distinctive criss-crossed beams. The kitchen consistently delivers top-notch British dishes. Expect innovative creations with a strong emphasis on local ingredients: risotto of Sand Hutton asparagus and Yoadwath oak-smoked salmon perhaps, or steamed suet pudding of beef with a deep-fried Loch Fyne oyster.

HAROME, Nr Helmsley, North
Yorkshire YO62 5JE
Tel: 01439 770397
Email: starinn@bt.openworld.com
Website:
www.thestaratharome.co.uk
Chef: Andrew Pern
Owners: A & J Pern

Times: 11.30–3/6.30–11, Closed
25 Dec, 2 wks early spring, BHs,
Mon, D Sun
Directions: From Helmsley take
A170 towards Kirkbymoorside,
after 0.50m turn right towards
Harome. After 1.50m Inn is 1st
building on right

The Boar's Head Hotel

Modern British **v**

Charming British setting and food

Ripley Castle Estate, HARROGATE,
North Yorkshire HG3 3AY
Tel: 01423 771888
Email: reservations@
boarsheadripley.co.uk
Website:
www.boarsheadripley.co.uk
Chef: Marc Guilbert
Owners: Sir Thomas Ingilby &
Lady Ingilby

A former coaching inn with an aristocratic elegance, the Boar's Head is set in the private village of Ripley belonging to the Ripley Castle Estate. It's owned by the current castle occupiers, Sir Thomas and Lady Ingilby, who donated some of their paintings, including those of past Ingilby ancestors. The dining room walls fetchingly come in a vibrant deep red, while comfortable seating and well-trained staff all fit the bill. The kitchen's modern approach is fittingly inspired by traditional British cuisine and uses fresh, quality ingredients with flair in well-presented dishes. Think a classic beef Wellington, or perhaps grilled fillet of pork served with cider and thyme-scented fondant potatoes. (The Bistro here offers less formal surroundings and a simpler menu.)

Times: 12–2/7–9
Prices: Fixed D £30–£40
Directions: On A61 (Harrogate/
Ripley road). In village centre
Parking: 4

Clocktower

Modern British

Elegant, modern hotel with excellent dining to match

Rudding Park, Follifoot,
HARROGATE, North Yorkshire
HG3 1JH
Tel: 01423 871350
Email: sales@ruddingpark.com
Website: www.ruddingpark.com
Chef: Stephanie Moon
Owners: Simon Mackaness

You'll find the refurbished Clocktower restaurant in the converted stable block of Rudding Park House, an elegant and stylish modern hotel set in 200-year-old landscaped parkland. The striking, contemporary dining room has bare-wood tables with quality settings and glassware, modern artwork on the walls, and an adjacent lively bar area. A relaxed and happy air prevails and staff are friendly and professional. The seasonal menu uses oodles of fresh Yorkshire produce and offers modern British dishes with plenty of creativity. Think Nidderdale lamb shank with bubble-and-squeak mash and mulled wine braised red cabbage, or a bread-and-butter pudding finish, with Yorkshire clotted cream. The conservatory – with its 400-year-old olive tree – offers an informal area for Yorkshire tapas. There's a vast alfresco terrace, too.

Times: 12–3/7–9.30
Prices: Main £13–£19.50
Directions: A61 at rdbt with A658
follow signs 'Rudding Park'
Parking: 250

The Courtyard Restaurant

The Courtyard Restaurant

Modern British

Trendy venue in a former stable block

1 Montpelier Mews, HARROGATE
HG1 2TQ
Tel: 01423 530708
E-mail: info@
thecourtyardrestaurant.net
Chef: Ryan Sadler
Owners: Martin Wilks

This converted Victorian stable block in an attractive courtyard of trendy shops is complete with original Jacob's ladder leading to the hayloft upstairs. Nowadays the restaurant boasts contemporary pastel décor, beech furniture and candlelight in the evening. You can dine outside in the cobbled courtyard garden in summer. The menu offers contemporary British cuisine with classical influences and local, seasonal produce is sourced wherever possible. Expect dishes like Cornish crab, dill and sesame ballotine or garlic corn-fed chicken, thyme-roasted onions and chorizo cream. Early bird menus are also available.

Times: 12–2/6–9.30, Closed 25 Dec, 1 Jan, Sun
Prices: Main £12.50–20
Directions: City centre location, Montpelier Quarter next to Royal Baths
Parking: On street

Stone Trough Inn

Modern British

Satisfying gastro-pub dining amid splendid scenery

This red-roofed, yellow stone country inn occupies a wonderful elevated position close to KIrkham's romantic castle ruins. Log fires, flagstone floors, walls full of bric-à-brac or country-pursuit cartoons and comfortable seating fill its labyrinth of cosy rooms and restaurant, making this a popular dining destination. Service is thoughtful and friendly. The hard-working kitchen takes a modern approach producing dishes like pan-fried calves' liver on black pudding mash with crisp pancetta and sage and redcurrant jus, or roast rack of Flaxton lamb with crab apple sauce and mint, with a warm apricot and frangipane tart to finish. Home-made breads, brioches and petits fours bolster the accomplished act.

Kirkham Abbey, Whitwell on the Hill, KIRKHAM, North Yorkshire YO60 7JS
Tel: 01653 618713
Email: info@stonetroughinn.co.uk
Website:
www.stonetroughinn.co.uk
Chef: Adam Richardson
Owners: Adam & Sarah Richardson

Times: 12–2.15/6.45–9.30,
Closed 25 Dec, 2-5 Jan, Mon, L
Tue–Sat, D Sun
Prices: Main £10.95–£19.95
Directions: 1.50m off the A64,
between York & Malton
Parking: 100

The Appletree

Modern British

Quality food in cosy, country gastro-pub

Once a working farm, The Appletree evolved into a pub when the farmer's wife began serving beer to workers in the front room. Today, hundreds of candles and a roaring fire create a cosy ambience for diners, whose well-spaced tables are tucked away in private nooks and window alcoves throughout the ground floor. The daily-changing menu takes in some specials, offering simple and unfussy dishes with some unusual flavour combinations and good use of local seasonal produce. Start with brûléed English goat's cheese with tomato salsa perhaps, before moving on to braised thick flank of Marton beef with red onion marmalade and horseradish cream, or smoked haddock with lemon and pea risotto.

MARTON, nr Pickering, North Yorkshire YO62 6RD
Tel: 01751 431457
Email: appletreeinn@supanet.com
Website: www.appletreeinn.co.uk
Chef: TJ Drew
Owners: TJ & Melanie Drew

Times: 12–2/6–9.30, Closed
Xmas, 2 weeks Jan, Mon-Tue
Prices: Main £10–£19
Directions: 2m from
Kirkbymoorside on A170 towards
Pickering, turn right to Marton
Parking: 18

Vennell's

Modern British

Small, traditional-styled local with accomplished fare

This eponymous, small, shopfront-style restaurant (formerly the Floodlite) overlooks the main street through the village. The décor in this Grade II listed property is traditional and comes in muted shades of beige, with the wallpaper, carpet and swag-and-tail curtains offering a homely feel, while plenty of artwork adorns the walls. There's a snug-style lounge downstairs to peruse the sensibly concise, appealing, classically-inspired menus and, while wife Laura runs front of house, chef-patron Jon (who worked for many years at Haley's Hotel in Leeds) is at the stove. Quality local ingredients and assured skill are evident throughout; think cured belly pork served with mustard mash, velouté, crackling, broad beans and apple, or steak and oxtail suet pudding with glazed vegetables.

7 Silver Street, MASHAM,
North Yorkshire HG4 4DX
Tel: 01765 689000
Email:
info@vennellsrestaurant.co.uk
Website:
www.vennellsrestaurant.co.uk
Chef: Jon Vennell
Owners: Jon & Laura Vennell

Times: 12–2/7.15–9.15, Closed 26-29 Dec, 1-14 Jan, 1 wk Sep, BHs, Mon, L Tue–Thu, D Sun
Prices: 3 Course Fixed D £24.90
Directions: 8m from A1 Masham exit

Pepper's Restaurant

Modern, Traditional British

Carefully-sourced produce in a welcoming atmosphere

An imposing Georgian townhouse with split-level dining and a cellar bar area. The friendly team show you to generous wooden tables where you can enjoy the artwork on display while perusing the menu. Traditional British and European dishes are reinterpreted using classical techniques and taking advantage of the best seasonal produce from the local area. Freshly baked bread speaks volumes for the attention to detail, a simple white roll transformed with mushroom and thyme. Starters might include a special of marinated line-caught mackerel while seared Scarborough landed sea trout with crushed peas in vinaigrette, crab fritter and chilled hollandaise may be on offer as a seafood main course.

11 York Place, SCARBOROUGH,
North Yorkshire YO11 2NP
Tel: 01723 500642
Email:
peppers.restaurant@virgin.net
Website:
www.peppersrestaurant.co.uk
Chef: Jonothon Smith
Owners: Jonothon & Katherine Smith

Times: 12–2/6–10, Closed 5 days over Xmas, Sun–Mon, L Tue–Wed
Prices: 3 Course Fixed D £20 Main £13–£19

Rose & Crown

Modern British

Relaxed, country-dining pub

Main Street, SUTTON-ON-THE-FOREST, North Yorkshire
YO61 1DP
Tel: 01347 811333
Email: ben@rosecrown.co.uk
Website: www.rosecrown.co.uk
Chef: Adam Jackson, Danny Jackson
Owners: Ben & Lucy Williams

This dining pub in a village setting midway between York and Helmsley has a simple beamed interior with wooden floors and tables and open fires. The warm and cosy décor of the dining room has contemporary features and been extended into a conservatory. There are African-inspired thatched gazebos on the terrace where you can enjoy alfresco dining. Dishes are attractively presented and there is an emphasis on fresh fish and seafood. Expect the likes of monkfish wrapped in Parma ham with buttered asparagus and mixed herb pesto, or haunch of venison with braised red cabbage and red wine jus.

Times: 12–2/6–9.30, Closed 1st 2wks Jan, Mon, D Sun
Prices: 3 Course Fixed D £15–£30
Main £9.50–£26
Directions: 8m N of York towards Helmsley on B1363
Parking: 12

Melton's Restaurant

British

Carefully prepared dishes in a relaxed setting

7 Scarcroft Road, YORK, North Yorkshire YO23 1ND
Tel: 01904 634341
Email: greatfood@meltonsrestaurant.co.uk
Website: www.meltonsrestaurant.co.uk
Chef: Michael Hjort & Annie Prescott

The Victorian terraced frontage conceals a bright and modern dining room with a bustling ambience. Long and narrow, its walls are covered with mirrors and a couple of large murals depicting the chef and his customers going about their business to a backdrop of city scenes. Unclothed tables, polished-wood floors, banquette seating or chairs and friendly service contribute to the relaxing atmosphere. The kitchen's modern, intelligently simple approach delivers carefully prepared dishes where flavour is everything; think pan-fried fillet of grey mullet slashed with fresh herbs and served with fresh lovage pasta, and perhaps a hot summer berry soufflé for dessert.

Owners: Michael & Lucy Hjort
Times: 12–2/5.30–10, Closed 3 wks Xmas, 1wk Aug, Sun, L Mon
Prices: Main £12.50–£21.50
Directions: South from centre across Skeldergate Bridge, restaurant opposite Bishopthorpe Road car park

Middlethorpe Hall & Spa

Modern British v NOTABLE WINE LIST

Luxurious dining in an historic setting

Bishopthorpe Road, Middlethorpe,
YORK, North Yorkshire YO23 2GB
Tel: 01904 641241
Email: info@middlethorpe.com
Website: www.middlethorpe.com
Chef: Nicholas Evans
Owners: Historic House Hotels Ltd

Built for a prosperous master cutler keen to play the gentleman,
Middlethorpe is a magnificent example of a William and Mary
country house. It sits in red-brick splendour adjacent to York
racecourse amid 20 acres of carefully tended estate that includes
a kitchen garden and luxury spa. Quality glassware sparkles in
candlelight and long windows overlook the grounds in the elegant
oak-panelled restaurant. Expect accomplished cooking rooted
in classical and regional cuisine that's studded with a liberal
sprinkling of luxury ingredients; think roast lamb cutlet served
with shepherd's pie, braised lentils and a caramelised garlic jus,
or perhaps pan-fried zander with confit chicken, celeriac fondant,
salsify, baby spinach and a thyme jus.

Times: 12.30–2.15/7–9.45
Prices: 3 Course Fixed D £41.50
Directions: 1.50m S of York,
beside York racecourse
Parking: 70

Shibden Mill Inn

Modern British

Secluded inn with a menu to draw the crowds

Shibden Mill Fold, Shibden,
HALIFAX, West Yorkshire HX3 7UL
Tel: 01422 365840
Email:
enquiries@shibdenmillinn.com
Website: www.shibdenmillinn.com
Chef: Steve Evans
Owners: Mr S D Heaton

A world away from the hustle and bustle of Halifax, this popular
17th-century inn enjoys an appealing and peaceful setting in
the Shibden Valley beside Red Beck. You can dine in both the
beamed lounge-style bars, warmed by log fires, and the candlelit
loft conversion beneath a raftered ceiling and chandeliers, or even
outside on the riverside terrace in summer. Expect an appealing,
crowd-pleasing menu with imaginative modern twists to classic
combinations using quality produce; take sea bream served with
celeriac purée, a red wine sauce and crispy Parma ham. Quality bar
meals complete the culinary picture.

Times: 12–2/6–9.30, Closed
25 Dec (Eve), D 26 Dec, 31 Dec
Prices: 2 Course Fixed D £9.95
Main £11.50–£17.95
Directions: Telephone for
directions
Parking: 100

The Weavers Shed Restaurant

Modern British 🍷NOTABLE WINE LIST

Enjoyable regional dining with home-grown ingredients

This converted 18th-century wool mill has undergone refurbishment. Contemporary in style, there are still plenty of original features, including stone and bare wood. The comfortable lounge leads on to an atmospheric, barn-style dining room with banquettes and chairs and clothed tables. There's a wonderful kitchen garden to drive the kitchen, which provides fowl, fruit, vegetables and over 70 varieties of wild edibles. Dishes are cooked in the modern British style and based almost without exception on home-grown and local produce. Expect chargrilled calves' liver served with cavolo nero cabbage, a cassoulet of haricot beans with parsley and pearl onions and roast veal jus, and to close, perhaps a bitter chocolate biscuit sandwich with malt ice cream and cocoa syrup.

86-88 Knowl Road, Golcar,
HUDDERSFIELD, West Yorkshire
HD7 4AN
Tel: 01484 654284
Email: info@weaversshed.co.uk
Website: www.weaversshed.co.uk
Chef: S Jackson, I McGunnigle,
C Sill
Owners: Stephen & Tracy Jackson

Times: 12–2/7–9, Closed 25 Dec–7 Jan, Sun, Mon, L Sat
Prices: Main £16.95–£25.95
Directions: 3m W of Huddersfield off A62. (Please telephone for further directions)
Parking: 30

Hey Green Country House Hotel

Modern British

Modern brasserie in elegant surroundings

Situated in a cosy country-house hotel set in landscaped gardens close to Huddersfield Canal, Crowther's Brasserie is located in the oldest part of the building, with a superb flagstone floor and open fire burning throughout winter. An archway leads into smaller dining areas creating a sense of intimacy. Expect a tempting selection of modern British dishes with a comforting feel – wild boar and Yorkshire beer sausages with onion gravy and mash perhaps – from a creative kitchen that delivers exquisite combinations of the freshest ingredients. You might start with black pudding with poached egg and a mustard sauce, followed by chargrilled tuna with olive mash, and Granny Smith crème brûlée with cinnamon shortbread. Booking is essential.

Waters Road, MARSDEN,
West Yorkshire HD7 6NG
Tel: 01484 848000
Email: info@heygreen.com
Website: www.heygreen.com
Chef: Nigel Skinkis
Owners: S Hunter, M Dolman

Times: 12–2.30/6.30–9.30,
Closed 1-4 Jan, L Mon–Sat
Prices: 3 Course Fixed D £20
Main £7.95–£16.95
Directions: M62 junct 22, equal distance from Oldham and Huddersfield on A62
Parking: 70

The Channel Islands

La Rocque, Jersey

Ocean Restaurant

Modern British

Sophisticated dining with Atlantic views

Adjoining the manicured fairways of the La Moye championship golf course, this luxury hotel enjoys breathtaking views over St Ouen's Bay. The air of understated luxury continues in the sophisticated Ocean Restaurant, while service achieves that perfect balance between professionalism and friendliness. The kitchen's modern approach combines intelligent simplicity alongside tip-top produce from the local Jersey larder, including the fruits of the sea. The cooking is accurate, consistent, innovative and full of flavour. Think a tranche of turbot with braised oxtail, baby gem lettuce, caramelised parsnips and girolle mushrooms, or perhaps cutlets of new season lamb served with a stilton soufflé, tarragon rôsti and lamb juices, and to finish, perhaps a crisp, thin mango tart with Bailey's reduction and coconut ice cream, while peripherals like amuse-bouche, breads and petits fours all hold form.

Atlantic Hotel,
Le Mont de la Pulente,
ST BRELADE, Jersey JE3 8HE
Tel: 01534 744101
Email: info@theatlantichotel.com
Website:
www.theatlantichotel.com
Chef: Mark Jordan
Owners: Patrick Burke

Times: 12.30–2.30/7–10,
Closed 5 Jan-8 Feb
Directions: From St Brelade take the road to Petit Port, turn into Rue de Sergente and right again, signed to hotel
Parking: 60

Longueville Manor Hotel

Modern British

Historic manor with sophisticated cuisine

Dating from the 13th century, this grand Norman manor house is an imposing dinner venue and a hotel of international renown. The two dining rooms cater for different moods, from the Jacobean dark-panelled Oak Room to the more relaxed and modern Garden Room, rich in fabrics and antiques. Whichever you choose, you're in for a treat; the cuisine at Longueville is confident and accomplished, and makes intelligent use of top-notch ingredients from the walled kitchen garden and local area (Taste of Jersey menu available). Combinations are deft and flavours balanced; the result is an assured menu of classical dishes. You might start with sesame-coated seared tuna, served with rocket salad, horseradish cream and caviar sauce, followed by best end of lamb with slow-roast plum tomatoes, French beans and sauté sweetbreads, and then finish with vanilla crème brûlée, Granny Smith sorbet and apple soup.

ST SAVIOUR, Jersey JE2 7WF
Tel: 01534 725501
Email: info@longuevillemanor.com
Website:
www.longuevillemanor.com
Chef: Andrew Baird
Owners: Malcolm Lewis

Times: 12.30–2/7–10
Prices: Fixed D £52.50–£64
Directions: From St Helier take A3 to Gorey, hotel 0.75m on left
Parking: 45

Hotel La Place

Modern British

Classic cooking in a beamed dining room

Route Du Coin, La Haule,
ST BRELADE JE3 8BT
Tel: 01534 744261
Email: hotlaplace@aol.com
Website:
www.hotellaplacejersey.com

This 16th-century farmhouse has been transformed into a comfortable hotel, and makes a good base for exploring the island. Take an aperitif in the cocktail bar overlooking the pool if the weather's clement, or by the log fire in the lounge in winter, and then head through to the Retreat Restaurant, a traditional, beamed affair which overlooks a pretty private courtyard. The menu suits the setting and makes good use of local produce – tuck into flash-fried Jersey scallops, chilli mange-tout and chorizo, and apricot-and-thyme-stuffed chicken breast with truffle risotto and Madeira jus.

Times: 12–2/7–9
Directions: Please telephone for directions

Water's Edge Hotel

Modern British

Stunning coastal setting for enjoyable cuisine

Bouley Bay, TRINITY, Jersey
JE3 5AS
Tel: 01534 862777
Email: mail@watersedgehotel.co.je
Website:
www.watersedgehotel.co.je
Chef: Gael Maratier
Owners: Water's Edge Hotel Ltd

There are breathtaking views over Bouley Bay from this art-deco style hotel, which certainly lives up to its name. You can even see as far as the French coastline on a good day. The split-level restaurant provides a wonderful setting in which to enjoy the carefully prepared dishes, but do try to get a window seat to make the most of the view. Choose from the carte or fixed-price market menu, both featuring local seafood, including live local lobster and Royal Grouville Bay oysters. For a touch of drama, try prime Angus sirloin fillet or crêpe Suzette from the flambé trolley. Formal service and crisp table linen complete the experience.

Times: 12.30–2/7–9.15, Closed Nov-Mar, L Mon–Sat
Prices: 3 Course Fixed D £23–£25
Main £16.50–£35
Directions: 10-15 mins from St Helier, A9 N to the A8 to the B31, follow signs to Bouley Bay
Parking: 20

Hotel Petit Champ

Modern British

Relaxed, country-house dining with amazing sea views

SARK, Channel Islands, GY9 0SF
Tel: 01481 832046
Email: info@hotelpetitchamp.co.uk
Website:
www.hotelpetitchamp.co.uk
Chef: Tony Atkins
Owners: Chris & Caroline Robins

This secluded hotel on Sark's west coast has a fascinating history, having served as a private home, boatyard and German observation post during the Occupation. These days, the only things guests come to watch are the magnificent sea views, which are particularly stunning at sunset. The restaurant delivers a menu of modern British dishes with an international twist: lemon- and truffle-roasted breast of chicken served with morel jus, for example, or treacle-marinated fillet of lamb with a casserole of creamy summer vegetables. Fresh crab and lobster from the harbour are a speciality, the latter offered with an array of sauces, including chilli, coriander and coconut cream, and garlic butter.

Times: 12.15–1.45/8,
Closed Oct-Etr
Prices: 5 Course Fixed D £20.75
Main £10.75–£19.25
Directions: 20 min walk from village, signed from Methodist Chapel

Loch Tummel, Perth & Kinross

Scotland

The Green Inn

Modern British v

Family-run restaurant in popular Deeside village

Trevor O'Halloran is a larger than life character at front of house, while son Chris is in charge of the kitchen – ably assisted by mum Evelyn – to make this a real family affair. A comfortable lounge leads to the splendid conservatory that looks out on to the small, secluded garden and, with only seven well-spaced tables, the atmosphere is comfortable and relaxed at this dinner-only affair. Chris's cooking has a contemporary approach underpinned by a classical theme, reflecting a learning stint at Le Manoir aux Quat' Saisons, with impressive technical skills and artistic presentation to the fore in dishes utilising fresh, local produce. Take pan-roasted Atlantic halibut fillet with truffle-scented potato, broad bean purée and carrot broth, and raspberry soufflé with mascarpone sorbet for dessert.

9 Victoria Road, BALLATER, Aberdeenshire AB35 5QQ
Tel: 013397 55701
Email: info@green-inn.com
Website: www.green-inn.com
Chef: Chris O'Halloran & Evelyn O'Halloran
Owners: Trevor & Evelyn O'Halloran

Times: 7–9, Closed 2 wks Jan & Nov, Sun, Mon
Prices: 3 Course Fixed D £36
Directions: Located in centre of Ballater

Meldrum House Hotel

Traditional British v

Elegant dining in a splendid country mansion

A baronial country mansion set in 350 acres of woodland and parkland with a golf course as the centrepiece. The hotel has been tastefully restored to highlight its original character. The traditional Scottish cooking – with international twists – has a flare for presentation in well-constructed dishes using quality Scottish produce. Expect roasted monkfish with garlic, red pepper chutney and saffron rice, or perhaps collops of beef fillet with a pickled walnut sauce. Desserts like rhubarb crumble and custard, or lemon tart with boozy fruits provide the finish.

OLDMELDRUM, Aberdeenshire AB51 0AE
Tel: 01651 872294
Email: enquiries@meldrumhouse.co.uk
Website: www.meldrumhouse.com
Chef: Gary Christie
Owners: Sylvia Simpson

Times: 12–2.30/6.30–9.30
Prices: 4 Course Fixed D £32.50
Directions: 11m N of Aberdeen, from Aberdeen to Dyce, follow A947 towards Banff, through Newmachen along outskirts of Oldmeldrum, main entrance is large white archway
Parking: 60

Castleton House Hotel

Castleton House Hotel

Traditional British v

Victorian country house with culinary flair

A sense of tranquillity pervades this charming 100-year-old house complete with delightful grounds and moat. A conservatory dining room with beautiful vases of seasonal flowers overlooks the gardens. With vegetables and herbs coming from the gardens too, the accomplished British cooking with French influences relies heavily on the quality and provenance of the ingredients, which if not home grown or home reared are sourced from the surrounding region. The result is simple, clear cooking with the flavours of the superb ingredients shining through at each course. The flawlessly-timed dishes might include a starter of tian of Skye salmon with lobster, caviar and hazelnut apple purée, followed by a main of roast loin of Glen Prosen venison with roast celeriac and muscovite sauce, and a dessert of warm plum tarte Tatin with caramel sauce and clotted cream ice cream.

Castleton of Eassie, GLAMIS, Angus DD8 1SJ
Tel. 01307 840340
Email: hotel@castletonglamis.co.uk
Website: www.castletonglamis.co.uk
Chef: Andrew Wilkie
Owners: David & Verity Webster

Times: 12–2/6.30–9, Closed New Year
Prices: 3 Course Fixed D £35 Main £5.95–£15.50
Directions: On A94 midway between Forfar & Coupar Angus, 3m W of Glamis
Parking: 50

Gordon's

Modern British v

Scottish cooking from a friendly family team

Main Street, INVERKEILOR,
Angus DD11 5RN
Tel: 01241 830364
Email: gordonsrest@aol.com
Website:
www.gordonsrestaurant.co.uk
Chef: Gordon Watson &
Garry Watson
Owners: Gordon & Maria Watson

The name of this family-run establishment only tells part of the story, as the eponymous Gordon is joined in the kitchen by son Garry whose cooking is now cutting edge with that all-important wow factor. The imaginative, modern cooking is underpinned by a classical theme and makes good use of seasonal produce from the abundant Scottish larder on its appealing, sensibly compact menus. Loin of venison with red cabbage and pear compôte, roast salsify and jus, or a raspberry and Drambuie iced parfait with raspberry soup might be just the thing. It's a cosy affair with bags of character – beamed ceiling, huge open fire and rugs on wooden floors.

Times: 12–1.45/7–9, Closed 1st 2 wks Jan, Mon, L Tue, D Sun
Prices: 4 Course Fixed D £39
Directions: On A92, turn off at signs for village of Inverkeilor, between Arbroath and Montrose
Parking: 6

Loch Melfort Hotel

Modern British v

Wonderful views specialising in fresh seafood

ARDUAINE, Oban, Argyll & Bute
PA34 4XG
Tel: 01852 200233
Email:
reception@lochmelfort.co.uk
Website: www.lochmelfort.co.uk
Chef: Colin Macdonald
Owners: Kyle & Nigel Schofield

In a spectacular location on the West Coast, this popular, family-run hotel enjoys outstanding views across Asknish Bay towards the islands of Jura, Scarba and Shuna, a perfect complement to the wonderful seafood on offer in the attractive dining room. An alternative dining choice, popular with visiting yachtsmen, the Skerry Bistro offers blackboard specials. Skilful cooking makes excellent use of local produce, particularly fresh fish and shellfish. Think grilled fillet of sea bream with chargrilled asparagus, Parisienne potatoes and a chive beurre blanc, or maybe pan-fried John Dory fillets with saffron-braised fennel and white wine, while meat-eaters might opt for pan-fried medallions of beef with Lyonnaise potatoes and green peppercorn sauce. Tantalising desserts include baked chocolate pudding with chocolate fudge sauce and vanilla ice cream. The wine list is also worth a look.

Times: 7–9, Closed 2 Jan-15 Feb, L all week
Directions: From Oban, 20 m S on A816; from Lochgilphead, 19 m N on A816
Parking: 65

Isle of Eriska

Isle of Eriska

British 🍷 NOTABLE WINE LIST

Flawless blend of service, style and good food

It's hard to beat the Isle of Eriska as a destination. Linked to the mainland by a causeway, it's a private island with stunning sea views and amazing sunsets. The restaurant maintains a fine balance of old-school formality and current dining sensibilities with highly professional staff offering knowledgeable and friendly service, particularly the sommelier. The menu is modern, utilising some of the finest Scottish produce. Seared dried Mull scallops with lobster charlotte, tomato and vanilla dressing and fine bean salad, followed by crisp duck breast, rillette pithivier, sweet red onions and thyme leaf jus are good examples of the daily-changing menu, with a hot chocolate madeleine, home-grown rhubarb compôte and gingerbread ice cream to finish. An impressive wine list pays due reverence to the memorable cuisine. Don't miss the badgers that come to feed at the terrace door in the evening.

ERISKA, Argyll & Bute PA37 1SD
Tel: 01631 720371
Email: office@eriska-hotel.co.uk
Website: www.eriska-hotel.co.uk
Chef: Robert MacPherson
Owners: Mr Buchanan-Smith

Times: 12.30–1.30/8–9,
Closed Jan
Prices: 4 Course Fixed D £39.50
Directions: A82 from Glasgow
to Tyndrum. A85 towards Oban;
at Connel bridge take A828 to
Benderloch village for 4m
Parking: 50

North West Castle Hotel

British v

Family-run hotel with a traditional menu

This imposing manor house has two unexpected claims to fame, both of a chilly nature. Built in 1820 for the celebrated arctic explorer Sir John Ross, it was also the first hotel in the world to have its very own indoor curling rink. Its spacious dining room is decorated in traditional style with well-spaced tables and sparkling chandeliers, and is adjoined by a comfy lounge where you'll find a blazing fire in winter. The menu is in keeping with the setting and features mains such as fillet of Isle of Bute rainbow trout, with parsley mashed potatoes and buttered spinach, followed by Scotch whisky and fruit tart with honey and whisky cream and vanilla ice cream.

STRANRAER, Dumfries
& Galloway DG9 8EH
Tel: 01776 704413
Email: info@northwestcastle.co.uk
Website:
www.mcmillanhotels.com
Chef: Bruce McLean
Owners: H C McMillan

Times: 12–2/6.30–9
Prices: 3 Course Fixed D
£23.50 Main £8–£15.85
Directions: From Glasgow N take
A77 to Stranraer. From S follow
M6 to Gretna then A75
to Stranraer. Hotel in town
centre opp ferry terminal
Parking: 50

Tower Restaurant and Terrace

Modern British

Cultural and culinary delights in a striking venue

Situated on the top floor of the Museum of Scotland, this elegant, contemporary restaurant enjoys impressive views over the castle and cathedral, with an outside terrace for summer dining. The colourful décor is chic and luxurious, with striking aluminium furniture and banquettes creating a clubby feel. The equally modern menu offers the likes of seared pigeon with beetroot jam and wilted chard, and gilt head bream with shiitake mushrooms and stir-fry bok choy. Superb quality beef comes prepared in a variety of ways. A couple of light menus at lunchtime and early evening offer terrific value.

Museum of Scotland, Chambers
Street, EDINBURGH, City of
Edinburgh EH1 1JF
Tel: 0131 225 3003
Email: reservations@tower-restaurant.com
Website:
www.tower-restaurant.com
Chef: Gavin Elder
Owners: James Thomson OBE

Times: 12/12–11, Closed
25-26 Dec
Prices: Main £15–£29
Directions: Above the Museum
of Scotland building at corner of
George IV Bridge & Chambers St,
on level 5

Norton House Hotel

Norton House Hotel

Modern British

Small, sophisticated restaurant in elegant hotel

Ushers restaurant is an intimate 22-seat affair, smartly decked out with pale walls, subdued lighting and maroon tablecloths with white runners. The kitchen's modern approach is underpinned by a classical theme, delivered via an appealing, sensibly compact carte. Skilled, precise cooking allows fine-quality Scottish ingredients to shine with deceptive simplicity and clean, clear, balanced flavours. Expect twice-baked Scottish crab soufflé served with langoustines and a soy and lime dressing to start, followed by a main course of pan-fried fillet of wild sea bass with langoustine tortellini, while a warm pear tarte Tatin served with red apple skin sorbet and a raisin anglaise might catch the eye at dessert.

A good cheese selection, first-class breads and interesting canapés hold up standards, and make a walk around the grounds almost mandatory.

Ingliston, EDINBURGH, City of Edinburgh EH28 8LX
Tel: 0131 333 1275
Email: nortonhouse@handpicked.co.uk
Website: www.handpicked.co.uk
Chef: Graeme Shaw & Glen Bilins
Owners: Hand Picked Hotels

Times: 7–9.30, Closed 26 Dec, 1 Jan, Sun-Mon
Prices: Main £18.50–£23.95
Directions: M8 junct 2, off A8, 0.5m past Edinburgh Airport
Parking: 100

Glenskirlie House and Castle

Modern British

Elegant hotel with an imaginative kitchen

Luxurious fabrics and striking wall coverings give the dining room of this refined country house an elegant feel, while well-spaced tables and unobtrusive staff make it an ideal destination for both romantic and business assignations. And the food's good too: a blend of classic and contemporary cuisine, conjured from the finest Scottish ingredients. Starters might include scallops with pea and mint gnocchi and cauliflower purée, or lobster thermidor baked in a soft pastry pie with baby capers, beetroot, daikon and shiso cress salad. Main dishes range from complex concoctions such as suprême of organic chicken stuffed with truffle butter, served with potato galette, turnip confit, kohlrabi, baby onion and fresh tarragon sauce, to simpler fare like fillet steak with sautéed mushrooms and onion rings.

Kilsyth Road, BANKNOCK, Bonnybridge, Falkirk FK4 1UF
Tel: 01324 840201
Email: macaloneys@ glenskirliehouse.com
Website: www.glenskirliehouse.com
Chef: Daryl Jordan
Owners: John & Colin Macaloney

Times: 12–2/6–9.30, Closed 26-27 Dec, 1-3 Jan, D Mon
Prices: Main £19–£25
Directions: Take A80 towards Stirling. Continue past Cumbernauld, at junct 4 take A803 signed Kilsyth/Bonnybridge. At T-junct turn r. Hotel 1m on r.
Parking: 100

Ostlers Close Restaurant

Modern British

Elegant restaurant making good use of local food

Tucked away down the eponymous close, this long-established, family-run restaurant attracts a loyal coterie of local food enthusiasts – as well as those drawn from further afield – with its well-deserved reputation for charming service and assured cooking. The owners have a passion for fresh, local ingredients (many of which are grown in their garden) and in particular for wild mushrooms which they pick themselves from local woodland, plus there's always locally-landed sea-fresh fish on the menu. Take a fillet of Pittenween halibut, for instance, served with St Andrews Bay lobster, or a saddle of roe venison teamed with wild mushrooms and a celeriac rösti, while an apple tart Tatin with apple ripple ice cream might head-up desserts.

Bonnygate, CUPAR, Fife KY15 4BU
Tel: 01334 655574
Website: www.ostlersclose.co.uk
Chef: James Graham
Owners: James & Amanda Graham

Times: 12.15–1.30/7–9.30, Closed 25-26 Dec, 1–2 Jan, 2 wks Oct, 2 wks Etr, Sun–Mon, L Tue–Fri
Prices: Main £11–£20
Directions: In small lane off main street, A91

Sangsters

Modern British

Enjoy great Scottish dishes in relaxed surroundings

A seaside village restaurant, Sangsters has a relaxed and peaceful atmosphere with a comfortable lounge for pre-dinner drinks and after-dinner coffees. The dining room has bright, clean and simple lines, the walls hung with local prints and watercolours. Cooking is precise, showing attention to detail and considerable skill in a menu of modern British cooking prepared from quality raw ingredients. Impressive dishes include Ross-shire diver scallops with ginger, lime and peppercorn butter, served with Thai coconut sauce, followed by oven-baked fillet of North Sea halibut, the sea-fresh fish complemented by an Arbroath smokie and chive crust with a vegetable risotto and vermouth sauce. Cinnamon pannacotta with apple vanilla and lemon compôte and an apple and cider sorbet might catch the eye at dessert, or chocolate-lovers might succumb to the chocolate cheesecake.

51 High Street, ELIE, Fife KY9 1BZ
Tel: 01333 331001
Email: bruce@sangsters.co.uk
Website: www.sangsters.co.uk
Chef: Bruce R Sangster
Owners: Bruce &
Jacqueline Sangster

Times: 12.30–1.30/7–9.30,
Closed 25-26 Dec, early Jan, mid
Feb/Oct, mid Nov, Mon, L Tue &
Sat, D Sun
Prices: 3 Course Fixed D £32.50
Directions: From St Andrews on
the A917, take the B9131 to
Anstruther, turn right at rdbt and
follow A917 to Elie 11m from St
Andrews

The Peat Inn

Modern British

The original restaurant with rooms

You only have to step inside this 300-year-old whitewashed coaching inn to discover a gastro-pub that pays serious homage to fine dining. Modest on the outside, inside sumptuous fabrics, gleaming crystal glasses and polished silver cutlery combine with high-backed chairs, tapestries and beams in a smartly decorated dining room. Recently refurbished, there are three separate dining areas, each with its own character in the style of a French auberge. The highly accomplished cooking shows great attention to detail with a focus on flavour, presentation and sourcing of quality produce, while intelligently simple, appealing, balanced combinations are delivered in fine style on the menu of the day, tasting option and carte. Take wild halibut served with wilted greens and a braised oxtail and horseradish velouté, and to close, perhaps a pavé of Amedei chocolates with praline ice cream.

PEAT INN, Cupar, Fife KY15 5LH
Tel: 01334 840206
Email: stay@thepeatinn.co.uk
Website: www.thepeatinn.co.uk
Chef: Geoffery Smeddle
Owners: Geoffery &
Katherine Smeddle

Times: 12.30–2/7–9.30, Closed
25-26 Dec, 1-4 Jan, Sun-Mon
Prices: 3 Course Fixed D £32
Main £16–£20
Directions: At junction of B940/
B941, 6m SW of St Andrews
Parking: 24

The Road Hole Grill

The Road Hole Grill

British ♦ NOTABLE WINE LIST

Sumptuous dining in golfing heaven

On the fourth floor of the Old Course Hotel, one of the most famous golfing hotels in the world, this elegant, traditional grill room commands stunning views over the course and St Andrews Bay. The friendly staff deliver exacting service and advice as befits the five-star setting. Well-balanced menus make full use of quality seasonal, local Scottish produce, with a welcome focus on luxury ingredients – foie gras, langoustines, scallops, oysters and Glen Lochry venison might make an appearance on the impressive carte. Beautifully presented, traditional classics are given a modern twist; take a fillet of Speyside beef with braised oxtail, root vegetables and a red wine and horseradish fumet, or perhaps pan-roast, line-caught sea bass with fennel gnocchi, while a warm Dundee marmalade cake – served with clotted cream ice cream and Dalwhinnie sabayon – might catch the eye at dessert.

Old Course Hotel, Golf Resort & Spa, ST ANDREWS, Fife KY16 9SP
Tel: 01334 474371
Email: reservations@ oldcoursehotel.co.uk
Website: www.oldcoursehotel.co.uk
Chef: Drew Heron
Owners: Kohler Company

Times: 7–10, Closed 23-26 Dec (residents only), L all week
Prices: 3 Course Fixed D £43–£45 Main £19–£28
Directions: M90 junct 8, close to A91. 5 mins from St Andrews
Parking: 100

Ubiquitous Chip

Traditional Scottish ⚫NOTABLE WINE LIST

Modern Scottish cuisine in a unique setting

A Glasgow institution for over 30 years, this unusual restaurant is set in a spectacular glass-covered courtyard in a cobbled mews with a fabulous array of lush green plants. A mezzanine level overlooks the tables and foliage below, and there's also a more formal dining room. There are three bars, too, each with its own atmosphere. The cooking is a mixture of traditional and original Scottish recipes using local ingredients. Menus are constantly evolving with the seasons, but three favourite dishes are tartare of finnan haddie with avocado and poached grapes, organic Orkney salmon marinated in honey and tamari with mashed potatoes and spinach sauce, and whisky and green ginger parfait with poached rhubarb to finish.

12 Ashton Lane, GLASGOW, City of Glasgow G12 8SJ
Tel: 0141 334 5007
Email: mail@ubiquitouschip.co.uk
Website: www.ubiquitouschip.co.uk
Chef: Ronnie Clydesdale
Owners: Ronnie Clydesdale

Times: 12–2.30/5.30–11, Closed 25 Dec, 1 Jan
Prices: 3 Course Fixed D £39.85
Directions: In the West End of Glasgow, off Byres Rd. Beside Hillhead subway station

---

The Summer Isles Hotel

Modern British

Food from land and sea in stunning location

This one-time fishing inn has retained a friendly and informal feel despite its transformation into a chic and comfortable hotel. Run by the same family since the late 1960s, it's a perfect base for exploring the stunning scenery of Achiltibuie, particularly during the summer when the long northern days stretch until 10.30pm. A single five-course menu is served every night, but with cooking this good you're in safe hands; flavours are clean, combinations refreshingly straightforward, and almost all the ingredients are home produced or locally caught. Warm scallop mousse with herb and tomato loaf, followed by grilled fillet of Lochinver halibut with local mussels steamed in saffron and white wine are fine examples of the fare.

ACHILTIBUIE, Highland IV26 2YG
Tel: 01854 622282
Email: info@summerisleshotel.co.uk
Website: www.summerisleshotel.co.uk
Chef: Chris Firth-Bernard
Owners: Mark & Gerry Irvine

Times: 12.30–2/8, Closed mid Oct-Etr
Prices: 5 Course Fixed D £51
Directions: 10 m N of Ullapool. Turn left off A835 onto single track road. 15m to Achiltibuie. Hotel 100 yds after post office on left
Parking: 15

Inverlochy Castle Hotel

Modern British 🍷 NOTABLE WINE LIST

Luxurious Highland castle setting for fine dining

This majestic castle, set in over 500 acres of gardens, is a truly impressive setting for fine dining. Genuine comfort and luxury abound, while service is professional but friendly. The kitchen's accomplished modern approach – underpinned by a classical theme – makes fine use of the abundant Highland larder and the estate's walled garden, on its daily-changing, five-course dinner and tasting menus. Expect high-level technical skill and clear flavours in dishes like caramelised Skye scallops with onion compôte and Puy lentils, followed perhaps by grilled tranche of turbot with truffled Jerusalem artichoke and caviar velouté, or truffle-crusted shoulder of beef with buttered spinach and wild mushrooms. Finish with a pineapple tarte Tatin, with pistachio ice cream and caramel sauce. The wine list has an extensive range of half bottles. Gentlemen are required to wear jackets and ties.

Torlundy, FORT WILLIAM, Highland PH33 6SN
Tel: 01397 702177
Email: info@inverlochy.co.uk
Website: www. inverlochycastlehotel.com
Chef: Matthew Gray
Owners: Inverlochy Ltd

Times: 12.30–1.15/6.30–10
Prices: 4 Course Fixed D £65
Directions: 3m N of Fort William on A82, just past Golf Club
Parking: 20

Inverlochy Castle Hotel

The Glass House Restaurant

Modern British v

Ambitious cooking in a conservatory setting

Grant Road, GRANTOWN-ON-SPEY, Highland PH26 3LD
Tel: 01479 872980
Website: www.theglasshouse-grantown.co.uk
Chef: Stephen Robertson
Owners: Stephen and Karen Robertson

Tucked away down a quiet residential street, this conservatory restaurant has attracted some rave local reviews. Its clean lines, leafy plants and large windows create a light, contemporary setting for an accomplished menu of modern British dishes. The range is limited – only three or four choices per course – but you're in safe hands; the food here is full of flavour and makes good use of seasonal local produce. Better still, it's great value for money even in the evening, when the cooking gets more adventurous. Kick off with seared scallops with pak choi and sorrel cream perhaps, followed by confit duck leg with roast butternut squash, and bread-and-butter pudding with ginger ice cream.

Times: 12–1.45/7–9, Closed 2 wks Nov, 1 wk Jan, 25-26 Dec, 1-2 Jan, Mon, L Tue, D Sun
Prices: Main £15.95–£18.95
Directions: Turn off High St between the bank and Co-op into Caravan Park Rd. First left onto Grant Rd.
Parking: 10

Culloden House Hotel

Traditional British

Serious Scottish cuisine in historic setting

Culloden, INVERNESS, Highland IV2 7BZ
Tel: 01463 790461
Email: info@cullodenhouse.co.uk
Website: www.cullodenhouse.co.uk
Chef: Michael Simpson
Owners: Culloden House Ltd

'Bonnie' Prince Charlie lodged at this grand Palladian mansion before the battle of Culloden Moor in 1746. High ceilings and intricate cornices are particular features of the public rooms, including the elegant Adam dining room. Scottish produce is served in a five-course extravaganza, commencing with canapés and finishing with hand-made petits fours. Perfectly cooked risotto of smoked haddock is served with a lemon dressing, to cut through the strong fish flavour, and another well balanced dish is grilled fillet of halibut set on courgette provençale with tomato jus. For dessert, an interesting combination of flavours comes together in an attractively presented lemon crème brûlée with cardamom and pistachio ice cream.

Times: 12.30–2/7–9, Closed 2 wks Jan/Feb
Directions: From A96, take left turn at junction of Balloch, Culloden, Smithton. Continue for 2m, hotel is on right
Parking: 50

Greywalls Hotel

Modern British

Fine cooking in a quintessential country house

Greywall's enviable location overlooking the famous Muirfield golf course has long made it a destination hotel for sporting types, and these days it also lures foodies from far and wide with its imaginative Scottish cuisine. The restaurant is comprised of two rooms with well-spaced, well-appointed tables and comfortable chairs. Traditional formalities mean jackets and ties for gentlemen and formal, though friendly, service. The kitchen's modern Scottish approach is underpinned by classical French techniques and combinations, the cooking focusing on high-quality produce from the abundant Scottish larder. You might start with honey and lime roast quail with pea purée, bacon and lettuce, or a salad of rare roast beef with gherkins, olives and pesto, followed by roast organic salmon with a lentil cassoulet, foie gras and Sévruga caviar, or saffron and gold leaf risotto with langoustines, fine beans and cress.

Muirfield, GULLANE,
East Lothian EH31 2EG
Tel: 01620 842144
Email: hotel@greywalls.co.uk
Website: www.greywalls.co.uk
Chef: David Williams
Owners: Mr & Mrs G Weaver

Times: 12–2/7–9.30, Closed Jan-Feb, L Mon–Thu, D Sun
Prices: 4 Course Fixed D £45
Directions: From Edinburgh take A1 to North Berwick slip road, then follow A198 along coast to far end of Gullane - Greywalls in last road on left
Parking: 40

La Potinière

Modern British

Ambitious cooking in cottage-style restaurant

A delightful cottage style restaurant of fairytale proportions, La Potinière is a two-partner operation, both sharing the kitchen, while Keith also acts as host and wine waiter. Accordingly, the meal is a leisurely four-course affair at dinner, plus an amuse-bouche and pre-dessert, and three courses at lunch. Smart, crisp linen and quality tableware reinforce the kitchen's serious intent, while the cooking lends a contemporary touch with artistic presentation and makes fine use of local seasonal produce. There are just two choices at each course, perhaps featuring cream of Jerusalem artichoke soup followed by warm guinea fowl timbale with wild mushrooms, or roast loin of Scottish venison with a truffle dauphinoise and beetroot fondant. Round things off in style with champagne rhubarb or white chocolate and Bailey's mousse.

Main Street, GULLANE,
East Lothian EH31 2AA
Tel: 01620 843214
Website: www.la-potiniere.co.uk
Chef: Mary Runciman & Keith Marley
Owners: Mary Runciman

Times: 12.30–1.30/7–8.30, Closed Xmas, BHs, Mon-Tue, D Sun (Oct–Apr)
Prices: 4 Course Fixed D £38
Directions: 20m SE of Edinburgh. 3m from North Berwick on A198
Parking: 10

Champany Inn

Traditional British

Unrivalled steak restaurant in a country lodge

Several cottages and an ancient watermill comprise this unusual hotel. The restaurant itself is an octagonal affair with exposed stone walls and timbered ceiling, while tapestries, gleaming copper and elegant portraits abound alongside an open kitchen. The small lounge boasts leather seating and antiques, while the extensive wine choice is stored on a mezzanine floor. A temple to prime beef and the Rolls Royce of steakhouses, Champany specialises in cuts from cattle sourced and prepared by the restaurant's own butchery and hung for three weeks. West Coast seafood also finds its place, but it's the full-flavoured, tender beef that takes pride of place, such as Aberdeen Angus sirloin, fillet or rib-eye. The farmer's cottage has now been converted into a shop selling Champany produce, while the Chop and Ale House serves a bistro-style menu.

LINLITHGOW, West Lothian
EH49 7LU
Tel: 01506 834532
Email: reception@champany.com
Website: www.champany.com
Chef: C Davidson & D Gibson & C Hart
Owners: Mr & Mrs C Davidson

Times: 12.30–2/7–10,
Closed 25-26 Dec, 1-2 Jan,
Sun, L Sat
Prices: Main £20–£42
Directions: 2m NE of Linlithgow. From M9 (N) junct 3, at top of slip road turn right. Champany is 500yds on right
Parking: 50

Livingston's Restaurant

Modern Scottish

Superb Scottish cooking in a delightful rural restaurant

Tucked away at the end of a semi-hidden 'ginnel' or lane, Livingston's provides an authentic Scottish experience. Ruby red fabrics, tartan carpets and soft candlelight conspire to create a relaxed and intoxicatingly Caledonian atmosphere that enhances the offerings on a menu which trumpets local ingredients such as Inverurie lamb, Highland venison and Stornoway black pudding. Among the highlights are dishes such as warm Stornoway black pudding tart with crispy pancetta and herb salad, roast halibut on wilted spinach with rosemary and red wine jus or try saddle of wild Highland venison with red cabbage and bitter chocolate sauce. Make room for the assiette of Livingston's puddings. The well-chosen wine list has interesting tasting notes.

52 High Street LINLITHGOW
EH49 7AE
Tel: 01506 846565
Email: contact@livingstons-restaurant.co.uk
Website: www.livingstons-restaurant.co.uk
Chef: Julian Wright
Owners: Ronald & Christine Livingstone

Times: 12–2.30/6–9.30,
Closed 1 wk Jun, 1 wk Oct, 2 wks Jan, Sun (except Mothering Sun)–Mon
Prices: Fixed D £33.95
Directions: Opposite post office
Parking: NCP Linlithgow Cross on street

Royal Hotel

Traditional British

Traditional food in an elegant environment

Melville Square, COMRIE,
Perth & Kinross PH6 2DN
Tel: 01764 679200
Email: reception@royalhotel.co.uk
Website: www.royalhotel.co.uk
Chef: David Milsom
Owners: The Milsom Family

Behind the façade of this 18th-century coaching inn, on Comrie's central square, lies an elegant interior of polished-wood floors, stylish soft furnishings, log fires and antique pieces. There's a choice of dining venues, including the lounge bar, a colonial-look conservatory brasserie, the open-hearthed library and the beautifully appointed formal dining room. In fine weather you can eat outside in the walled garden. Scottish fare is skilfully prepared from local produce, with prime Scottish beef, venison, salmon, game and seafood figuring strongly.

Times: 12–2/6.30–9, Closed Xmas
Prices: Fixed D £19
–£26.50 Main £9.75–£17.50
Directions: In main square, 7m from Crieff, on A85
Parking: 25

Taymouth Restaurant

Traditional British

Tay views and quality Scottish fare

The Kenmore Hotel, The Square,
KENMORE, Perth & Kinross
PH15 2NU
Tel: 01887 830205
Email: reception@kenmorehotel.co.uk
Website: www.kenmorehotel.co.uk
Chef: Peter Backhouse
Owners: Kenmore Estates Ltd

Built in 1572, the Kenmore is Scotland's oldest inn. The historic building has a cosy bar with a log fire, while the modern restaurant is surrounded by glass and enjoys panoramic views over the River Tay and the surrounding forests. Seasonality plays a big part in the menu composition, and dishes prepared from fresh local ingredients are simply and cleanly presented, as in oven-roasted Scottish salmon filled with Islay whisky-flavoured haggis soufflé and leek sauce, or roast breast of duckling with a nice crisp skin, coated with lemongrass and honey sauce and accompanied by stir-fried pak choi. For dessert, try baked rice pudding, with scented vanilla, pineapple compôte and coconut ice cream.

Times: 12–17/17–9.30
Prices: 3 Course Fixed D £18–£31
Main £10.25–£18.95
Directions: A9 N, A827 Ballinluig, A827 into Kenmore, hotel is at centre of village
Parking: 40

Dunalastair Hotel

Modern British

Accomplished cuisine in traditional Highland hotel

KINLOCH RANNOCH,
Perth & Kinross PH16 5PW
Tel: 01882 632323
Email: info@dunalastair.co.uk
Website: www.dunalastair.co.uk
Chef: Kevin Easingwood
Owners: R Gilmour

This traditional Highland hotel was built as a retreat for soldiers. The magnificent wood-panelled Schiehallion restaurant, complete with roaring log fire and lighting made from red deer antlers, has a real baronial feel. The kitchen adds a modern touch to traditional dishes making use of excellent Scottish ingredients. The cooking and presentation are beautiful in their simplicity with a great balance of flavours and no superfluous elements. Try roast celeriac soup followed by Scottish lamb rump set on red cabbage with port jus or wild mushroom and parmesan risotto.

Times: 12–2.30/6.30–9
Prices: 3 Course Fixed D £29.50
–£36 Main £12.95–£19.95
Directions: From Pitlochry N, take B8019 to Tummel Bridge then B846 to Kinloch Rannoch
Parking: 50

Dalmunzie House Hotel

Traditional, British

Cooking worthy of the laird in a highland mansion

SPITTAL OF GLENSHEE,
Blairgowrie, Perth & Kinross
PH10 7QG
Tel: 01250 885224
Email:
reservations@dalmunzie.com
Website: www.dalmunzie.com
Chef: Michelle Metten
Owners: Scott & Brianna Poole

A former Highland laird's mansion, complete with turrets, set on an estate of 6,500 acres. Within easy reach of the ski slopes at Glenshee, this could be the perfect destination after a hard day on the piste. The house is furnished with antiques, and logs burn in the original fireplaces. The spacious dining room has well-appointed tables and a classic blue and cream colour scheme where you can soak up the fine-dining experience, or have a more relaxed bite in the bar. Top-quality, seasonal ingredients are sourced for dishes with a British approach, underpinned by classic French influences. Take chargrilled venison loin served with baby spinach, cauliflower purée and an elderflower wine jus, or perhaps a sticky toffee pudding with butterscotch sauce and malt whisky ice cream to finish.

Times: 12–2.30/7–9,
Closed 1-28 Dec
Prices: 4 Course Fixed D £36
Directions: 30m N of Blairgowrie on A93 at the Spittal of Glenshee
Parking: 40

Burt's Hotel

Modern British

Contemporary cooking in a sophisticated setting

The Square, MELROSE,
Scottish Borders TD6 9PL
Tel: 01896 822285
Email: burtshotel@aol.com
Website: www.burtshotel.co.uk
Chef: David McCallum
Owners: The Henderson Family

Set in Melrose's picturesque 18th-century market square, with a distinctive white-painted façade, Burt's has been in the same family for 35 years and its hospitality is a byword locally. Originally home to a local dignitary, today it still retains much of its period charm, and the elegant restaurant has a smart, clubby feel, with dark green striped wallpaper, sporting prints, and high-backed chairs. Here the modern British menu takes in the likes of salmon and crayfish ravioli, with étuvée of leek and céviche of scallop, or perhaps a tranche of halibut, saffron mash, langoustine tortellini and bouillabaisse sauce. There's a great choice of grills boasting matured Scottish lamb and beef, and an excellent cheeseboard including a number of local and speciality products. Lunch and supper are also served in the relaxing Bistro Bar.

Times: 12–2/7–9, Closed 26 Dec, 3-5 Jan
Prices: 3 Course Fixed D £32.75
Main £16.50–£28
Directions: Town centre in Market Sq
Parking: 40

Bosville Hotel

Modern British

Masterful cooking of truly local produce

Bosville Terrace, PORTREE,
Isle of Skye, Highland IV51 9DG
Tel: 01478 612846
Email:
bosville@macleodhotels.co.uk
Website: www.macleodhotels.
co.uk/bosville
Chef: John Kelly
Owners: Donald W Macleod

A popular hotel with fine views over Portree Harbour, the Bosville offers stylish public areas including a smart bar, bistro and the Chandlery Restaurant. The restaurant draws on an abundance of fresh local produce, especially seafood and game. Great produce, skilful cooking techniques and inspirational combinations are evident in dishes such as hand-dived scallops from Loch Sligachan on a carrot purée with roast beetroot, garnished with lardons of Stornoway black pudding accompanied by an apple and lemon emulsion, or pan-seared estate venison loin served on a confit of tomatoes, beans and Orbost garlic chives, Glendale wilted greens, a little rabbit bridie and Waternish shiitake mushroom fricassée.

Times: 6.30–9.30
Prices: 4 Course Fixed D £40, Closed all week
Directions: 200mtrs from bus station, overlooking Portree Harbour
Parking: 10

Restaurant Index

Location Index

Credits

The Automobile Association would like to thank the following photographers, companies and picture libraries for their assistance in the preparation of this book.

Abbreviations for the picture credits are as follows: (t) top; (b) bottom; (l) left; (r) right; (AA) AA World Travel Library.

12/3 AA/C Jones; 22/3 AA/R Moss; 31b AA/N Hicks; 44b AA/S L Day; 50/1 AA/J Miller; 71 AA/S L Day; 78/9 AA/R Victor; 87 AA/M Moody; 93 AA/J A Tims; 100/1 AA/W Voysey; 107b AA/N Jenkins; 113 AA/C Molyneux; 126/7 AA/T Mackie; 139 AA/T Mackie; 158/9 AA/P Sharpe; 171 AA/C Jones; 180/1 AA/M Kipling; 190/1 AA/S Abrahams; 196/7 AA/S L Day.

6b & 35b copyright 2007 to www.RichardBudd.co.uk http://www.RichardBudd.co.uk

Mallory Court Hotel